INDIVIDUAL PLACEMENT AND SUPPORT

EVIDENCE-BASED PRACTICES SERIES

SERIES EDITORS:

David E. Biegel, Ph.D.
Elizabeth M. Tracy, Ph.D.
Mandel School of Applied Social Sciences,
Case Western Reserve University

Family Psychoeducation for Serious Mental Illness
Harriet P. Lefley

School Social Work
An Evidence-Informed Framework for Practice
Michael S. Kelly, James C. Raines, Susan Stone, and Andy Frey

Mental Health Treatment for Children and Adolescents
Jacqueline Corcoran

Individual Placement and Support
An Evidence-Based Approach to Supported Employment
Robert E. Drake, Gary R. Bond, and Deborah R. Becker

The Evidence-Based Practices Series is published in collaboration with the Mandel School of Applied Social Sciences at Case Western Reserve University.

INDIVIDUAL PLACEMENT AND SUPPORT

AN EVIDENCE-BASED APPROACH TO SUPPORTED EMPLOYMENT

Robert E. Drake
Gary R. Bond
Deborah R. Becker

OXFORD
UNIVERSITY PRESS

OXFORD
UNIVERSITY PRESS

Oxford University Press is a department of the University of Oxford.
It furthers the University's objective of excellence in research, scholarship,
and education by publishing worldwide.

Oxford   New York

Auckland   Cape Town   Dar es Salaam   Hong Kong   Karachi
Kuala Lumpur   Madrid   Melbourne   Mexico City   Nairobi
New Delhi   Shanghai   Taipei   Toronto

With offices in

Argentina   Austria   Brazil   Chile   Czech Republic   France   Greece
Guatemala   Hungary   Italy   Japan   Poland   Portugal   Singapore
South Korea   Switzerland   Thailand   Turkey   Ukraine   Vietnam

Oxford is a registered trademark of Oxford University Press
in the UK and certain other countries.

Published in the United States of America by
Oxford University Press
198 Madison Avenue, New York, NY 10016

Library of Congress Cataloging-in-Publication Data
Drake, Robert E., 1949-
Individual placement and support : an evidence-based approach to
supported employment / Robert E. Drake, Gary R. Bond, and Deborah R. Becker.
p. cm. — (Evidence-based practices)
Includes bibliographical references and index.
ISBN 978–0–19–973401–6 (pbk. : alk. paper)
1. People with mental disabilities—Employment—United States.
2. People with mental disabilities—Services for—United States.
I. Bond, Gary R.   II. Becker, Deborah R.   III. Title.
HD7256.U5D73 2012
362.4′04840973—dc23
2012003714

Printed in the United States of America
on acid-free paper

This book is dedicated with deep appreciation to all of the courageous people who have gained employment through IPS supported employment.

Bob Drake
Gary Bond
Debbie Becker

CONTENTS

PREFACE

Researchers are fundamentally students, striving to clarify the nature of a problem, to assemble knowledge in a coherent picture, to formulate useful questions, to answer these questions using rigorous scientific methods, and to disseminate new information. After studying employment for people with mental illness for many years, we summarize our journey thus far: where we started, what we currently know about helping people succeed in work, what we are trying to learn now, and where we think the field is headed. By sharing our thinking as well as summarizing research, we hope to stimulate other researchers, for much remains to be done. The book is primarily for the students and researchers who will advance the fields of psychiatric disability and rehabilitation. Others with interests in mental health services research—the process of developing evidence-based interventions, conducting the research, understanding the research findings, and the dissemination of research—are welcome to join the journey.

When we began this effort over 20 years ago, several facts were clear: People with mental illnesses expressed a desire for regular employment but rarely entered the mainstream workforce. Professionals, families, and the public were pessimistic about employment as a legitimate goal. After focusing for centuries on the deficits related to mental illnesses, professionals emphasized all the reasons that people with mental illness could not work. Families feared that work would be too stressful for their relatives, perceiving that symptom remissions were fragile, recognizing that disability insurance and meager benefits were critically important, and accepting that stability was a sufficient goal. The public view of mental illness was fearful and inaccurate, consistently misinformed by the media's attention to horrific but rare anecdotes.

In this rather bleak context, we have endeavored to improve employment prospects for mental health clients because so many expressed the goal of meaningful employment in regular work settings. We listened to people describe what they needed, what they found helpful, and what they found hurtful. We studied successful clients, clinicians, and programs. We gathered expert opinions and used scientific methods to test conflicting ideas. Our journey has challenged conventional wisdom, public prejudice, and dysfunctional policies at every step. This book summarizes our thinking up to 2011.

Before we begin, we want to acknowledge that the book reflects the thinking and work of many people. When Drake and Becker began to study employment in New Hampshire in the 1980s (in 1994 joined by Bond, who had been independently researching vocational services in various psychiatric rehabilitation programs), numerous clients and family members, many of whom prefer to remain anonymous, met with us and described their disappointing and occasionally constructive experiences in the service system when they attempted to find and keep employment. Don Shumway, who got us started, and Jim Musumeci, Tom Fox, and Paul Gorman from the New Hampshire Division of Behavioral Health encouraged us to improve vocational services in New Hampshire and supported our research, as did Bruce Archimbault, Paul Leather, and others from the New Hampshire Division of Vocational Rehabilitation. Jess Turner and Phil Wyzik of West Central Services, and Nick Verven, Ken Snow, Bill Rider, and Ed Bailey of the Mental Health Center of Greater Manchester gave their time and supported our efforts to study employment in natural and planned experiments.

Numerous mental health and rehabilitation professionals with experience and expertise in vocational services met with us, generously gave us advice, and assisted us in defining and studying programs. Among those professionals were Len Stein, Mary Ann Test, Jana Frey, Bill Knoedler, and Deborah Allness from the Program for Assertive Community Treatment in Madison, Wisconsin; Bob Liberman, Jim Mintz, and Chuck Wallace from UCLA; Bill Anthony, Marianne Farkas, Karen Danley, and Sally Rogers from the Boston University Center for Psychiatric Rehabilitation; Morris Bell and Bob Rosenheck from Yale University; Tony Lehman and Howard Goldman from the University of Maryland; Charlie Rapp and Linda Carlson from the University of Kansas; and Paul Wehman from Virginia Commonwealth University.

Over the years, many colleagues and students at Dartmouth have collaborated with us in developing and studying Individual Placement and Support (IPS). We particularly thank Greg McHugo and Haiyi Xie, our constant muses as methodologists and statisticians on all studies. Other valued Dartmouth colleagues over the years have included Hoyt Alverson, Marianne Alverson, Phil Bush, Elizabeth Carpenter-Song, Mike Cohen, Robin Clark, Pat Deegan, Laura Flint, Lindy Fox,

Crystal Glover, Paul Gorman, Will Haslett, David Lynde, Susan McGurk, Matt Merrens, Kim Mueser, Saira Nawaz, Sandy Reese, Michelle Salyers, David Strickler, Karin Swain, Sarah Swanson, Will Torrey, Rob Whitley, Rosemary Wolfe, and Emily Woltmann. Over the years, Bond's graduate students at Indiana University-Purdue University Indianapolis, including Kikuko Campbell, Laura Dietzen, Melody Dilk, Kim Dreher, Lisa Evans, Amanda Jones, Colleen Katuin, Marina Kukla, Alan McGuire, Piper Meyer, Jeff Picone, Sandy Resnick, Angie Rollins, Michelle Salyers, Amanda Taylor, and Kathleen Vogler have also contributed through dissertations, masters theses, publications, and other work to our understanding of vocational services for people with serious mental illness. We are also indebted to our colleagues at Thresholds in Chicago, including Jerry Dincin, Ginnie Fraser, Rochelle Frounfelker, Sheila O'Neill, Sandra Wilkniss, and Tony Zipple, where we have conducted a series of recent IPS studies. Many colleagues and collaborators around the United States and in other countries have helped with IPS studies. Among these colleagues are Susan Azrin, Tom Burns, Nicole Clevenger, Angelo Fioritti, Lisa Dixon, Bill Frey, Shirley Glynn, Howard Goldman, Mustafa Karakas, Eoin Killackey, Eric Latimer, Janice Machado, Steve Marder, John McGrew, Harry Michon, Roline Milfort, Alec Miller, Keith Nuechterlein, Oshie Oshima, Ernest Quimby, Jarnee Riley, Miles Rinaldi, David Salkever, Peggy Swarbrick, Rich Toscano, and Jaap van Weeghel. Finally, we are indebted to our funders, the National Institute of Mental Health, the National Institute of Disability and Rehabilitation Research, the Substance Abuse and Mental Health Services Administration, the Social Security Administration, and the Johnson & Johnson Office of Corporate Contributions, especially to our friend and collaborator Rick Martinez, whose support, vision, and encouragement over many years have been invaluable.

Bob Drake, Gary Bond,
and
Debbie Becker

BACKGROUND AND CONCEPTS

INTRODUCTION

Simply stated, here is the situation we confront as clients, family members, professionals, researchers, advocates, and policy makers: Most people with serious mental illnesses (about 70%) want to work. Like others, they want the responsibility, status, dignity, regular activity, income, challenge, social connections, opportunity to contribute, satisfaction, and all of the other things that employment provides. Despite these interests, only 10–15% of people with serious psychiatric illnesses in community treatment programs in the United States are competitively employed (Bertram & Howard, 2006; Henry, 1990; Lindamer et al., 2003; Pandiani & Leno, 2011; Rosenheck et al., 2006; Salkever et al., 2007). Rates are even lower, typically less than 5%, in follow-up surveys of people discharged from psychiatric hospitals (Farkas, Rogers, & Thurer, 1987; Honkonen, Stengård, Virtanen, & Salokangas, 2007). National and international surveys of community samples, which include respondents with less serious disorders, have reported employment rates of 20%–25% for people with schizophrenia and related disorders (Marwaha et al., 2007; Mechanic, Bilder, & McAlpine, 2002). Traditional vocational programs of many kinds have demonstrated little success in improving these dismal rates of employment (Bond, 1992; Bond, Drake, Becker, & Mueser, 1999).

In the 1980s supported employment began to emerge in many forms as an intervention for people with psychiatric disabilities. Supported employment for people with psychiatric disabilities has been standardized and studied as the Individual Placement and Support (IPS) model. As we review below, the research on IPS has been remarkably robust and consistent. Most people who participate in IPS find satisfying employment, typically improving over time as they gain experience and become steady workers. Currently, IPS helps approximately two-thirds of participants in clinical trials to achieve competitive employment. We are learning more about how to help the other third.

Nevertheless, after nearly two decades, the spread of IPS in the United States has been slow. One recent survey (SAMHSA, 2009) estimated that only 2% of people with serious mental illness receive any form of supported employment—a far cry from the 70% who want to work!

Furthermore, new challenges have emerged. Health care financing continues to emphasize medications rather than psychosocial services and rehabilitation supports. More people with mental illnesses receive psychotropic medications, but people with the most serious psychiatric illnesses get fewer and fewer needed psychosocial services (Frank & Glied, 2006). Partly as a result of these trends, people with serious mental illnesses are increasingly shunted into the criminal justice system, thereby complicating their employment goals (Fisher et al., 2006; Teplin, Abram, & McClelland, 1996; Tschopp, Perkins, Hart-Katuin, Born, & Holt, 2007). In addition, the national recession and high rates of local unemployment have created new barriers to employment for people with disabilities (Fogg, Harrington, & McMahon, 2010; Kaye, 2010).

What can researchers do to address these problems and to move the field ahead? In this book we invite all stakeholders to think with us about psychiatric rehabilitation, examining the challenge from different perspectives, considering the state of current research, and planning for the future. People with mental illnesses themselves have become an important force—in politics, advocacy, clinical services, peer supports, and research. Similarly, family members, professional advocates, policy makers, and other stakeholders have important roles to play in reforming mental health care in the United States. All stakeholders need reliable and valid data to make good decisions. Producing such data is the fundamental job of researchers.

After more than two decades working on these issues, we are eager to share how we have considered these problems, what we have learned about doing research in the process, and what may be helpful in the future. For those of you who are students, we encourage you to become researchers who make a difference in people's lives. Publishing papers that have no impact is easy; pursuing promotions and the trappings of academia can be false goals; and following the money from industry or consulting can be even more dangerous. But producing data that actually help people with mental illness to improve their lives should be our goal in mental health services research. We have a boundless opportunity: little is known, services are poor, many people need our help, and our work is directly practical.

DEFINITIONS

Let's begin with a few definitions to make sure we are speaking the same language. We will endeavor throughout to use everyday English and to avoid mental health jargon, but clarifying a few basic terms is necessary.

Supported employment is a generic term with a federal definition but without specific guidelines (Federal Register, 1992). IPS is the only evidence-based approach to supported employment for people with serious mental illnesses. IPS has evolved over two decades and continues to evolve as the evidence develops. The standard for change is the evidence base for improving vocational outcomes.

Serious mental illness is often used synonymously with the term severe and persistent mental illness. It denotes people whose lives are derailed by mental health problems for significant periods of time—people who have significant impairments in major life roles, such as self-care, employment, and intimate relationships (Bhugra, 2006; U.S. Department of Health and Human Services, 1999). Adults with serious mental illnesses usually have psychotic disorders, such as schizophrenia, or severe forms of mood disorders, such as bipolar disorder or chronic depression. Although some people rebound from these illnesses quickly and avoid long-term impairments, many others are affected for years. Because definitions and counts of mental illness and impairment vary (Schinnar, Rothbard, Kanter, & Jung, 1990), exact numbers are uncertain. But most government reports, across many countries, estimate that 3% – 5% of adults between ages 18 and 65 have a serious mental illness (OECD, 2009). Serious mental disorders have been noted throughout recorded history (Torrey, 2001), are relatively common in all parts of the world, and produce an enormous disease burden (World Health Organization, 2001b). The rates of impairment may differ in less industrialized countries (Harrison et al., 2001), but many individuals nevertheless struggle in relation to culturally defined roles. Serious mental illnesses comprise a major proportion of the global burden of disease (Prince et al., 2007; Wang et al., 2005). Societal costs include health and social care, amplified significantly by the impact of disability on employment status, income, and need for subsidized housing (Saxena, Thornicroft, Knapp, & Whiteford, 2007).

Disability is a status based on personal, environmental, and social factors as well as level of impairment (Bartlett, Lewis, & Thorold, 2006). Illness or injury is only a component. For example, an individual with the impairment of paraplegia might require a wheelchair for mobility but would become disabled only if his or her work, income, health care, housing, transportation, and interpersonal environments created unnecessary barriers. The situation is more complicated for people with mental illnesses because the conditions themselves are often unobservable, are highly stigmatized, tend to fluctuate, and have only a minimal direct relationship to functional status (Institute of Medicine, 2002; World Health Organization, 2001a).

Mental health disability produces individual and societal costs. Individual costs include the pain and suffering related to secondary disablement in addition to the primary illnesses, as well as the impact on the ability to work and earn an income. Societal costs encompass all of the negative effects related to having a large group of individuals become socially and economically marginalized, often with long-term dependency on services. In the era of long-term institutionalization, these effects were predominantly the costs of running the institutions, whereas today psychiatric disablement impinges on society in more complex ways.

People with serious mental illnesses are people first. They are not diagnoses—they are not schizophrenics, bipolars, or depressives. They are people with a diagnosis or a disorder. The distinction is important. It reminds us all to relate to, help, support, and treat the person, not the diagnosis.

People who use the mental health system are variously referred to as *clients, patients, consumers, survivors, users,* and other terms. We use these terms interchangeably, recognizing the validity of common usage.

Recovery is a multifaceted concept—simultaneously an ideology, a movement, a vision, a personal process, a set of principles, a set of standards for care, and a banner of hope (Whitley & Drake, 2010). In psychiatric rehabilitation, we generally use the term to refer to a process in which people with illnesses or disabilities move beyond preoccupation with illness, become hopeful about the future, and pursue their own journeys and goals (Deegan, 1988).

Values are also important—from the perspectives of people with mental disorders, professional caregivers, and society. People with the most serious and disabling mental disorders are experts on their own personal experiences, their own individual aspirations, and their own preferences regarding health outcomes and interventions. Honoring their views and autonomy—often in the form of shared decision making—is a theme we develop throughout this book. Professional caregivers have clearly articulated values (Beauchamp & Childress, 2001), simply stated as respect for the individual (being honest), beneficence (trying to do good), avoiding malfeasance (not doing harm), and justice (treating everyone fairly). These are also themes throughout our book. And what about society? Perhaps the clearest statement of societal values in relation to psychiatric rehabilitation is the Americans with Disabilities Act, which states that people with disabling conditions have civil rights and protections in employment and other public settings (Americans with Disabilities Act of 1990). Again, this theme reverberates throughout our book.

THE PRIMARY GOAL: PEOPLE WITH SERIOUS MENTAL ILLNESS WANT TO WORK

Why is this surprising? People with mental illnesses want the same things that the rest of us want: to live freely, to have friends and companions, and to be productive. Evolution and society have selected for these traits because they are consonant with survival, adaptation, and procreation. People with impairments and illnesses are fundamentally human and want to pursue these goals as well.

Freedom and relationships are important aspects of recovery, but this book is about productive activity. People with mental illnesses want to be productive. Early in the course of mental illness, nearly all people want to remain in or return to school or work. The only exception might be a small minority of young people who have been socialized into antisocial lifestyles very early in life, before they develop mental illness. Yet even these misdirected youths typically maintain the hope of returning to legitimate employment (Bourgois, 2003; Robins, 1966). Somewhat more surprising is the fact that the majority of older people with long-term mental disorders still want to work (Twamley, Narvaez, Becker, Bartels, & Jeste, 2008). Surveys of people with serious mental illness typically show rates of expressed interest in employment at about 70% (Frounfelker, Wilkniss, Bond, Drake, & Devitt, 2011; McQuilken et al., 2003; Mueser, Salyers, & Mueser, 2001; Ramsay et al., 2011). This high figure is only surprising because of the pervasive acculturation process that most people with serious mental illnesses have endured: early school or work failures, ubiquitous social stigma, low expectations of professionals, the often lengthy and humiliating process of declaring oneself permanently and totally disabled in order to obtain a poverty-level income and health insurance, and the grinding experience of unemployment, poverty, disenfranchisement, and marginalization. And yet people still want to work! The drive to be productive is human, innate, and almost inextinguishable.

The barriers to employment for people with serious mental illness are legion (Braitman et al., 1995; Cook, 2006; Henry & Lucca, 2004; Rosenheck et al., 2006; Secker, Grove, & Seebohm, 2001; Stuart, 2006). The acculturation process described above is overwhelming (Estroff, Patrick, Zimmer, & Lachicotte, 1997). Imagine spending three years proving to the Social Security Administration that you are permanently disabled in order to get health insurance: getting doctors' reports, signing documents, appealing decisions with even stronger arguments, maybe obtaining a lawyer who advises you to avoid work! It's no wonder that people sometimes believe that they are in fact disabled. Then the threat of losing Social Security benefits and health insurance looms. Clients at every mental health center hear horror stories about losing benefits, being asked to pay back money, and having difficulty getting back on Social Security. Maybe the process would be easier if the rules were clear. But nothing could be further from the reality. Even Social Security employees have difficulty understanding the complex rules, mostly geared to people with physical disabilities and often not easily applied to psychiatric disabilities, and people frequently get conflicting or incorrect information from official sources. In addition to fear of losing benefits, people with serious mental illness face multifarious barriers: lack of education and work history, fear of failure, fear of application forms, employers' bias, society's bias, lack of appropriate clothes, lack of transportation, lack of interviewing skills, low expectations of mental health professionals, rejection by state vocational rehabilitation agencies, and on and on. The traditional 10–15% employment rate begins to look high in relation to the barriers!

Why do people with serious mental illness want to work in the face of such great odds? Read their stories, talk with them, and listen carefully. Their reasons are diverse, but one motivation is consistent. Like people with other serious illnesses, they strive to conduct their lives in as normal a fashion as possible. People with a highly stigmatized illness like schizophrenia still have a strong desire for normalcy—to pursue a meaningful life, to be part of the community, to avoid being defined by the illness. For reasons of identity, self-esteem, and social confidence, they would prefer to say, "I work at the recreation department" or "I'm an assistant at the nursing home" rather than "I'm unemployed due to mental illness." In addition, they want the other things that employment provides to everyone: extra income, a structure for the day, social opportunities, a feeling of accomplishment, the chance to contribute to society, and so on. Literally thousands of published recovery stories document the importance of work in overcoming illness and re-establishing a sense of hope and accomplishment (Bailey, 1998; Clevenger, 2008; Rogers, 1995; Steele & Berman, 2001). As Josie Bailey (1998) wrote, "Now that I'm working, I really notice the difference when I get up in the morning and go out. I say to myself, 'Hey, nobody knows that I have a mental illness. I'm just a person going to work.' It makes me feel good."

Longitudinal follow-up studies (10 years or more) confirm that clients perceive the benefits of working (Harding, Brooks, Ashikaga, Strauss, & Breier, 1987). A large proportion in one study reported that working helped them with self-confidence, hopefulness, boredom, loneliness, relationships, physical health, and energy (Salyers, Becker, Drake, Torrey, & Wyzik, 2004). In another study, a large majority reported that they sought mental health care less often while working and that their feelings about life and about themselves were more positive (Becker, Whitley, Bailey, & Drake, 2007). In a third study, many clients reported that steady work helped them to manage anxiety, stress, depression, psychosis, and substance use; and enhanced their moral, material, cognitive, structural, and emotional lives (Strickler, Whitley, Becker, & Drake, 2009).

To summarize, people with mental illness offer several insights that constitute the phenomenological core of IPS research. The reasons that most want to work are similar to what people in the general population report: pursuing normal adult roles, participating fully in society, having something meaningful to do, meeting other people, having more income, and so on. Like others, they want jobs that are competitive, interesting, and challenging, not sheltered jobs and not jobs that are incongruent with their interests and preferences. We know less about people who choose not to work. Young people often have age-appropriate educational goals rather than work goals. Some people consider themselves retired. Others have found niches in the casual labor market, working when they want, avoiding taxes, perhaps working for family. Still others are overwhelmed by mental illness and/or addiction and believe that they cannot work. They have accepted, adapted to, or been socialized into a disabled role in society.

People also report that they need help becoming employed, staying employed, and changing jobs. The help they need involves encouragement, finding an appropriate job match, adjusting initially to a job, coping with the job, and sometimes changing jobs. All of these steps correspond closely with the principles and practices of IPS (Swanson & Becker, 2010), not accidentally of course because IPS has been shaped by feedback from thousands of participants.

People who become steady workers report myriad benefits from working. These testimonies almost always include income, structure, self-esteem, social contacts, citizenship, and recovery. They often involve illness management—the ability to control anxiety, symptoms, substance use, and medication side effects. From humanistic or recovery perspectives, the number and consistency of these reports certainly should cause policy makers to question the predominance of pharmacology and economic analyses searching for cost offsets.

Steady workers also report that working part-time generally fits their needs. It allows them to increase income and psychosocial benefits without creating too much stress or threatening their Social Security status. We do not know whether or how much this balance would shift if the Social Security regulations were to be different.

Some people with mental illness believe that they are permanently disabled by illness, that work would be too stressful, and that they cannot work. How much of this defeatism can be attributed to genuine impairment, how much to negative experiences trying to work, and how much to the socialization process of applying for and feeling trapped by disability benefits? The answer is unknown. We do know that young people in the early phases of illness rarely have these attitudes. Instead, they want to return to school or work, to peer friendships, and to live a life that they see as normal. We also know that many people try to return to school or work without the supports they need. The experience of illness, the disability process, and failures lead to pessimism for a small portion of people. What is more remarkable is that so many others continue to want to work despite barriers.

INTERNATIONAL TRENDS

The Organization for Economic Co-operation and Development (OECD) recently summarized disability statistics and trends across its 30 member countries, which represent democracies committed to free market economics (OECD, 2009). Data from all countries were derived from self-report and disability-related costs and refer to all health-related disabilities. The following trends were similar across countries: (a) Despite a decade of economic growth preceding the current recession, employment among persons with disabilities has not increased and has often decreased. People with self-reported disabilities are twice as likely as those without disabilities to be unemployed and are much more likely to be living in poverty. (b) Over half of the OECD countries have experienced significant increases in rates of disability beneficiaries among working-age adults in the past decade. The costs of disability benefits alone average 1.2% of gross domestic product and are as high as 5% in some countries. (c) Across OECD countries, the annual rate of leaving disability status due to employment is below 2%. Thus, disability benefits constitute a de facto involuntary retirement plan for the great majority of beneficiaries. (d) The proportion of disability claimants with mental health problems is increasing and now constitutes about one-third of claimants across OECD nations. (e) People with mental illnesses are 30–50% less likely to be employed than persons with other health or disability conditions in these countries.

Healthcare financing systems also powerfully shape who can access treatment and care. Prepayment systems, such as social insurance, voluntary health insurance, or tax-based arrangements, are generally seen as better than out-of-pocket payments because they pool risks, have the potential to redistribute benefits toward people with greater needs, and may be made progressive, so that poorer individuals pay less for equivalent health care than wealthier people. Out-of-pocket-payment systems cannot be as effective in targeting need, nor are they as equitable, but they are still widely used (Dixon, McDaid, Knapp, & Curran, 2006). While at the global level, the most common method of financing mental health care as a whole is through taxation (60%), more than a third of low-income countries rely on out-of-pocket payments as a primary source of finance (Saxena, Paraje, Sharan, Karam, & Sadana, 2006).

COSTS OF MENTAL HEALTH DISABILITY

Mental illnesses, although usually defined by clinical symptoms, have consequences across many life domains, leading to multiple needs for support. The costs of mental illness therefore range well beyond the health system, and their precise distribution between individuals, families, and society more generally varies from country to country, depending on how support is structured, coordinated, and financed. Common across all countries, however, are the substantial impacts for individuals and families (lost income because of disrupted employment, out-of-pocket payments), for employers (through lost productivity because of sickness absences and underperformance), and for governments (lost taxes, criminal justice system impacts, welfare payments). Indeed, health service costs are often dwarfed by these wider economic impacts (Andlin-Sobocki, Jönsson, Wittchen, & Olesen, 2005; Sainsbury Centre, 2003; U.S. Department of Health and Human Services, 1999). Moreover, because serious mental illnesses tend to be persistent, these economic burdens persist for many years (Knapp, McCrone, Fombonne, Beecham, & Wostear, 2002; Scott, Knapp, Henderson, & Maughan, 2001).

Aside from the perennial question of the affordability of good quality care and support for people with serious mental illnesses, the main challenges stem from 'silo budgets' and the disincentives and dislocations they cause. Resources are locked up within tightly controlled budgets, and difficulties in achieving greater overall effectiveness or cost-effectiveness are exacerbated by professional rivalries, increasingly rigorous performance assessments, and bureaucratic processes. For example, better treatment for serious mental illness could have its biggest resource impact not in the health sector but in helping patients to access employment and reduce absenteeism (Lerner et al., 2004), but unless resources are moved from that part of government that funds welfare support to health care providers and employment services, the dominant incentives militate against the overall well-being of already disadvantaged individuals (Bejerholm, Larsson, & Hofgren, 2011).

THE DISABILITY TRAP AND THE DISABILITY BENEFITS CULTURE

People with severe and persistent mental illnesses face an untenable dilemma. In the United States, many desperately need mental health services and temporary income support when they leave school or work due to illness, and for many the only opportunity to attain these benefits is through one of the two federal disability programs, Social Security Disability Insurance or Supplemental Security Income. Currently, adults with mental illness constitute the largest and fastest growing group of participants in Social Security disability programs (Danziger, Frank, & Meara, 2009; McAlpine & Warner, 2000). As of 2007, 29% of Social Security Disability Insurance beneficiaries (approximately 2.0 million people) and 39% of Supplementary Security Income recipients (also approximately 2.0 million people) were classified as having a mental disorder (SSA, 2008). Applying for and being approved for these programs is an arduous process, confounded by complex rules, and often takes years of trying to prove that one is severely disabled (Bilder & Mechanic, 2003; Burkhauser, Butler, & Weathers, 2002; Estroff, Patrick, Zimmer, & Lachicotte, 1997; Zola, 1992). Nearly all beneficiaries live below the poverty line (Cook, 2006; Draine, Salzer, Culhane, & Hadley, 2002; Stapleton, O'Day, Livermore, & Imparato, 2006), but they are understandably reluctant to do anything that threatens their benefits and health insurance once they have attained disability status (MacDonald-Wilson, Rogers, Ellison, & Lyass, 2003; Rosenheck et al., 2006). A substantially higher percentage of beneficiaries express a desire to return to work (~50%) than actually agree to participate in return-to-work programs (~5%) (Ruiz-Quintanilla, Weathers, Melburg, Campbell, & Madi, 2006). In fact, less than 1% per year leaves disability status for any reason except death or aging (Rupp & Scott, 1996). This situation has been variously called the "disability trap" (Ramsay, Stewart, & Compton, 2012), "benefits trap" (Burns et al., 2007), or "poverty trap" (Stapleton, O'Day, Livermore, & Imparato, 2006).

Even when individuals have a very strong desire to overcome disability and achieve independence, they are highly unlikely to be able to obtain the effective services that they need to do so (Drake, Essock, & Bond, 2009). Public mental health spending in the United States, for example, has not increased since 1996 (Frank, Goldman, & McGuire, 2009). Public mental health services are relatively ineffective (Drake, Essock, & Bond, 2009), poorly accepted (Kreyenbuhl, Nosse, & Dixon, 2009), and currently deteriorating (Bogira, 2009; Cunningham, McKenzie, & Taylor, 2006). The majority of persons with severe and persistent mental illnesses report receiving no mental health treatments at all (Mojtabai et al., 2009; Wang, Demler, & Kessler, 2002). Because public insurance payments are not aligned with evidence-based practices, few of those in treatment receive effective interventions (Drake, Essock, & Bond, 2009). In essence, the system pays people to remain disabled and gives them little or no support to escape disability. Individuals therefore become accustomed to and socialized into a life of poverty and disability. This situation constitutes what is called the "disability benefits culture." The OECD data cited earlier suggest that the situation is similar in other developed countries.

IMPACT OF DISABILITY ON GENERAL WELL-BEING

The disability benefits culture engenders demoralization and passivity. Certainly part of the reason is unemployment, which leads to negative outcomes, including depression, social isolation, reduced self-esteem, substance use, and a general decline in mental health for everyone (Warr, 1987). Conversely, numerous advantages accrue to individuals with serious mental illnesses who do gain steady employment. These advantages include increased self-esteem, decreased psychiatric symptoms, reduced social disability, and overall greater subjective quality of life (Bond, Resnick et al., 2001; Burns et al., 2009; Kukla, Bond, & Xie, 2012; Mueser et al., 1997). For those who become steady workers, mental health treatment costs decline dramatically over the long term after adjusting for morbidity/needs (Bush, Drake, Xie, McHugo, & Haslett, 2009). In essence, employment helps people to escape from the disabled mental patient role and establish a new identity as a working, contributing citizen.

Despite this, plentiful international evidence indicates that rates of employment among people with mental illness are especially low. In Europe, for example, one international study of people with schizophrenia found that the rates of those in work ranged between 5% (London, UK) and 23% (Verona, Italy) (Thornicroft et al., 2004). These very low work participation rates have important consequences. The loss of the opportunity to work is by far the single greatest contributor to the costs of mental health in Europe, for example, accounting for two-thirds of the total mental health care–related costs in Sweden, and 59% of the total costs in Switzerland (Salize et al., 2009).

The interrelationships between mental health problems and employment are many and various. As well as the link with individual well-being, employment is a major contributor to national productivity and competitiveness, and also has implications for the sustainability of social welfare systems. Indeed, the challenge is growing: increasing rates of absenteeism, earlier retirement, and exclusion from the workforce due to mental health problems, particularly stress and depression, now account for an ever greater share of long-term social welfare benefits (Dewa, McDaid, & Ettner, 2007).

HOW CAN SCIENCE HELP?

Throughout the history of health care, not just mental health care, incorrect and often harmful clinical traditions, theories, and treatments have dominated. The only way to avoid or correct these mistakes and to ensuring that interventions are improving valued health outcomes is to use the scientific method. Are people doing better? This question cannot be answered by appeals to authority, intuition, clinical experience, theory, or any untested beliefs. As the enormous achievements in cancer therapies attest (Mukherjee, 2010), a scientific approach to evidence-based health-care is the only valid alternative. We argue throughout this book that we should be able to measure whether or not people are reaching their employment goals.

Traditionally, mental health and rehabilitation interventions have been based on theories, values, assumptions, innovations, and so on. These were all good sources of ideas, but they were not tempered by scientific testing. A scientific approach establishes specific procedures for developing and testing interventions and measuring processes and outcomes—in this case employment—in a stepwise fashion. Each new idea is tested in an unbiased fashion to see if it adds something to meaningful outcomes. For example, does a procedure improve the time to first job, performance on the job, satisfaction with the job, tenure on the job, long-term employment, wages, social supports, or some other intrinsically meaningful outcome?

As in medicine, we want to be certain that we are focused on the correct outcomes. Improving a physiological measure, a symptom score, or performance in a training setting can be misleading unless it also enhances something that the individual values. Ability to walk to the dining hall is meaningful; an increased spirometer performance is not. Similarly, having a job that one enjoys is meaningful; improving performance in a training situation may not be.

Interventions that help people to achieve meaningful goals are called evidence-based practices. Simply put, evidence-based practices are demonstrably effective—interventions that produce measurable outcomes under scientific conditions. Most people think that science has always been the criterion for medicine, psychology, and mental health care. Doesn't everyone want interventions that are effective? But other goals, such as profits, have often determined care. Furthermore, a variety of objections have impeded the development and use of evidence-based practices, as we will discuss in future chapters.

In the final section of this chapter we identify a set of criteria for evaluating the value and utility of a mental health intervention. These criteria are far broader than the parochial standards commonly used to establish a practice as "evidence-based." Too many so-called evidence-based practices in the mental health field are so narrow and specialized to be of little value, while other practices may be powerful but require clinical training and sophistication beyond the reach of most practitioners in the U.S. public mental health system (Drake & Bond, 2010). The criteria we list below have provided a template for shaping our research program over the past two decades and serve as a guide to the contents of this book.

IDEAL COMPONENTS OF AN EVIDENCE-BASED PRACTICE

Many frameworks have been proposed for identifying evidence-based practices. All emphasize empirical support from methodologically rigorous studies (Chambless & Ollendick, 2001). Meta-analysis is often used (Bero & Drummond, 1995). While both the evidence for the effectiveness of an intervention and methods used to evaluate this evidence are fundamental to identifying an evidence-based practice, such frameworks fall short of encompassing ideal criteria for a mental health intervention. For example, certain types of skills training have been designated as evidence-based practices based on evidence from multiple randomized controlled trials that use behaviors commonly measured in the therapy session (e.g., response to role plays) rather than measures of intrinsically valued community functioning.

Here we draw on evidence-based practice formulations that employ a broader set of practical and policy relevant criteria. Leff (2005) suggested 11 guidelines, including *availability of fidelity scales, inclusion of outcomes that have clinical and policy significance, measurement of long-term outcomes, and collection of information on dissemination efforts.* Mueser and Drake (2005) noted the following key elements: *transparency of the review process, standardization of the intervention, controlled research, replication, and meaningful outcomes.* Schutz, Rivers, and Ratusnik (2009) argued for a balance between rigor and relevance, while Baker, McFall, and Shoham (2009) highlighted *efficacy, effectiveness, cost-effectiveness,* and *scientific plausibility.* Bond and Campbell (2008) proposed these criteria: *clearly defined, designates the target group for whom it is intended, shown effective in a set of rigorous research studies, independently replicated by at least two research groups, addresses important needs in the target population,* and *capable of implementation in a wide range of settings.* Finally, the

"RE-AIM" framework considers the *reach, efficacy, adoption, implementation,* and *maintenance* of an intervention in assessing its practical utility (Glasgow, Vogt, & Boles, 1999).

Drawing from these formulations, we have proposed that an ideal mental health intervention should (1) be well defined, (2) reflect client goals, (3) be consistent with societal goals, (4) demonstrate effectiveness, (5) yield durable outcomes, (6) produce minimal side effects, (7) have reasonable costs, (8) be adaptable to diverse communities and client subgroups, and (9) be relatively easy to implement (Bond, Drake, & Becker, 2010).

(1) *Be well defined.* Until recent years, investigators rarely provided adequate descriptions of program models (Brekke, 1988; Michie, Fixsen, Grimshaw, & Eccles, 2009). Typically interventions were underspecified or based primarily on broad value statements. In such circumstances, understanding the research findings or building a cumulative science was impossible. A minimum requirement for an evidence-based practice is that it is operationally defined. The definition must articulate the staffing, structure, and operation of the model, and specify the interventions used. To meet this criterion, a practice manual should specify model components. In addition, ensure that a particular program follows practice standards requires a valid fidelity scale that measures adherence to a program model (Bond, Evans, Salyers, Williams, & Kim, 2000).

From its inception, the IPS model has always included articulation and refinement of model principles and operational definitions of model components. We discuss this conceptual work and related empirical studies in Chapter 4.

(2) *Reflect client goals.* A program model should align with the goals of the clients receiving the services. This criterion addresses the pervasive problem of disengagement from mental health services; over half of the population of individuals with serious mental illness receive no services whatsoever. The reasons are complex and diverse but include unacceptability of the services (Drake & Essock, 2009). For example, day treatment and group homes are contrary to most clients' preferences and aspirations (Corrigan, Mueser, Bond, Drake, & Solomon, 2008). Mental health practices should reflect client goals and preferences and be delivered within a shared decision making framework (Edwards & Elwyn, 2009).

The primacy of client preferences is a theme throughout this book. In the first three chapters we summarize the many surveys documenting the central role of employment in the goal hierarchy of people with serious mental illness. In our long-term studies, as reviewed in Chapter 5, we document the central role of work in recovery stories, mirroring what many others have reported.

(3) *Be consistent with societal goals.* The goals of an evidence-based practice should also be congruent with societal goals. When a practice has positive societal consequences, its value is greatly enhanced. For example, a program providing housing to homeless individuals not only improves their quality of life, but also enhances the community at large.

Society includes employers, the general public and its interest in public safety, and family members. Societal goals are imperfectly represented in laws, governmental policies, and cultural norms, as we discuss in Chapter 12. In the area of employment, the Americans with Disabilities Act reflects the societal goal that everyone deserves a chance to work. The IPS model is congruent with this legislation. In some cases, policies are misaligned to the implementation of evidence-based practices, but in these cases, the problem often resides in the policy, not in the evidence-based practice.

(4) *Demonstrate effectiveness.* The criteria for establishing effectiveness (and efficacy) have been widely discussed in the literature; they include use of rigorous research designs and credible control groups, replication by different research groups, studies conducted in real world settings, low dropout rates, large effect sizes, and consistency of findings across studies.

Program effectiveness obviously lies at the heart of what it means to be an evidence-based practice. Although relatively recently developed as a model, IPS has amassed a considerable body of research evaluating its effectiveness of IPS, as reviewed in Chapter 5.

(5) *Yield durable outcomes.* The impact of psychosocial interventions commonly attenuates over time, especially once the intervention ends. One partial solution is to offer an intervention on a time-unlimited basis (Test, 1992). However, interventions are clearly most valuable if they lead to stable and enduring changes. In the recovery ideology, interventions should reduce dependence on the mental health system over time (Anthony, Cohen, Farkas, & Gagne, 2002). In Chapter 5 we also examine long-term outcomes from IPS.

(6) *Produce minimal side effects.* Many medical interventions (such as medications) successfully alleviate symptoms but also unfortunately produce undesirable side effects. Psychosocial programs can also have unintended negative effects. For example, day programs segregate people from society and convey messages that clients do not belong in integrated settings and need professionals to help them function. For a psychosocial program to be considered an evidence-based practice, its side effects should not offset its benefits.

In Chapter 6 we review the body of research examining the broader impact of IPS on non-vocational outcomes, that is, the broader impact of IPS beyond the work place. The findings regarding the "spread" of influence of IPS are complicated, but the good news is that IPS exceeds the minimal standard in many areas of medicine of avoiding intolerable side effects.

(7) *Have reasonable costs*. Providers in public mental health must consider the financial risks associated with adopting a new practice (Hyde, Falls, Morris, & Schoenwald, 2003; Panzano & Roth, 2006). For state mental health policy, cost-effectiveness and cost offsets are critically important. We review the economic impact of IPS in Chapter 7.

(8) *Be adaptable to diverse communities and client subgroups*. Practices should also be transportable to diverse communities and acceptable to a wide range of client subgroups. Many evidence-based practices have been studied narrowly, e.g., in urban areas, predominantly with Caucasian clients, or in a single country. Some European researchers have questioned whether evidence-based practices developed in the United States are applicable in their health care systems (Burns, 2000). With regard to different ethno-racial client groups, research is often nonexistent. Evidence-based practices are often implemented in diverse ethnic groups without modification and without consideration of culture (Carpenter-Song et al., 2010). In Chapter 8 we review an extensive literature on the generalizability of the IPS model.

(9) *Be relatively easy to implement*. A useful intervention must be relatively easy to implement. It should also be capable of broad implementation—termed *scalability*. By contrast, if the model is too clinically complex, its wide-scale adoption is more difficult, especially in service systems in which most practitioners lack advanced clinical training. One factor influencing ease of implementation is acceptability of the program model to practitioners (Addis, Wade, & Hatgis, 1999). Ease of implementation has become even more important with the rapid turnover of the mental health workforce (Woltmann et al., 2008). In Chapter 10 we examine the growing body of evidence regarding implementation of IPS and its sustainability over time.

2

EVOLUTION OF PSYCHIATRIC
REHABILITATION SERVICES
IN THE UNITED STATES

Not until the passage of the Barden–LaFollette Act of 1943 was psychiatric disability recognized as a condition eligible for vocational rehabilitation (Rubin & Roessler, 2001). Even after that legislation was passed, people with psychiatric disabilities had difficulty accessing vocational rehabilitation services (Andrews et al., 1992; Marshak, Bostick, & Turton, 1990). But starting in the 1950s, when deinstitutionalization led to increasing numbers of people with serious mental illness returning to the community, the need for vocational services became apparent. Even through the late 1980s (and even to the present!), however, many mental health and rehabilitation professionals resisted the notion that competitive employment was a viable option for people with mental illness.

Following deinstitutionalization, vocational rehabilitation for people with psychiatric disorders went through several phases (Bond, 1992). In the 1950s and 1960s, vocational programs arose in a variety of institutional settings: hospitals, sheltered workshops, and halfway houses (Black, 1988). People demonstrated the ability to work in these settings, but they rarely transitioned to regular jobs in the community. In parallel, the optimism that created these facility-based efforts never produced a focus on competitive employment. Institutional work settings—segregated and stultifying, and with low expectations—would seem to be a vestige of the institutionalization era. Nevertheless, they survive in many places, particularly day hospital settings, sheltered workshops, and work enclaves within hospitals, because they are easy to supervise and easy to bill for.

In the 1970s and early 1980s, community mental health centers and comprehensive rehabilitation centers appeared throughout the United States. The pioneers of this era, however, were psychosocial rehabilitation centers such as Fountain House in New York (Malamud & McCrory, 1988; Vorspan, 1992), Thresholds in

Chicago (Dincin, 1975), and the Club in Piscataway, NJ (Lehrer & Laniol, 1977). Following the innovations first developed by John Beard at Fountain House in New York (Beard, Propst, & Malamud, 1982), these centers implemented transitional employment programs. Transitional employment jobs were in community businesses but were temporary, part-time, managed by the psychosocial rehabilitation program, and intended for training. The goal was that after one or usually more of these training experiences, people would transition to regular employment. These programs eventually became part of the services offered by a minority of community support programs and community mental health centers around the United States. Although the transitional employment model was never validated by controlled research, it provided an important transition for mental health programs toward the idea of community inclusion. Psychosocial rehabilitation centers using transitional employment continue to flourish in several states. They often provide supported employment now as well as other valued services such as social and housing supports.

In the 1990s optimism regarding vocational rehabilitation increased again as a number of vocational models appeared. In addition to transitional employment, influential vocational models included the psychiatric rehabilitation model, the job club model, the assertive community treatment model, and others.

The Center for Psychiatric Rehabilitation at Boston University developed a conceptually grounded approach with roots in client-centered therapy and skills training; the vocational aspect of the model followed a "choose-get-keep" sequence, with skills training at each step (Danley & Anthony, 1987). The emphasis on pre-employment career exploration might be questioned now, and the only randomized controlled study of the model was unsuccessful (Rogers, Anthony, Lyass, & Penk, 2006). Nevertheless, several aspects of the approach have been influential, especially its emphasis on respect for the client and the client's preferences regarding work. Clients understandably feel more satisfied with individualized job searches based on their preferences, and honoring their preferences can result in longer job tenure (Becker, Drake, Farabaugh, & Bond, 1996).

The job club was an intensive behavioral counseling approach based on instrumental learning principles, emphasizing interpersonal skills, a social information network, and motivational factors (Azrin & Philip, 1979). The model prioritized activities close to the job search (Vandergoot, 1987), but relied on a self-directed job search and did not address job retention. The lack of professional intervention in the job search and follow-along in this model probably accounted for poor outcomes among clients with serious mental disorders (Bond, 1992; Corrigan, Reedy, Thadani, & Ganet, 1995).

Assertive community treatment emphasized training in the community on practical skills, including vocational skills, and long-term supports in the community (Stein & Test, 1980). Most studies of assertive community treatment have not demonstrated superior competitive employment outcomes (Bond, Drake, Mueser, & Latimer, 2001; Kirsh & Cockburn, 2007; Lurie, Kirsh, & Hodge, 2007), perhaps because the vocational aspect of the model was not clearly specified. But in the 1990s, the assertive community treatment program in Madison, WI, began to move toward supported employment approaches by directly helping people find regular jobs in the community, and the Madison program has reported better employment outcomes (Russert & Frey, 1991).

OTHER INFLUENCES

In addition to vocational models, other social, political, clinical, and economic factors affected the development of supported employment. We briefly overview several of these factors to establish the context for supported employment research. For clients, the recovery movement symbolized this sea change. For family members, the formation of the National Alliance on Mentally Illness was pivotal. For professionals, new psychosocial approaches based on promoting strengths rather than treating deficits, new medicines with the promise of less disabling side effects, and a focus on evidence-based medicine began to promote optimism regarding treatment outcomes. All of these forces influenced the development of IPS supported employment.

Advocacy. The central figures in community mental health care are of course people with mental illnesses. Spurred by bleak biomedical models that emphasized chronic illness and poor prognosis, inadequate community-based treatment systems, widespread stigmatization, and psychiatry's preoccupation with medications, mental health care recipients began to organize in the 1940s to provide mutual support and to seek more effective services in the community (Dincin, 1975). The consumer movement has taken myriad forms, but personal stories of recovery have been a consistent and dominant theme (Deegan, 1988; Fergeson, 1992; Glater, 1992; Leete, 1993; Ralph, 2000). Recovery stories emphasize finding meaningful activities that reinforce a sense of purpose and accomplishment. They provide different and unique voices, but most endorse the opportunity to work. As Nicole Clevenger (2008) wrote, "Work is not part of my recovery; work is my recovery."

Although mental health service users have been at center stage, families have been their primary supporters and the primary political advocates for changes in the mental health system (Hall, Edgar, & Flynn, 1997; Hall, Graf, Fitzpatrick, Lane, & Birkel, 2003; NAMI, 2006, 2011; Noble, Honberg, Hall, & Flynn, 1997). With political empowerment, families have stimulated numerous positive changes. First, families have emphasized the need to provide mental health services that are oriented toward independence, functioning, and quality of life, not just stabilization of illness or living outside of the hospital. Second, families have demanded access to accurate information regarding mental illnesses and treatments for themselves and for their client family members, and collaborative participation in the treatment process and service system planning process. Information is of course empowering because it reveals the problems that clients have had accessing effective rehabilitative services. For example, families long ago identified vocational services as their relatives' most common unmet need (Steinwachs, Kasper, & Skinner, 1992). Third, family organizations decried the ineffectiveness of traditional vocational services (Noble, Honberg, Hall, & Flynn, 1997). Finally, families have been concerned with helping their relatives to become self-sufficient so that they can provide for themselves and pursue satisfying lives when parents and other family members are no longer available (Lefley, 1987). Family organizations have recognized the potential of supported employment to promote competitive jobs, decent wages, real independence, and true community integration rather than segregation and dependence on the mental health system.

Innovative approaches to community mental health. The developers of assertive community treatment emphasized the importance of integrating a variety of services through the vehicle of the multidisciplinary treatment team (Test & Stein, 1976). To avoid service fragmentation and diffusion of responsibility, the teams provided nearly all services by including clinicians from different disciplines on the team, by providing different work shifts to ensure 24-hour access to clients, and by daily communication. Over time, as other components of community-based care have evolved and been refined, they are easily integrated into the structure of the 24-hour multidisciplinary team because the team provides appropriate services directly rather than by referral. That is, as approaches to crisis intervention, family psychoeducation, treatment of co-occurring substance abuse, supported employment, and other interventions have evolved, they have been rapidly and successfully incorporated into the multidisciplinary team model (Allness & Knoedler, 2003; Liberman, Hilty, Drake, & Tsang, 2001; Stein & Santos, 1998). Employment has for years been a central concept of the assertive community treatment approach, as more clients became interested in working and succeeded in competitive jobs (Test, 1992; Test, Allness, & Knoedler, 1995). Reviews of assertive community treatment do indicate, however, that the vocational component is often omitted from replication efforts and that employment outcomes do not improve without the supported employment component (Bond, Drake, Mueser, & Latimer, 2001; Mueser, Bond, Drake, & Resnick, 1998; Phillips et al., 2001).

At the same time that Stein and Test were pioneering a community-based approach to combining mental health and social services, Charles Rapp and his colleagues from the field of social work were innovating an even more radical departure from traditional approaches (Rapp, 1993; Rapp & Goscha, 2011). Recognizing that values, language, concepts, roles, and all of the other determinants of stigma combined to reinforce the negative aspects of having an illness, they attempted to reverse the long-standing medical focus on psychopathology by emphasizing strengths—the client's own abilities as well as the positive potential of his or her living environment—rather than weaknesses. The client (or mental health service user) was conceptualized as the citizen with rights to be the director of services. Traditional emphasis on training, treating, and changing the recipient of mental health care was eschewed in favor of a new emphasis on integration, normalization, resilience, hope, environmental strengths, and recovery. Among the fundamental tenets of the strengths model is the belief that people with mental illness can use their own strengths and the natural strengths of community environments to achieve their personal goals; to develop hope, confidence, and self-esteem; and to attain success, satisfaction, independence, and quality of life. This process occurs one step at a time, and people need access to resources, opportunities, and social supports to succeed. According to the strengths approach, ensuring that these facilitative elements are available should be the central task of the mental health system. Because most people with mental illness identify competitive work as one of their primary goals, the strengths model has emphasized supported employment for years (Rapp & Goscha, 2011).

Shared decision making. The movement toward client education, informed choice, and shared decision making has received even more attention and research support in general medicine than in psychiatric rehabilitation (Wennberg, 2010). In a wide variety of medical areas, such hypertension, back pain, breast cancer, prostate disease, and diabetes, clinical approaches have moved away from the "doctor as authority" model toward an approach that involves providing patients with all available information about their illnesses and treatments so that they can be actively involved in choosing their treatments. Moreover, research indicates that involving clients in the process of making medical decisions leads to better outcomes, not just in terms of satisfaction and adherence but also in terms of biomedical parameters, e.g., blood pressure and blood sugar levels. Mental health providers have been relatively paternalistic in the area of shared decision making, possibly due to the belief that people with mental illness have impaired decisional capacity much more often than this is actually true.

Even some approaches to supported employment have implied incompetence on the part of clients by, for example, assuming that months of counseling are needed to help the client choose a realistic work goal. As we discuss below, research shows that nearly all people with serious mental illness who express an interest in employment already have a realistic work goal. Furthermore, and in support of the shared decision making model, employment in jobs that match their goals results in greater satisfaction and longer job tenure than when they are placed in available but non-matching jobs.

Outcomes research. Research on the long-term outcomes of mental illness, even the most severe illness of schizophrenia, has never been totally bleak

(Bleuler, 1911). As an antidote to misinformation regarding the course of mental illness, Strauss, Harding, McGlashan, and others have attempted to educate the mental health field to the finding that schizophrenia, like other psychiatric disorders, has a variable course with many good outcomes and a likelihood of functional recovery for many clients (Harding, Strauss, Hafez, & Liberman; McGlashan, 1988; Strauss, Hafez, Lieberman, & Harding, 1985). Furthermore, Desisto et al. (1995) have also argued from long-term follow-up studies that an emphasis on community-based rehabilitation rather than hospital-based care substantially affects functional outcomes. That is, clients who are in systems of care that emphasize community integration, continuity of familial and social supports, and access to competitive work roles have better long-term outcomes.

New medications. The advent of a series of new antipsychotic drugs, starting with clozapine, energized the field of psychiatry with a more hopeful view of recovery (Weiden, Aquila, & Standard, 1996). Many clients reported substantial improvements with the new medications (Mellman et al., 2001). The possibility that new medications would enable people to benefit more substantially from rehabilitative and recovery-oriented approaches received great publicity, but thus far research has not shown that the newer antipsychotic medications produce functional improvements (Percudani, Barbui, & Tansella, 2004; Resnick et al., 2008).

3

ORIGINS OF INDIVIDUAL PLACEMENT AND SUPPORT

The Individual Placement and Support model was inspired by the supported employment model of the 1980s, which developed as a reaction to "train–place" models that dominated the vocational rehabilitation field. "Train–place" or "step-wise" vocational models assume that the individual benefits from some form of training, instruction, or practice in a protected but artificial setting before entering a competitive work role. Competitive jobs are defined as: paying at least minimum wage and the wage that others receive performing the same work, based in community settings alongside others without disabilities, and not reserved for people with disabilities.

Up until the late 1980s, stepwise models of vocational services were widely accepted as best practices in the vocational rehabilitation field. As described by Black (1988), these included sheltered workshops, transitional employment, and set-aside jobs. In the United States, a federal agency, the National Institute for the Severely Handicapped, funds a substantial number of set-side jobs each year. "Social firms"—businesses employing people with and without disabilities and receiving government subsidies—have been popular in Europe and other parts of the world since the late 1960s. Over the past half-century, traditional approaches to vocational rehabilitation have also included other stepwise approaches, such as pre-employment training of various types (e.g., skills training, trial work programs, work adjustment jobs, enclave jobs, and businesses run by mental health programs). The rationale for all of these programs was that clients with serious mental illness and other disabilities were ultimately capable of working but that they needed a gradual introduction because of their lack of skills and experience in the work sphere. Another argument made by stepwise proponents was that competitive employment was too stressful. The assumption was that after gaining

24

experience in protected work or vocational training settings clients would be more capable of succeeding in competitive employment.

Stepwise approaches have been criticized on several fronts. People are often not motivated in practice settings; work tasks rarely match their interests; skills do not generalize; predicting the skills one will need before the job is identified is impossible; people tend to lose interest and motivation during the training; and there is little or no evidence that these types of experiences really help people move on to competitive employment (Bond, 1992, 1998).

Wehman and colleagues first described supported employment as a "place–train" approach to vocational rehabilitation in the early 1980s (Wehman, 1986; Wehman & Moon, 1988). Working in the developmental disabilities field, they were able to demonstrate that the approach of seeking rapid placement into competitive employment, followed by specifically targeted job training and support, was superior to pre-employment "train–place" approaches. The supported employment approach was soon adopted in the mental health field by a number of leaders in the psychiatric rehabilitation movement (Anthony & Blanch, 1987; Danley & Anthony, 1987; Fabian, 1989a; Mellen & Danley, 1987; Noble, Conley, Banerjee, & Goodman, 1991; Trotter, Minkoff, Harrison, & Hoops, 1988).

The basic rationale for a place–train approach is simple and straightforward. Without knowing ahead of time what type of job an individual will obtain, training the person for specific skills, including social skills, that might be needed for success on a particular job may be inefficient. For example, practicing food preparation skills may give little benefit to an individual who obtains a gardening job, and practicing social skills will be largely irrelevant (at least in the work environment) for another person who obtains work as a housekeeper. In other words, the use of pre-employment training assumes that learned skills transfer to different situations and different tasks, but for individuals with major mental illness, this turns out to be inaccurate.

Another problem with preparatory skills training is the unappealing nature of the training situation. Many pre-employment training or work adjustment sites are frankly boring, unchallenging, and unrealistic (Dincin, 1975). Clients know these are not competitive jobs, not the jobs they want, and not the skills they need (Estroff, 1981; Quimby, Drake, & Becker, 2001). Hence they appear to be uninterested or unmotivated. Vocational staff members often misinterpret clients' disinterest as representing personality traits (e.g., "laziness") or illness (e.g., negative symptoms) rather than understandable reactions to unchallenging and artificial work environments (Schultheis & Bond, 1993). On the other hand, it commonly happens in supported employment programs that an individual who previously showed no interest in job training situations surprises everyone by performing at a much higher level in a competitive job of her choice.

Determining needed skills and supports in the context of an intact competitive job is relatively straightforward. The individual has a job he is interested in doing, he has real demands for performance, he can see that he needs specific skills to do the job successfully, and he experiences a real social situation on the job. At this point an employment specialist and a team can be more helpful. Along with the client, they can identify and develop the needed skills and supports.

Wehman (1986) clearly described the place–train approach as fundamental to supported employment. As a result of lobbying efforts by proponents of traditional vocational services invested in defining supported employment as broadly as possible, however, the Rehabilitation Act Amendment of 1986, which codified supported employment in law, specified competitive employment, follow-along supports, and emphasis on the most severely disabled clients, without requiring a place–train approach. Thus, a wide variety of programs claimed to offer supported employment, many of which continued to rely on train–place methods.

COLLABORATIVE EMPIRICISM

As Becker and Drake began to implement supported employment programs in New Hampshire in the late 1980s (joined by Bond in 1994), we received enormous amounts of help not only from clients but also from colleagues who were already doing supported employment. One problem, however, was that we often received conflicting advice. This situation is not atypical in the field of mental health services because there is often so little solid information available to guide service developments. The task therefore is to clarify opposing ideas, to collect data from natural experiments, to measure outcomes carefully in relation to services, and to set up controlled experiments when the field is ready to focus on specific questions. In each of these steps, clients, families, practitioners, and mental health administrators are considered full partners with the research team. We share all data with our partners and make collaborative decisions about next steps and needed studies. This is the method of collaborative empiricism – improving services through continuous feedback and the interplay between practice ideas and actual outcome data (Mueser & Drake, 2005). The approach of collaborative empiricism parallels continuous quality improvement methods except that it is more formal, using research-quality data (Dickey & Sederer, 2001).

In regard to supported employment, the field was ripe for this approach. Political pressures from many sources focused attention on improving employment outcomes for clients with serious mental illness. In New Hampshire, leaders of the Division of Behavioral Health responded to the demands from clients and family members by identifying employment outcomes as a priority area and providing small financial incentives to regional mental health programs to improve rates of employment (Rapp et al., 2005). Beginning in 1989, the Division of Behavioral

Health asked our group of mental health services researchers at Dartmouth to help by clarifying service models, documenting changes in the vocational service system, studying outcomes, conducting controlled clinical trials, and suggesting policy changes.

THE EVOLUTION OF THE IPS RESEARCH PROGRAM

One of the hallmarks of the IPS model, setting it apart from many psychiatric rehabilitation practices, has been the close connection between model development and expansion and rigorous research evaluation. A quality improvement feedback loop has been part of the evolutionary process.

By way of introduction to the remaining chapters in this book, we briefly review in this section the history of IPS research from its initial stages of development in the early 1990s to the present. In Chapter 9 we offer a paradigmatic description for the development of evidence-based practice. But in practice, stages of research on a program model do not evolve linearly in a tidy fashion. Research on real world problems is "messy." It proceeds on the basis of serendipity and a host of other nonscientific considerations. Nevertheless, we propose that the IPS research program is notable for its breadth and to a large extent its orderly development, as suggested by Table 3-1.

The IPS model was developed in response to a statewide need for vocational services within the New Hampshire public mental health system (Becker & Drake, 1993; NIMH, 1999). The first formal evaluation of the IPS model evaluated the replacement of day treatment with IPS (Drake et al., 1994). This initial pre-post study established proof of concept, demonstrating the effectiveness of IPS and also the lack of unintended negative outcomes (Torrey, Becker, & Drake, 1995). Fortuitously, in this initial study, it was possible to compare the converting site to a similar site that did not convert. As discussed in Chapter 5, these evaluations of day treatment conversions were replicated in several subsequent studies. Replication is the hallmark of scientific advances, and this feature of IPS research is one of its strengths.

The positive outcomes in the initial IPS demonstration study laid the foundation for the first randomized controlled study, which was conducted in two community mental health centers (Drake, McHugo, Becker, Anthony, & Clark, 1996). Another distinguishing feature of IPS research has been its firm grounding in real world settings; virtually all of the research has been conducted under these conditions. Subsequently, over a dozen high-quality replication studies of IPS have been conducted, as discussed in Chapter 5. These have not been exact replications, although most have shared some common methodological features. The trade-offs between exact replication and modification in methods is a key issue, which we discuss below. Another distinctive feature of most of the

TABLE 3-1 EVOLUTION OF THE IPS RESEARCH PROGRAM

Type of Research	Purpose	Example
Needs assessments	Identify need	(NIMH, 1999)
Pre-post studies	Establish proof of concept	(Drake et al., 1994)
Quasiexperimental studies	Evaluate effectiveness	(Drake et al., 1994)
Initial randomized controlled trials	Evaluate effectiveness	(Drake, McHugo, Becker, Anthony, & Clark, 1996)
Fidelity scale development	Assess model integrity	(Bond, Becker, & Drake, 2011)
Ethnographic studies	Understand client experiences and sociocultural context	(Alverson, Becker, & Drake, 1995)
Replication studies	Establish generalizability	(Drake et al., 1999)
Large-scale registries	Assess generalizability	(Becker et al., 2011)
Large-scale multi-site studies	Demonstrate scalability	(Frey et al., 2011)
Long-term follow-up	Evaluate durability of effects	(Becker, Whitley, Bailey, & Drake, 2007)
Implementation studies	Evaluate implementation	(Bond, McHugo, Becker, Rapp, & Whitley, 2008; Marshall, Rapp, Becker, & Bond, 2008)
Process studies	Understand how IPS works	(Bond & Kukla, 2011a)
Economic studies	Assess costs and cost-effectiveness	(Clark, Xie, Becker, & Drake, 1998; Latimer, Bush, Becker, Drake, & Bond, 2004)
Systematic reviews	Synthesize the IPS literature	(Bond, Drake, & Becker, 2008; Kinoshita et al., 2010)
Augmentations of IPS	Refinement of model	(McGurk, Wolfe, Pascaris, Mueser, & Feldman, 2007)
Policy analyses	Study societal and governmental factors	(Drake, Bond, Thornicroft, Knapp, & Goldman, 2011)

IPS randomized controlled trials is that they have compared newly established IPS programs to alternatives that have been in existence. To some extent, these comparisons have been dictated by the realities in the field; as a newly developed program, established IPS programs simply were not in existence when the initial IPS studies were conducted. As IPS enters its third decade, mature programs are now available in many areas. One issue that needs examining is the relative effectiveness of mature IPS programs compared to those in start-up. Our hypothesis would be that mature programs would be more effective, all things being equal, though newly established programs probably benefit from the enthusiasm and optimism generated by Hawthorne effects (McCarney et al., 2007).

While most research has examined the effectiveness of IPS in improving competitive employment outcomes, there has always been keen interest in the impact of IPS and of employment more broadly on recovery in other life domains, that is, the impact on non-vocational outcomes, as examined in Chapter 6. The study of non-vocational outcomes has been a continuing component in the ongoing program of research evaluating the effectiveness of IPS (e.g., Mueser et al., 1997).

An early and important methodological step was the development and validation of a scale to measure fidelity of IPS implementation (Bond, Becker, Drake, & Vogler, 1997). As discussed in Chapter 4, a validated fidelity scale is crucial for advancement of research on a program model.

From the beginning, IPS researchers have used mixed methods, complementing quantitative research with qualitative methods, including ethnographies (Alverson, Becker, & Drake, 1995). We discuss the importance of this methodological combination below.

A further stage in evaluating IPS programs was to extend the evaluation to multiple sites, if not nationally. Paralleling the distinction in single-site studies between non-experimental and experimental designs, multisite evaluations can be uncontrolled program evaluations, for example, registries, and multisite randomized controlled trials. The outcome reporting in the IPS Learning Collaborative described in Chapter 10 represents one such example (Becker, Drake, & Bond, 2011; Becker et al., 2011). To date, there have been only a couple of large-scale randomized controlled trials (Frey et al., 2011). Such studies are understandably expensive and risky in that it is far more difficult to maintain quality in a multisite study than in a smaller-scale study. But large multisite studies contribute to policy planning, because these studies demonstrate scalability.

The literature on the long-term impact of psychosocial interventions is generally negative. That is, outcomes usually attenuate over time. Given these general findings, the need for long-term follow-up studies of IPS is apparent, as discussed in Chapter 5. As IPS research has matured, we have begun to see long-term follow-up studies (Becker, Whitley, Bailey, & Drake, 2007; Salyers, Becker, Drake, Torrey, & Wyzik, 2004), but larger studies are needed.

In addition to outcome studies, IPS researchers have been examining the barriers and strategies to implementing IPS (Marshall, Rapp, Becker, & Bond, 2008), as discussed in Chapter 10. Relatively few process studies examining specific aspects of the IPS model have been conducted (Bond & Kukla, 2011a).

A crucial consideration for program managers in the wide scale adoption of any evidence-based practice is its cost, as discussed in Chapter 7. Thus economists have studied financial considerations for providing IPS services (Latimer, Bush, Becker, Drake, & Bond, 2004; Salkever, 2011). Another obvious area for further development is in cost-effectiveness research (Clark, 1998). Economic considerations are but one part of the broader domain of policy analysis, such as societal factors, disability and labor laws, and governmental structures promoting or inhibiting the development and sustainment of IPS (Drake, Bond, Thornicroft, Knapp, & Goldman, 2011), as we discuss in Chapter 10.

Throughout its development, IPS research has been subjected to rigorous reviews, as summarized in the Chapter 5. These reviews are critical to ensuring progress in the research program by assessing overall effects, identifying gaps, and suggesting future directions, as discussed in Chapter 11. One byproduct of these reviews has been the recognition of areas of model development and augmentation. The work on adding cognitive remediation to IPS is one example (McGurk, Wolfe, Pascaris, Mueser, & Feldman, 2007).

CHAPTER SUMMARY

In this chapter we have reviewed the historical roots of IPS. The core principles of IPS can be traced back from evidence-based practices in other areas of psychiatric rehabilitation and health care. But for nearly every principle for which we can identify a precedent, we can also identify a tradition that held the exact *opposite* viewpoint. With regard to stepwise models of employment services, this was a deeply held view at the onset of the development of IPS. In particular, the Choose–Get–Keep model of supported employment, which was regarded as the best practice model at the time, strongly encouraged a stepwise approach, asserting that people with serious mental illness needed an extended period of time in vocational preparation before entering a competitive job in order to become work ready and to identify career goals (Anthony & Blanch, 1987). Regarding the separation of vocational and rehabilitation services, advocates for the clubhouse model, which was widely viewed as the prevailing best practice model of psychiatric rehabilitation, strongly asserted the crucial role of separating treatment and rehabilitation, on the theory that clients and practitioners should not confuse treatment services (focused on symptoms and deficits) with rehabilitation (focused on personal goals and functional outcomes) (Noble, Honberg, Hall, & Flynn, 1997). A third example of prevailing wisdom was the belief that clients had unrealistic job preferences, and that the job market should drive the job placement, because it was fruitless to try to arrange job matches. As we note throughout this book, the arbiter of IPS model development has been and will continue to be the empirical evidence rather than theory or clinical wisdom.

II

RESEARCH ON IPS

In Section II we review IPS research. Chapter 4 examines the evidence for the principles of IPS. In the chapters that follow, we examine the employment outcomes and then consider non-vocational outcomes, economic outcomes, generalizability, and research methods.

4

IPS PRINCIPLES

In this chapter we describe the principles of IPS and the research that helped to establish these principles. The pertinent research supporting each of these principles has been reviewed several times over the last two decades (Bond, 1994, 1998, 2004). Over time we have added two new principles to the original set of six principles, based on research and feedback from the field. In 2004, we added a principle emphasizing the role of benefits counseling (Bond, 2004). Recently, we added an eighth principle, identifying systematic job development as critical to ensuring effective IPS services.

The evidence for some IPS principles is well established; for others the evidence is weaker. Moreover, the justification for these principles also derives from a strong value base undergirding the field of psychiatric rehabilitation (Corrigan, Mueser, Bond, Drake, & Solomon, 2008). These principles also reflect the philosophy of shared decision making (Edwards & Elwyn, 2009), as we have discussed in the first part of this book. The principles are as follows:

1. **Competitive Employment:** *Agencies providing IPS services are committed to competitive employment as an attainable goal for clients with serious mental illness seeking employment.*

The competitive employment principle means that IPS programs assist clients to enter into competitive jobs directly. IPS employment specialists do not encourage clients to obtain noncompetitive jobs, which include volunteer jobs, unpaid internships, sheltered work, and set-aside jobs. The focus on direct entry into competitive employment runs counter to the stepwise approach to employment that has long dominated the vocational rehabilitation field, as discussed in the last chapter. Put simply, stepwise approaches are not effective.

Most stepwise approaches have never been evaluated systematically. But the empirical literature on stepwise approaches has consistently demonstrated that they do not lead to competitive employment outcomes, in either the short or long term (Bond, 1992; Bond & Boyer, 1988; Bond, Drake, Becker, & Mueser, 1999; Penk et al., 2010). The two most common outcomes from stepwise programs are that clients prematurely drop out of services, or if they remain, they rarely graduate but instead develop an institutional dependency on the vocational program.

Many studies have raised doubts about the effectiveness of psychiatric rehabilitation day programs for promoting competitive employment (Bond & Dincin, 1986; Dincin & Witheridge, 1982). Studies also have shown that day treatment programs could be discontinued and replaced with IPS with positive outcomes (Drake et al., 1994; Drake, Becker, Biesanz, Wyzik, & Torrey, 1996).

In contrast to stepwise approaches, employment programs focusing on direct entry into competitive employment are congruent with client preferences (Bedell, Draving, Parrish, Gervey, & Guastadisegni, 1998). And, as the remainder of this book documents, competitive employment leads to better outcomes in other life domains.

2. Eligibility Based on Client Choice: *Clients are not excluded on the basis of readiness, diagnoses, symptoms, substance-use history, psychiatric hospitalizations, level of disability, or legal system involvement.* The only requirement for admission to an IPS program is a desire to work in a competitive job. Starting IPS is based on client choice. Agencies develop a culture of work so that all practitioners encourage clients to consider work as a possibility. They ask about work during intake, treatment planning, mental health assessments, and updates. Agencies create opportunities for clients to share their back-to-work stories with other clients and staff, for example in treatment groups, agency-wide meetings, and newsletters. Posters and brochures about work are put in waiting areas and staff offices. When the culture values work, people have the greatest opportunity to develop the confidence to consider work. But clients always determine the timing.

Historically, the vocational rehabilitation system invested heavily in vocational assessment on the assumption that screening for readiness for vocational services would yield a more cost-effective use of federal funding for rehabilitation services (Courtney, 2005). Moreover, many vocational rehabilitation counselors believed that clients with psychiatric disabilities could not work, and their decisions regarding eligibility determination reflected those beliefs (Andrews et al., 1992; Marshak, Bostick, & Turton, 1990). In a landmark article, Anthony and Jensen (1984) reviewed the empirical literature and decisively rebutted widely held assumptions that clinicians could predict who was able to work, and that standardized assessments were an effective means for identifying work readiness.

Starting with the Rehabilitation Act of 1986, the vocational rehabilitation system has embraced the notion of "zero exclusion," which refers to the removal of any precondition for participating in supported employment services related to clinical or work history, substance use, readiness, or any other background factor. One early proponent of the zero exclusion principle was John Beard, founder of the Fountain House clubhouse. In the clubhouse model, the belief is that everyone deserves a chance to work, regardless of history or background (Beard, Propst, & Malamud, 1982). Although the roots of this principle derive from a statement of values, the research has also overwhelmingly supported its validity (Campbell, Bond, & Drake, 2011; Campbell, Bond, Drake, McHugo, & Xie, 2010).

3. Integration of Rehabilitation and Mental Health Services: *IPS programs are closely integrated with mental health treatment teams.* This principle means that IPS specialists participate regularly in treatment team meetings to review client progress. During these meetings, IPS workers review clients on their caseload who are working, people who are seeking work, and also help team members think about work for those who have not been referred to the IPS program. Through frequent communication outside of meetings, IPS workers and treatment team members share information and develop ideas to help clients improve their functional recoveries. Practitioners give clients consistent messages. To facilitate communication, IPS workers and treatment team members share office space.

Historically, mental health and vocational services were separate. One innovation in the IPS model that differentiated it from conventional thinking at the time was that it is a service model embedded within the community mental health system, not the vocational rehabilitation system. This principle was drawn from the multidisciplinary team approach, the guiding principle of the assertive community treatment model (Stein & Test, 1980).

The principle of integrating services has proved to have broader applicability across many areas of mental health, including the integration with substance abuse treatment, physical health care, and many other domains (Corrigan et al., 2008). True integration of vocational services with mental health treatment has been hard for mental health agencies to attain (Campbell et al., 2007), but its role in enhancing employment outcomes is well documented (Cook, Lehman et al., 2005; Drake, Becker, Bond, & Mueser, 2003).

4. Attention to Client Preferences: *Services are based on clients' preferences and choices, rather than providers' judgments.* Staff and clients conduct an individualized job search, based on client preferences, strengths, and work experiences. Clients list jobs they have done in the past, identifying what they liked about previous jobs and how that may relate to other types of jobs. The IPS worker makes suggestions to expand their options. Clients make choices about job types, work settings and environments, wages and hours, and also about services. Clients discuss with their IPS workers the advantages/disadvantages of disclosing to an employer that they have a disability. Clients determine whether the IPS worker will have direct contact with employers on their behalf. Clients communicate the kind of support they want to help keep a job. IPS workers make suggestions about services and support, and they come to an agreement with the client.

Historically, the IPS principle of client choice in vocational services can be traced to the Chose-Get-Keep vocational model (Danley & Anthony, 1987). Predating this perspective was the shared decision making principle in health care (Adams & Drake, 2006), which leads to the same conclusion, that client preferences concerning type and location of employment, as well as the services they receive, are paramount in the vocational process. Federal rehabilitation legislation also affirms the primacy of client self-determination in the Rehabilitation Act Amendments of 1992 (P.L. 102–569).

Within the vocational literature, the research suggests client choice has an important influence on employment outcomes. Several studies have shown that most clients with serious mental illness hold specific occupational preferences, and that these preferences are usually realistic and fairly stable over time (Becker, Bebout, & Drake, 1998; Becker, Drake, Farabaugh, & Bond, 1996; Mueser, Becker, & Wolfe, 2001). Consistent with the IPS model, most IPS clients do obtain jobs consistent with their occupational preferences (Becker, Bebout, & Drake, 1998; Becker et al., 1996; Mueser, Becker, & Wolfe, 2001). Three studies have supported the *occupational matching hypothesis*, which states that clients who obtain jobs matching their initial preferences will be more satisfied with their jobs and will continue working longer than those who are not matched (Becker et al., 1996; Gervey & Kowal, 1994; Mueser, Becker, & Wolfe, 2001).

Occupational preference is but one factor in preferences for employment. A broad construct widely studied within the personnel psychology literature as a predictor of employment outcomes is *person–job fit*, defined as "the compatibility between an individual and a work environment that occurs when their characteristics are well matched" (Kristof-Brown, Zimmerman, & Johnson, 2005, p. 281). Other aspects of the person–job fit besides occupational preferences, such as job location, hours of employment, and wage rate, have been found related to job satisfaction (Abrams, DonAroma, & Karan, 1997; Beveridge & Fabian, 2007). Studies suggest that worker perceptions of job match and job satisfaction soon after beginning a job predict job tenure (Carpenter & Perkins, 1997; Huff, Rapp, & Campbell, 2008; Kukla & Bond, 2012; Resnick & Bond, 2001; Xie, Dain, Becker, & Drake, 1997).

5. Personalized Benefits Counseling: *Employment specialists help clients obtain personalized, understandable, and accurate information about their Social Security, Medicaid, and other government payments.* IPS workers encourage all clients to learn how different work scenarios (i.e., hours and wages or changing jobs) would affect their benefits. A specially trained person provides benefits counseling. IPS workers sometimes provide these services, but full-time benefits counselors are often available through other community agencies.

In Chapter 1 we discussed the benefits trap as a major barrier to employment. In fact, fear of losing benefits is the single most common barrier to seeking employment (MacDonald-Wilson, Rogers, Ellison, & Lyass, 2003; O'Day & Killeen, 2002). Conversely, benefits counseling is a commonly mentioned job-related support (Henry & Lucca, 2002). Practitioners and researchers recognize the importance of the provision of benefits counseling as part of a supported employment program (Evans & Bond, 2008).

Although the crucial role of benefits counseling in IPS is widely recognized, the direct evidence documenting its impact is surprisingly weak. In one study, clients with serious mental illness significantly increased employment earnings after receiving benefits counseling (Tremblay, Smith, Xie, & Drake, 2006). An unpublished program evaluation of benefits counseling also reported positive outcomes (Bailey, Rubin, Fox, & Ley, 2007). Despite the dearth of research, it is nonetheless apparent that benefits counseling is a necessary component of effective IPS services. Studies show that IPS is an effective model for clients receiving Social Security disability benefits (Bond, Xie, & Drake, 2007; Frey et al., 2011).

6. Rapid Job Search: *IPS programs use a rapid job search approach to help clients obtain jobs directly, rather than providing lengthy pre-employment assessment, training, and counseling.* In the first few sessions after program entry, the IPS worker and client build a career profile of the client's preferences, skills, strengths, and previous employment and education. This profile provides direction for the job search and job support. IPS workers, clients, or both start making face-to-face contacts with employers (hiring managers) within a month of starting the IPS program. A rapid job search conveys to the client that the IPS worker is taking his or her goals seriously. It also demonstrates that the IPS worker believes the person has skills and strengths to work a job. Additionally, a rapid job search is direct action toward achieving the client's concrete goal. If the client is uncertain of the type of work he or she wants, the search may begin by directly exploring different types of jobs.

The rapid job search principle has sometimes been incorrectly stated as, and understood to mean, *rapid placement.* But this principle focuses on the process of looking for a job, not the end result. Agencies that establish rapid placement as their goal run the risk of compromising client preferences in the type of job obtained. Obtaining a quick job start simply because a job is available is counterproductive in the long run, because a poor job fit usually leads to job dissatisfaction and ultimately to job loss.

Historically, Wehman (1986) was among the first to contrast the prevailing "train–place" model with a "place–train" model, arguing that work skills taught in a classroom or clinic did not transfer to specific community jobs. In the psychiatric field, Stein and Test (1980) had similarly concluded that transfer of training did not occur from hospital settings to the community. Bond and Dincin (1986) found that prevocational training was not only an unnecessary step in employment process but also was harmful by creating an institutional dependency. Rapp and his colleagues have also documented the dispiriting, demeaning, and infantilizing culture fostered by day treatment centers that organize services around training clients for life outside the day center (Rapp & Goscha, 2011).

The superiority of rapid job search approaches over stepwise preparatory models has been replicated in many studies, including several randomized controlled trials reviewed in Chapter 5. This principle is firmly grounded empirically.

7. Systematic Job Development: *Employment specialists build an employer network based on clients' interests, developing relationships with local employers by making systematic contacts.* Job development is more than contacting employers for job availability, it involves cultivating a relationship. Typically, the purpose of the first employer contact is for the IPS specialist to introduce herself/himself to the hiring manager and request another meeting. The second contact is to learn about the employer's business and human resources. Future contacts are to discuss potential employees when there might be a good job match. People who are new to the position of employment specialist often have not developed skills in making face-to-face employer contacts. Instead they try to find job leads on the Internet or make cold calls to employers and ask directly about job openings.

Historically, clients were encouraged to find jobs on their own. The evidence is quite clear, however, that many people with serious mental illness get discouraged and give up with self-directed job searches (Bond, 1992; Corrigan, Reedy, Thadani, & Ganet, 1995). Many vocational studies suggest that vocational counselors and IPS employment specialists who devote more time to employer contacts have higher job acquisition rates (Leff et al., 2005; Rosenthal, Dalton, & Gervey, 2007; Vandergoot, 1987; Zadny & James, 1977). In recent years, IPS specialists have defined specific job development strategies (Carlson, Smith, & Rapp, 2008; Swanson & Becker, 2010; Swanson, Becker, Drake, & Merrens, 2008), including for clients with criminal justice histories (Swanson, Langfitt-Reese, & Bond, in press). Successful employment specialists devote considerable time to building a network of employers with whom they maintain contact for the sake of matching clients to specific jobs.

8. Time-Unlimited and Individualized Support: *Follow-along supports are individualized and continued for as long as the client wants and needs the support.* IPS workers and other members of the treatment team provide work support.

For example, the psychiatrist might make medication adjustments and the case manager might talk about strategies for managing anxiety on the job in certain situations. Each client has his/her own support needs. One person might need training to follow different bus routes and another client might need to negotiate a job accommodation to work in a quiet area. IPS workers also help clients end jobs and develop a career path. IPS programs provide ongoing support and remain committed to the support of clients long after they have achieved employment, avoiding artificial deadlines for program terminations that may be dictated by funding sources. IPS workers have frequent contact with people as they start a job by meeting weekly and then every other week. Once a client has worked steadily (e.g., for a year), the IPS worker and client discuss transitioning from IPS services. Another team member who regularly meets with the client becomes the key person to ask about work during their routine meetings and helps to solve work problems. The client can return to IPS services if they need additional support in their work lives.

Historically, within the state–federal vocational rehabilitation system, the goal for counselors has been to obtain successful closures, defined primarily in terms of achievement of 90 days of employment. Funding provided by the vocational rehabilitation system has been correspondingly brief. As a consequence, support for clients seeking employment has often been time-limited. Yet the evidence has consistently suggested that clients continue to need support beyond artificial deadlines (Bond & Kukla, 2011a; McHugo, Drake, & Becker, 1998). One of the core elements in the supported employment legislation was the recognition of the importance of ongoing support (Courtney, 2005). Within the psychiatric rehabilitation field, researchers have long recognized that services should be individualized and that long-term supports are necessary (Corrigan et al., 2008).

The principle of ongoing and individualized support has been one of the pillars of supported employment and of IPS. Until recently, the supporting evidence was fragmented, but as reviewed later in this chapter, the evidence base has been growing.

PUTTING IT ALL TOGETHER: THE IPS FIDELITY SCALE

Our explanation of the core principles of IPS gives a broad profile of the IPS model, but a more detailed operational description of program elements is given by the 25-item IPS Fidelity Scale ("IPS-25") (Becker, Swanson, Bond, & Merrens, 2008) (also known as the Supported Employment Fidelity Scale), as shown in Appendix A. The scale presented in Appendix A is a revision of the original 15-item scale first published in 1997 (Bond, Becker, Drake, & Vogler, 1997).

The development of the current scale was prompted by the emerging research over a period of nearly two decades. Although the original scale continues to be widely used, the new scale is more comprehensive, detailed, and research-based. In Chapter 10 we discuss the rationale for the use of fidelity scales for both research and quality improvement purposes (Bond, Evans, Salyers, Williams, & Kim, 2000). We next review the literature supporting the predictive validity of the original 15-item IPS fidelity scale.

Fidelity. As shown in Table 4-1, 10 studies have assessed the predictive validity of the 15-item IPS Fidelity Scale (Becker, Smith, Tanzman, Drake, & Tremblay, 2001; Becker, Xie, McHugo, Halliday, & Martinez, 2006; Bond, 2011; Catty et al., 2008; Henry & Hashemi, 2009; Hepburn & Burns, 2007; McGrew, 2007, 2008; McGrew & Griss, 2005; Resnick, 2009). All of these studies used independent fidelity assessors, typically at least two assessors. In four studies, all the participating sites were explicitly seeking to implement IPS (Becker et al., 2006; Bond 2011; Catty et al., 2008; Resnick, 2009). Although the methodological details varied, the common goal of these studies was to assess the correlation between program fidelity and concurrent site-level employment rates. The most common outcome measure used was competitive employment rate for clients with psychiatric disabilities enrolled in employment services (Becker et al., 2001; Becker, Xie, McHugo, Halliday, & Martinez, 2006; Bond, 2011; Catty et al., 2008; Henry & Hashemi, 2009; Resnick, 2009). Other outcome measures used as criteria for successful employment were successful closure rates from the state vocational rehabilitation agency (Hepburn & Burns, 2007; McGrew, 2007, 2008; McGrew & Griss, 2005), percentage employed 20 hours or more per week (Henry & Hashemi, 2009), and hourly wages (Henry & Hashemi, 2009). As shown in Table 4-1, 6 of the 10 studies reported statistically significant measures of association between fidelity and employment outcome, and two others had results approaching statistical significance. One study did not test for statistical significance, while the remaining study found no differences.

More recently, we have examined the relationship between IPS fidelity and employment outcome using the 25-item IPS fidelity scale (Bond et al., 2012). Findings suggest that the predictive validity is similar for the original and revised scales.

In summary, despite the small number of sites in most studies, the results are relatively consistent. Some of the studies found a significant correlation even though their samples were restricted to sites within a relatively narrow range from moderate to high fidelity (because all were seeking to implement IPS). The finding of a significant positive association between IPS fidelity and employment outcome has been replicated by several research groups, who have found that individual items are positively associated with outcome and that the scale as a whole is a dependable tool for guiding effective practice (Bond, Becker, & Drake, 2011).

TABLE 4-1 ASSOCIATIONS BETWEEN IPS FIDELITY AND COMPETITIVE EMPLOYMENT OUTCOMES

Location	# Sites	Sample Characteristics	Findings	Reference
Vermont	10	Mixed group of employment programs	$r = .76$ ($p < .01$)	Becker et al. (2001)
7 states	26	Sites receiving technical assistance in IPS	$r = .51$ ($p < .01$)	Becker et al. (2006)
National	32	Sites receiving technical assistance in IPS	$r = .35$ ($p < .05$)	Bond (2011)
Indiana	20	SE programs (not specifically IPS)	$r = -.07$ (n.s.)	McGrew & Griss (2005)
Indiana	17	SE programs (not specifically IPS)	$r = .37$ ($p < .06$, one-tailed)	McGrew (2007)
Indiana	23	SE programs (not specifically IPS)	$r = .39$ ($p < .05$, one-tailed)	McGrew (2008)
Maryland	Statewide	Two program types: IPS and other vocational (non-IPS)	Successful VR closures: IPS (60%), Non-IPS (36%)	Hepburn & Burns (2007)
Europe	6	Sites receiving technical assistance in IPS	Meta-regression contrasts with usual services ($p = .08$)	Catty et al. (2008)
Massachusetts	21	SE programs (not specifically IPS)	Odds ratio = 1.24 ($p < .03$)	Henry (2009)
National	21	Sites receiving technical assistance in IPS	Odds ratios 1.09, 1.10, 1.11 (all $p < .05$) at 6, 12, & 18 months	Resnick (2009)

Note: IPS = Individual Placement and Support, SE = supported employment, VR = state vocational rehabilitation agency. From Bond, G. R., Becker, D. R., & Drake, R. E. (2011). Measurement of fidelity of implementation of evidence-based practices: Case example of the IPS Fidelity Scale. *Clinical Psychology: Science and Practice, 18*, 126–141. Reprinted with permission from John Wiley and Sons.

INTENSITY OF IPS SERVICES

Conceptually, the two types of IPS interventions most directly associated with successful employment are job development and follow-along support. Surprisingly, while program fidelity has been widely studied, very little research has been conducted on these two components, even though intuitively one would hypothesize that job development activity would lead to more job starts, while follow-along support would lead to longer job tenure. In part, the lack of research has been a result of the difficulty defining an appropriate statistical model for separating out these two component activities from all the services provided by an employment specialist. In addition, because the individual client patterns of job searching, job starts, and job endings are highly variable, statistically evaluating the association between service intensity (i.e., frequency of employment specialist contacts) and employment outcomes is difficult. In this section we discuss the current knowledge base concerning the relationship between intensity of job development activity and job acquisition, and between follow-along support and job tenure.

Job development. Within the vocational rehabilitation literature, one consistent finding has been amount of contact with employers is the most important factor differentiating clients who gain employment from those who do not (Rosenthal, Dalton, & Gervey, 2007; Vandergoot, 1987; Zadny & James, 1977). This general finding has been shown in the supported employment literature as well. Several studies have found a significant association between intensity of employment specialist assistance during the job finding phase and rate of job starts (Bond, Miller, & Dietzen, 1992; Jones, Perkins, & Born, 2001; Leff et al., 2005; McGuire, Bond, Clendenning, & Kukla, 2011). Leff et al. (2005) found a positive correlation between job development and job acquisition in a multisite study with 1340 clients receiving either supported employment or services as usual. The McGuire et al. (2011) study found a delayed effect in which the positive influence of employment services was not realized until several months later. The authors interpreted this time-lag finding to reflect intensive early job development and initial job acquisition, followed by a tapering off of contacts. In another supported employment study, number of job leads and employer contacts was positively associated with job offers (Larson, Barr, Kuwabara, Boyle, & Glenn, 2007).

None of the preceding studies examined the quality of job development contacts as predictors of outcome. An evaluation of a training program teaching employment specialists techniques to build employer relationships found that the rate of job starts doubled after the training (Carlson, Smith, & Rapp, 2008).

Follow-along support. Ongoing support from employment specialists has been hypothesized as a key to enhancing job tenure after clients obtain competitive work. But empirically based standards for what supports are needed, for how long, at what intensity, and for which kinds of clients have not been established. According to the IPS-25 the standards for frequency of contact are flexible, usually starting with weekly contacts and reducing contacts after stabilization on a job, as appropriate, in accordance with client choice, with increased contact in response to stresses on the job and job losses (Becker et al., 2008). These standards are based on clinical experience; ideally they would be grounded in normative data from successful IPS programs.

Unfortunately, most of the literature on follow-along service in supported employment programs is obsolete. Early supported employment studies reporting frequency of employment specialist contact have limited value for setting benchmarks, because these early programs only remotely resembled the IPS model (Bond, Miller, & Dietzen, 1992; Bybee, Mowbray, & McCrohan, 1995; MacDonald-Wilson, Revell, Nguyen, & Peterson, 1991; Rogers, MacDonald-Wilson, Danley,

Martin, & Anthony, 1997). Somewhat more relevant is a secondary analysis of a study of supported employment and other vocational models, which found two hours of contact per month over a two-year follow-up (Cook et al., 2005). The heterogeneity of programs included in this study makes these data unsuitable for IPS benchmarks.

Another important question is the trajectory of employment services. Based on the original conceptualization of supported employment, the job coaching model, the job coach provided intensive training at the job site and reduced these supports over time as clients learned to perform their job responsibilities (Wehman, 1986). This model was developed for and is applicable to clients with intellectual disabilities, but it is not well suited to most clients with serious mental illness. IPS research has found that few clients require intensive onsite job coaching (Becker & Drake, 2003). While supported employment studies have found a decline in the intensity of supported employment services over time, the timing and extent of this decline has varied across studies (Anderson, 1999; Bond & Kukla, 2011a; Cook et al., 2005; McGuire et al., 2011). One IPS study examining frequency of contact after a client obtained a competitive job found that employment specialists made weekly contact immediately after a job start, within a few months reduced this to monthly, and maintained this frequency thereafter (Bond & Kukla, 2011a).

Some studies have reported a positive association between ongoing support and job tenure. McHugo et al. (1998) found that clients who were working at follow-up were more likely to be receiving follow-along support from the IPS team than those who were unemployed. But follow-along support averaged only about 15 minutes per week. In two long-term studies, clients maintaining steady employment reported that ongoing professional support was a primary factor in their continued success (Becker, Whitley, Bailey, & Drake, 2007; Salyers, Becker, Drake, Torrey, & Wyzik, 2004).

The optimal level of job support undoubtedly fluctuates across time for each client and differs greatly across clients. For example, some clients keep a job over an extended period of time with little assistance from an IPS team, whereas others constantly need the team's assistance. Some research has suggested that additional ongoing support is needed to compensate for severe cognitive impairments and psychiatric symptoms (McGuire et al., 2011; McGurk, Mueser, Harvey, La Puglia, & Marder, 2003; Zito, Greig, Wexler, & Bell, 2007). Consistent with a compensatory hypothesis, an analysis of a state administrative data set concluded that services often increased prior to job loss (Hannah & Hall, 2006).

Finally, one recent IPS study found a small but significant positive correlation ($r = .27$) between frequency of employment specialist contacts and months worked for 142 clients over a two-year follow-up (Bond & Kukla, 2011a). Because this study enrolled clients after they had obtained employment, it eliminated the confounding effects of initial job development.

In summary, the relationship between intensity of employment specialist activity and employment outcomes has not firmly been established, although some studies are suggestive. Moreover, none of the studies reviewed in this section have examined the quality of services, which likely exerts a strong influence on outcome.

EMPLOYMENT SPECIALIST COMPETENCIES

A common finding within and across employment programs is wide variation in success rates for employment specialists, as measured by rates of new job starts, job tenure, and other employment outcome indicators. For example, one study found competitive employment rates among 57 employment specialists ranging from 0% to 80% (Taylor & Bond, submitted). Thus, employment specialist competence is likely a major source of variance in employment outcomes. Few studies, however, have examined this hypothesis.

Four qualitative studies have sought to identify competencies of effective employment specialists. One study contrasted practices in four high-performing mental health centers with four low-performing centers, using employment rates as the performance criterion (Gowdy, Carlson, & Rapp, 2004). The authors concluded that staff in the high-performing sites differed noticeably in their attitudes from those in the low-performing sites. In high-performing sites, the staff were much more hopeful that clients wanted to work and could work, and that stigma was not an insurmountable barrier. In low-performing sites, staff blamed the economy and a host of external factors for their poor performance. The authors also discovered behavioral differences, for example, staff at high-performing sites made more frequent contact with employers (Gowdy, Carlson, & Rapp, 2003). A second qualitative study was based on 22 qualitative interviews with specialists and their supervisors. They identified the following desirable attributes: (1) initiative; (2) outreach; (3) persistence; (4) hardiness; (5) empathy; (6) passion; (7) team orientation; (8) professionalism (Whitley, Kostick, & Bush, 2010). In the third study, the investigators used the method of extreme groups to characterize two subgroups within a large agency providing IPS at multiple sites—most effective and least effective employment specialists. They concluded that the most effective employment specialists managed their time efficiently, developed egalitarian relationships with clients, and collaborated well with other professionals. The least effective employment specialists understood the IPS model but lacked the skills to apply the principles (Glover & Frounfelker, 2011a). Finally, McGurk and Mueser (2006) examined strategies employed by 50 employment specialists. Finding that the more coping strategies suggested, the higher the proportion of clients working on their caseload.

A survey using an IPS knowledge quiz found that employment specialists employed by high-fidelity IPS programs were more knowledgeable about IPS principles than a comparison group of vocational counselors working in programs following other models (Dreher, Bond, & Becker, 2010). IPS supervisors were more knowledgeable than line staff, and respondents from the comparison group who believed their program followed the IPS model were no more knowledgeable than respondents who subscribed to another vocational model. This study suggests a role for IPS supervisors in imparting basic information about the IPS model. It also suggests that knowledge of IPS may be a necessary condition for implementing IPS with high fidelity.

A cross-sectional study of 57 employment specialists examining self-report and supervisor ratings found that employment specialists who spent more of their time in the community, had a higher rate of client contact, and had higher performance ratings, had better employment outcomes (Taylor & Bond, submitted). This study also found that many employment specialist characteristics, including knowledge of the IPS model, optimism, conscientiousness, and self-efficacy, did not predict better outcomes.

CHAPTER SUMMARY

Research has shaped IPS guidelines in the form of eight principles and a 25-item fidelity scale. The relationship between IPS fidelity and employment outcome is strong. But there is a lack of research to make recommendations on intensity of IPS services. Some research suggests a relationship between job development and job acquisition. A few studies have shown an association between job support and tenure. The timing and type of support is likely to be individualized. Employment specialist competencies are likely to influence outcomes, yet these have not been rigorously studied. Some studies have suggested that employment specialist characteristics, attitudes, and knowledge influence the quality of services and outcomes.

IPS developed not so much as a unique approach to supported employment but rather as an attempt to optimize and standardize supported employment for people with psychiatric disabilities by combining the information on services and outcomes from many research studies. Over the two decades of development of the IPS model, our goal has been to review clinical and research experience continuously and to synthesize the principles of supported employment that are empirically related to successful vocational outcomes.

5

EMPLOYMENT OUTCOMES

In this chapter we examine the evidence for the effectiveness of IPS, summarizing four lines of research: (1) a group of quasiexperimental studies of programs converting their services from day treatment to IPS; (2) 16 randomized controlled trials comparing IPS to alternative vocational programs; (3) a detailed analysis of a combined data set from four randomized controlled trials examining a comprehensive set of competitive employment measures; and (4) long-term follow-up studies of IPS, including two with a follow-up period of eight years or more.

DAY TREATMENT CONVERSION STUDIES

Three quasiexperimental studies in New England evaluated the impact of day treatment programs converting their rehabilitation services to IPS. The initial study was a natural experiment comparing two rural mental health centers in neighboring communities. One center closed its day treatment program and replaced it with IPS; the other continued day treatment along with traditional brokered vocational services (Drake et al., 1994b). The competitive employment rate increased substantially at the conversion site, while the rate was unchanged at the comparison site. Moreover, the conversion site had no increases in negative outcomes (e.g., hospitalization, incarceration, dropouts). Clients, their families, and mental health staff had favorable reactions to the conversion, though a minority identified loss of social contact as a drawback (Torrey, Becker, & Drake, 1995). Many clients who did *not* find work also reported that they benefited from the change because they developed valued activities *outside* the community mental health center. Based on the success of the initial conversion, the comparison site subsequently converted to IPS, also with favorable results (Drake, Becker, Biesanz, Wyzik, & Torrey, 1996). In another study involving the downsizing of a day treatment program, clients transferring to a newly established IPS program had better outcomes than those remaining in day treatment (Bailey, Ricketts, Becker, Xie, & Drake, 1998). A subsequent study compared two day treatment programs converting to IPS to one that did not (Becker et al., 2001) with equally positive findings.

The overall competitive employment rates were compiled from the combined samples from the conversion sites (N = 287 clients) and comparison sites (N = 184) in these studies. The pre–post time periods varied across studies, ranging from 3 to 12 months for baseline and from 3 to 24 months for follow-up. The competitive employment rate for the conversion sites more than doubled, from 15% to 38%. The employment rate for the comparison sites remained static (12% pre; 15% post) (Bond, 2004).

The findings from these studies of converting day treatment have had a major impact on the mental health field, because they demonstrated that IPS could replace segregated day services with a recovery-oriented program model. Subsequently, two other projects documented increased competitive employment outcomes with a movement from segregated day services, in one case with a shift from day services to a supported employment model (Gold & Marrone, 1998), and the other shifting services from a sheltered workshop to IPS (Oldman, Thomson, Calsaferri, Luke, & Bond, 2005). Further conversions of day treatment with promising outcomes, but lacking formal outcome evaluations, have been reported in the literature (Bond, McHugo, Becker, Rapp, & Whitley, 2008; Swanson et al., 2011).

REVIEW OF 16 RANDOMIZED CONTROLLED TRIALS OF IPS

The literature on the effectiveness of IPS has been reviewed by different research groups (Bond, 2004; Bond, Becker et al., 2001; Bond, Drake, & Becker, 2008, 2012; Bond, Drake, Mueser, & Becker, 1997; Burns et al., 2007; Crowther, Marshall, Bond, & Huxley, 2001; Kinoshita et al., 2010; Twamley, Jeste, & Lehman, 2003; Wang et al., 2011). While these systematic reviews have all concluded that IPS is effective, all are incomplete. Not all focused specifically on IPS, and none has comprehensively reviewed all the available outcomes. This chapter sought to address these gaps updating the findings from the most recent review (Bond, Drake, & Becker, 2012).

METHODS

Study inclusion criteria. The review used the following study inclusion criteria: (1) randomized controlled trial study design; (2) comparison of IPS to a control condition not providing IPS, (3) longitudinal competitive employment outcomes,

(4) systematic assessment monitoring of the IPS services using a standardized IPS fidelity scale (Bond, Becker, Drake, & Vogler, 1997).

Sample. As shown in Table 5–1, the review included 16 studies (Bond et al., 2007; Burns et al., 2007; Davis et al., 2012; Drake et al., 1999; Drake, McHugo, Becker, Anthony, & Clark, 1996; Gold et al., 2006; Heslin et al., 2011; Hoffmann Jäckel, Glauser, & Kupper, 2011; Killackey, Jackson, & McGorry, 2008; Latimer et al., 2006; Lehman et al., 2002; Michon, van Vugt, & van Busschbach, 2011; Mueser et al., 2004; Nuechterlein, 2010; Twamley, Narvaez, Becker, Bartels, & Jeste, 2008; Wong et al., 2008). Altogether, these studies enrolled 1,109 IPS participants (mean = 69.3 per study) and 1,171 control participants (mean = 73.2 per study). The mean length of follow-up was 18.8 months. Except for one three-group design (Mueser et al., 2004), all studies used a two-group design (IPS vs. control). Eleven studies were conducted at single site, while five studies had multiple sites (Bond et al., 2007; Burns et al., 2007; Drake, McHugo, Becker, Anthony, & Clark, 1996; Heslin et al., 2011; Michon, van Vugt, & van Busschbach, 2011). Two studies used nonintegrated supported employment control groups (Drake, McHugo, Becker, Anthony, & Clark, 1996; Mueser et al., 2004). Otherwise, all the control groups consisted of either treatment as usual or well-established alternative vocational models. Many other details of the study protocols, including sample inclusion criteria and measurement batteries, were the same or similar across studies.

In most studies, participants were recruited from clients receiving services from community mental health centers. In all the studies, participants were unemployed at the time of study admission. In all but one study (Lehman et al., 2002), the study inclusion criteria included an expressed desire to work. Another eligibility criterion common across most studies was the absence of significant medical conditions, such as end-stage cancer, that would preclude working during the follow-up period or participating in assessment interviews. The Los Angeles study (Nuechterlein et al., 2008) required a two- to three-month stabilization period before study entry because participants were often in a psychotic state at referral. The Swiss study (Hoffmann, Jäckel, Glauser, & Kupper, 2011) had unusually stringent admission criteria suggesting better vocational potential (e.g., requirement to attend the vocational assessment program at least 15 hours a week prior to enrollment and score above a certain level in work performance). In seven studies, participants were required to attend research information meetings explaining the study purpose as a condition for study enrollment (Drake, Becker, & Anthony, 1994a).

Outcome measures. Following the recommendation of Drebing et al. (2012), this chapter focuses on competitive employment outcomes. All 16 randomized controlled trials included multiple measures of competitive employment outcome, but the specific measures reported varied across studies. The one universally reported outcome was the competitive employment rate, defined as percentage of

TABLE 5-1 STUDY DESCRIPTIONS FOR 16 RANDOMIZED CONTROLLED TRIALS OF INDIVIDUAL PLACEMENT AND SUPPORT

PI	Pub Year	Study Sites	Graph Acronym	Follow-up (mos)	N (IPS)	N (Ctl)	Comparison Condition	Study Participant Pool	Research Information Group Requirement
Drake	1996	Manchester and Concord, NH	96 NH	18	73	67	*Group Skills Training:* Initial training in choosing, getting, and keeping a job, followed by competitive job placement services from a stand-alone rehabilitation program	CMHC clients	Attend 4 meetings
Drake	1999	Washington, DC	99 DC	18	74	76	*Enhanced Vocational Rehabilitation:* Facilitated by a vocational rehabilitation counselor assigned to the project; services provided by well-established rehabilitation agencies offering sheltered workshops	Intensive case management clients	Attend 4 meetings
Lehman	2002	Baltimore, MD	02 MD	24	113	106	*PSR Program* providing in-house evaluation and training, sheltered work	CMHC clients	None
Mueser	2004	Hartford, CT	04 CT	24	68	136	(1) *PSR* providing transitional employment; (2) *Brokered supported employment,* which included janitorial enclave and individual placements	CMHC clients	Attend 2 meetings
Gold	2006	Sumter, SC	06 SC	24	66	77	*Sheltered Workshop*	CMHC clients	Attend 1 meeting

(continued)

TABLE 5-1 (CONTINUED)

PI	Pub Year	Study Sites	Graph Acronym	Follow-up (mos)	N (IPS)	N (Ctl)	Comparison Condition	Study Participant Pool	Research Information Group Requirement
Latimer	2006	Montréal, Canada	06 QUE	12	75	74	*Traditional Vocational Services* that included skills training, sheltered workshops, and set-aside jobs	Outpatients at an academic hospital	Attend 2 meetings
Bond	2007	Chicago, IL	07 IL	24	92	95	*Diversified Placement:* vocational approach emphasizing a range of job options, including agency-run businesses, agency-contracted placements with local business and sheltered work options	87% were new admissions to PSR agency services	Attend 2 meetings
Burns	2007	6 European countries	07 EUR	18	156	156	*Train-place:* Best traditional vocational services available providing work skills training, selected on site-by-site basis	Clients at mental health clinics	Attend 1 meeting
Wong	2008	Hong Kong	08 HK	12	46	46	*Sheltered workshops:* work in planned environment, possibly advancing to placement	Hospital patients enrolled in occupational therapy	None
Killackey	2008	Melbourne, Australia	08 AUST	6	20	21	*Treatment as usual:* Referral to external vocational agencies and access to vocational groups	Patients in early psychosis program	None

Twamley	2008	San Diego, CA	08 CA	12	28	22	*VR referral:* vocational evaluation, employment preparation classes, job search assistance, and job retention support if needed	Outpatient clinic clients	None
Davis	2012	Tuscaloosa, AL	10 AL	12	42	43	*Standard VA vocational rehabilitation:* Stepwise model providing sheltered and transitional employment, variable integration with treatment team, limited help with competitive placements	Veterans receiving VA services	None
Nuechterlein	2010	Los Angeles, CA	10 CA	18	46	23	*Brokered VR:* referrals to traditional vocational rehabilitation agencies	Referrals from local psychiatric hospitals and outpatient clinics	None
Heslin	2011	London, UK	11 UK	24	93	95	*"Usual Care":* existing psychosocial rehabilitation and day programs	CMHC clients	None
Michon	2011	4 cities in the Netherlands	11 HOL	30	71	80	*Traditional Vocational Service:* job placement based on available jobs, no integration with MH services	MH agency clients	None
Hoffmann	2011	Bern, Switzerland	12 SWZ	24	46	54	*Traditional Vocational Rehabilitation:* "high-quality, train-place vocational rehabilitation programs." Clients typically begin in sheltered workshops	Referrals from Bern University Hospital of Psychiatry	None

(continued)

TABLE 5-1 (CONTINUED)

PI	Pub Year	Study Inclusion Criteria	Baseline Characteristics of Study Participants	Follow-up Rate
Drake	1996	SMI, out of hospital for ≥ 1 month, local residence of 6 months, age 20–65, unemployed ≥ 1 month, absence of significant cognitive or medical impairment, interest in work	Mean age 37.5 ± 9.5 years, 49% male, 96% Caucasian, 74% ≥high school, 51% never married, 22% homelessness during past yr, 46% schizophrenia-spectrum, 11% substance use disorder	98%
Drake	1999	SMI, unemployed ≥ 1 month, absence of significant cognitive or medical impairment, interest in work	Mean age 40.0 ± 7.1 years, 39% male, 83% African American, 65% ≥high school, 65% never married, 26% homeless in past year	95%
Lehman	2002	SMI and unemployed ≥ 3 months. Not required to express desire to work	Mean age 41.5±8.5 years, 57% male, 75% African American or other minority, 51% ≥high school, 62% never married, 6% currently homeless, 75% psychotic disorder, 40% substance use diagnosis with current use	69%
Mueser	2004	SMI, receiving services at CMHC study site, unemployed, desire for competitive employment	Mean age 41.2 ± 9.1 years, 62% male, 45% African American, 31% Latino, 48% ≥high school, 73% never married, 75% schizophrenia-spectrum, 25% substance use disorder	81%
Gold	2006	SMI, ≥ 18 years of age, unemployed at study entry, current and/or future interest in competitive employment, ≥ 6 months receiving CMHC services	71% between 26 & 45 years of age, 62% female, 83% not married currently, 52% ≥ high school, 69% schizophrenia-spectrum, 9% alcohol use disorder with current use, 8% drug use disorder with current use	80%
Latimer	2006	SMI, 18—64 years of age, interest in competitive employment, unemployed on date of consent.	Mean age 40.3 ± 10.0 years, 59% male, 43% ≥high school, 79% never married, 17% schizoaffective, 59% other schizophrenia-spectrum, 20% bipolar disorder	83%
Bond	2007	SMI, ≥ 18 years of age, admitted to day program at agency, interest in paid employment, ≥ 30 days enrollment at agency, ≥ 30 days unemployed, no DPA services in last 3 months, no physical illness preventing participation, no previous IPS	Mean age 38.8 ± 9.6 years, 64% male, 51% African American, 8% Latino, 82% ≥high school, 74% never married, 19% homelessness during past yr, 58% schizophrenia-spectrum, 11% substance use disorder	88%

Author	Year	Inclusion criteria	Sample characteristics	%
Burns	2007	SMI, between 18 years of age and local retirement age, living in the community at baseline, ≥ 1 year unemployed, interest in competitive employment	Mean age 37.8 years, 60% male, 26.6 years of age at first psychiatric contact, 80% schizophrenia/schizoaffective disorder, 17% bipolar disorder, 3% other, 56% > 1 month work in past 5 years, 11.9 years of education, 34% live independently	81%
Wong	2008	Mental illness lasting ≥ 2 years, of working age, between 18 & 55 years of age, interest in competitive employment, absence of significant medical illness	Mean age 33.6 ± 9.2 yrs, 60% male, 22% ≥high school, 90% never married, 76% schizophrenia-spectrum	99%
Twamley	2008	≥ 45 years of age, schizophrenia or schizoaffective disorder, unemployed at baseline, absence of co-morbid substance dependence, absence of dementia	44% 45–49 years of age, 60% male, 64% Caucasian, 60% schizoaffective disorder	79%
Davis	2012	Veterans with PTSD, 20–60 years of age, medically cleared to work, unemployed, interest in competitive employment, intent to remain in local residence, absence of significant cognitive or medical impairment, absence of schizophrenia-spectrum disorder/bipolar I disorder, absence of need for substance detoxification, absence of pending legal charges	40.2 ± 12.1 years of age, 88% male, 72% African American, 26% never married, 89% ≥high school, 89.4% co-morbid major depressive disorder, 7.1 ± 5.6 yrs of military services	84%
Nuechterlein	2010	First psychotic episode <2 years before, schizophrenia spectrum, between 19 & 60 years of age, local residence, English primary language, interest in work or school, absence of significant cognitive impairment, ≥6 months no substance abuse, psychosis not accounted for by substance abuse, not contraindicated with risperidone	25.2 ± 4.0 years of age, 67% male, 13.2 ± 1.9 yrs education, 83% schizophrenia, 1.2 ± 0.9 psychiatric hospitalizations	No report

(continued)

TABLE 5-1 (CONTINUED)

PI	Pub Year	Study Inclusion Criteria	Baseline Characteristics of Study Participants	Follow-up Rate
Heslin	2011	SMI, 18–65 years of age, proficient in English, unemployed ≥ 3 months	38.4 ± 9.4 years of age, 72% male, 57% living alone, 46% African American, 77% psychotic disorder, 30% mood disorder	86%
Michon	2011	SMI, interest in work	35 yrs of age, 74% male, 82% not married, 64% living independently, 67% psychoses	77%
Hoffmann	2011	Stabilized mental disorder, unemployed, interest in employment, 18–64 years of age, judged eligible for vocational services by governmental agency. Exclusion criteria: IQ < 70, primary substance abuse disorder, unwilling to attend outpatient therapy, work performance <50% normal, attend vocational program < 15 hours/week	33.8 ± 9.5 years of age, 65% male, 74% never married, 75% completed vocational training or had university degree, 38% schizophrenia spectrum, 1.7 ± 2.6 psychiatric hospitalizations	93%

Table 5-1. Acronyms

PI—Principal Investigator; IPS—Individual Placement and Support; Ctl—control group; CMHC—community mental health center; MH—mental health; SE—supported employment; PSR—psychosocial rehabilitation; SMI—serious mental illness; VR—State-federal vocational rehabilitation system; VA—Veteran Affairs; PTSD—posttraumatic stress disorder total sample working a competitive job at any time during follow-up. Some studies also reported: percentage working at least 20 hours a week, days to first job (i.e., time from study entry to first job start), and weeks worked (which we standardized by converting to annualized weeks worked). We calculated annualized weeks worked for both the full intent-to-treat sample (everyone enrolled in the study) and the worker sample only (those who obtained at least one competitive job during follow-up).

Data collection and analyses. Data were either recorded directly from published reports or hand-calculated from information presented in the published studies. Effect size for each study for the difference in employment rate between supported employment and controls was calculated using the arc sine approximation (Lipsey, 1990). An unweighted overall effect size was calculated as the simple mean of the individual effect sizes. For all other outcome measures, means are reported without standard deviations, which were not always available from the published studies. Overall means were calculated weighting individual means by sample sizes.

FINDINGS

Competitive employment outcomes. The competitive employment rate was significantly higher for the IPS condition than for controls in every one of the studies, as shown in Figure 5–1. In total, 619 (55.8%) of IPS participants obtained employment, compared with 267 (22.8%) control participants. Averaging the rates across studies, the mean competitive employment rate was 58.9% (median = 62.2%) for IPS compared to 23.4% (median = 26.0%) for controls. The mean difference in percentage

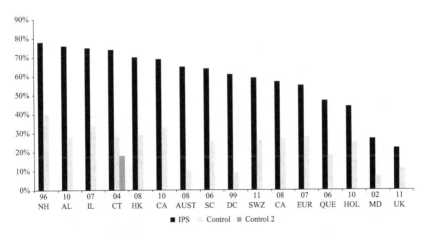

FIGURE 5–1 Competitive employment rates in 16 randomized controlled trials of Individual Placement and Support (IPS)

employed between IPS and controls was 35.5%, ranging from 11.0% to 55.5%. The individual study effect sizes ranged from .30 to 1.18. The overall unweighted mean effect size was .77.

Among the nine U.S. studies, the competitive employment rate of 27% for the Maryland IPS sample (Lehman et al., 2002) was an outlier—less than half the rate for IPS in the other eight U.S. studies and close to the mean competitive employment rate for the control groups. With this study removed, the unweighted mean competitive employment rate for U.S. studies increased to 69% for IPS and 28% for controls.

Number of days to first competitive job was reported in 10 studies, as shown in Table 5-2. The UK study was an extreme outlier (Heslin et al., 2011), with mean of 708 days to first job for IPS clients who obtained work. Excluding this outlier, the average time to first competitive job was 50% faster for IPS participants compared to controls (134 days versus 205 days).

The findings for mean hours worked per year in competitive employment for seven studies are shown in Table 5-3. The variability across studies was substantial, ranging from a mean of 656 hours for the Alabama study (Davis et al., 2012) to 126 hours for the Québec study (Latimer et al., 2006). Nonetheless, the overall unweighted effect size was large ($d = .58$), and the ratio of mean hours worked for IPS to controls was threefold. Table 5-3 does not include the Swiss study (Hoffmann et al., 2011), which calculated hours worked for the second year only of follow-up. However, this study also found that the

TABLE 5-2   MEAN NUMBER OF DAYS TO FIRST COMPETITIVE JOB IN 10 IPS STUDIES

Study	IPS	Control
08 HK	72 (N = 32)	118 (N = 13)
06 Qué	84 (N = 51)	89 (N = 39)
08 CA	93 (N = 16)	171 (N = 6)
11 SWZ	116 (N = 27)	214 (N = 14)
99 DC	126 (N = 45)	293 (N = 7)
06 SC	133 (N = 42)	322 (N = 20)
07 IL	156 (N = 69)	193 (N = 32)
02 MD	164 (N =47)	287 (N = 12)
04 CT	197 (N = 51)	277 (N= 31)
11 UK	708 (N =21)	698 (N = 11)
Total	**164.3 (N = 401)**	**234.6 (N = 185)**
Total without 11 UK	**134.2 (N = 380)**	**205.3 (N = 174)**

Table adapted from Bond, G. R., Drake, R. E., & Becker, D. R. (2012). Generalizability of the Individual Placement and Support (IPS) model of supported employment outside the US. *World Psychiatry, 11*, 32–39. Reprinted with permission from Elsevier.

TABLE 5-3 MEAN HOURS WORKED PER YEAR IN COMPETITIVE JOBS IN SEVEN IPS STUDIES (TABLE ADAPTED FROM (BOND, DRAKE, & BECKER, 2012))

	Follow-up (months)	IPS		Control		Ratio IPS/ CTL	Effect size
		Mean	SD	Mean	SD		
10 AL	12	656	661	236	494	2.78	.72
96 NH	18	405	843	137	400	2.96	.60
07 IL	24	298	836	143	723	2.09	.40
07 EUR	18	286	707	79	312	3.61	.57
99 DC	18	215	569	19	125	11.48	.72
04 CT	24	187	516	36	231	5.22	.86
06 QUE	12	126	267	73	252	1.73	.20
Mean, all studies		**284.3**		**86.1**		**3.30**	**.58**

Table adapted from Bond, G. R., Drake, R. E., & Becker, D. R. (2012). Generalizability of the Individual Placement and Support (IPS) model of supported employment outside the US. *World Psychiatry, 11*, 32–39. Reprinted with permission from Elsevier.

IPS group averaged significantly more hours worked than did the control group (628.0 vs. 316.9).

The findings for annualized weeks worked in competitive employment are reported for eight studies in Table 5–4. Overall, the mean weeks worked per year in competitive employment for IPS participants was more than twice the mean weeks for controls. When the comparisons were limited to participants who obtained competitive employment during follow-up, the mean weeks worked were virtually the same for IPS and controls.

On the measure of weeks worked, the Swiss study again reported findings for the second year only. In the comparisons between the total enrolled samples, this study also found for that the IPS group averaged more than twice the number of weeks worked as the control group (24.5 vs. 10.2) (Hoffmann et al., 2011).

Other outcomes. Outcomes for all paid employment, including noncompetitive jobs, were reported in eight studies (Bond et al., 2007; Drake et al., 1999; Drake, McHugo, Becker, Anthony, & Clark, 1996; Gold et al., 2006; Hoffmann et al., 2011; Latimer et al., 2006; Mueser et al., 2004; Wong et al., 2008). In six of these studies, the rate of noncompetitive employment for IPS participants was 11% or less. Two studies reported substantially higher rates: 20% in the Québec study (Latimer et al., 2006) and 26% in the Swiss study (Hoffmann et al., 2011). Consideration of all paid employment (i.e., inclusion of both competitive and noncompetitive employment) did not materially affect the employment findings in five of the eight studies (Drake, McHugo, Becker, Anthony, & Clark, 1996; Gold et al., 2006; Hoffmann et al., 2011; Mueser et al., 2004; Wong et al., 2008). Considering all paid

TABLE 5-4 ANNUALIZED WEEKS WORKED IN COMPETITIVE JOBS IN EIGHT IPS STUDIES (TABLE ADAPTED FROM (BOND, DRAKE, & BECKER, 2012))

	All study participants		Working participants	
	IPS	*Control*	*IPS*	*Control*
10 AL	21.6 (N =42)	6.8 (N = 43)	28.4 (N =32)	24.4 (N = 12)
06 Qué	17.0 (N = 75)	14.1 (N = 74)	25.0 (N = 51)	26.8 (N = 39)
07 IL	16.2 (N = 92)	8.2 (N = 95)	21.6 (N = 69)	24.3 (N = 32)
04 CT	14.9 (N = 68)	2.3 (N = 136)	19.8 (N = 51)	9.8 (N = 31)
08 HK	13.0 (N = 46)	7.0 (N = 46)	18.6 (N = 32)	24.9 (N = 13)
99 DC	10.1 (N = 74)	0.8 (N = 76)	16.6 (N = 45)	8.7 (N = 7)
06 SC	10.0 (N = 66)	2.9 (N = 77)	15.8 (N = 42)	11.3 (N = 20)
02 MD	6.0 (N = 113)	1.6 (N = 106)	14.4 (N = 47)	14.1 (N = 12)
Total	**12.8 (N=576)**	**4.9 (N=653)**	**20.0 (N=369)**	**19.3 (N=166)**

Table adapted from Bond, G. R., Drake, R. E., & Becker, D. R. (2012). Generalizability of the Individual Placement and Support (IPS) model of supported employment outside the US. *World Psychiatry, 11,* 32–39. Reprinted with permission from Elsevier.

employment outcomes, two studies showed no differences between IPS and controls in employment rates and on several other employment measures (Bond et al., 2007; Latimer et al., 2006), while another study reported no differences in overall earnings between IPS and controls (Drake et al., 1999).

Early program dropouts refer to clients who either discontinue vocational services within an early time period or never make an initial contact. Studies reporting early dropout rates have not had a standardized time period or common method of assessing discontinuation. For example, Drake et al. (1999) and Hoffmann et al. (2011) reported dropout rates for clients discontinuing services within the first 2 months Bond et al. (2007) used the first 6 months as the time period for defining early dropouts, and Latimer et al. (2006) defined early dropouts as failing to have at least one contact with vocational staff in both of the first and the second 3-month follow-up periods. Averaging across seven studies (Bond et al., 2007; Burns et al., 2007; Drake et al., 1999; Drake et al., 1996; Hoffmann et al., 2011; Latimer et al., 2006; Mueser et al., 2004), 8% of IPS participants were early program dropouts, compared to 38% of controls.

Ten studies included in the review also examined non-vocational outcomes, which most often included psychiatric symptoms, quality of life, and psychiatric hospitalizations (Bond et al., 2007; Burns et al., 2009; Drake et al., 1999; Drake et al., 1996; Gold et al., 2006; Hoffmann et al., 2011; Latimer et al., 2006; Lehman et al., 2002; Mueser et al., 2004; Twamley, Narvaez, Becker, Bartels, & Jeste, 2008). Some also included measures of self-esteem, social functioning, and social network.

With rare exception, IPS participants did not differ from controls on any of these measures.

Studies excluded in current review. We found nine randomized controlled trials comparing a non-IPS supported employment program to some other vocational model. Four had significant findings suggesting superior competitive employment findings for supported employment (Bond, Dietzen, McGrew, & Miller, 1995; Gervey & Bedell, 1994; McFarlane et al., 2000; Test, Allness, & Knoedler, 1995), while two reported significantly better employment outcomes for their supported employment intervention but did not clearly differentiate between competitive employment and set-aside jobs, so that the interpretation of their competitive employment results is clouded (Chandler, Meisel, Hu, McGowen, & Madison, 1997; Tsang, Chan, Wong, & Liberman, 2009). Two studies found no differences in competitive employment outcomes between supported employment and the comparison group (Rogers, Anthony, Lyass, & Penk, 2006; Shafer, 2005). Finally, one study had mixed results, with some findings favoring the comparison group (which used a clubhouse model) over supported employment (Macias et al., 2006).

SUMMARY: RANDOMIZED CONTROLLED TRIALS OF IPS

Rigorous evaluations of IPS suggest that about 60% of IPS clients obtain competitive jobs, compared to 20%–25% of those who receive other types of vocational assistance. One way of interpreting this finding is that approximately 25% of clients who express an interest in competitive employment will succeed in obtaining a job with the help of a traditional (non-evidence-based) vocational program, but IPS helps an additional 35% of the target group who otherwise would remain unemployed. The finding of a large and statistically significant beneficial impact of IPS is robust, upheld in all 16 studies. The effectiveness of IPS is also suggested by other measures of competitive employment outcome, including time to first job, job duration, and total hours employed during the follow-up period. Most IPS clients work part-time, typically half-time; about two-thirds of those who obtain competitive employment work 20 hours or more per week. Few IPS clients work full-time, likely due to preferences, limited stamina, and/or fear of losing health insurance or other benefits. Consistent with the principle of rapid job search, the time to first competitive job for IPS participants is nearly 10 weeks sooner than for controls. The mean length of time to first job for IPS participants (19 weeks) is nonetheless lengthy for a model that prescribes rapid job search.

Some comment is warranted about the inclusion of the two studies with clearly substandard IPS outcomes (Heslin et al., 2011; Lehman et al., 2002). The Lehman et al. (2002) study deviated from the other IPS studies in that it was the only study among those reviewed that did not require participants to have a goal of competitive employment. Many participants apparently joined the study to receive the research payments and not because of their interest in employment. This study's poor competitive employment outcomes are consistent with its lenient admission criteria. Regarding the UK study (Heslin et al., 2011), we concur with two commentaries (Campbell, 2010; Latimer, 2010) that noted this study's shortcomings in adhering to the IPS model, according to descriptions provided by the investigators (Howard et al., 2010).

Conversely, an outlier on the upper end was the IPS study of veterans with posttraumatic stress disorder (Davis et al., 2012). This study had outstanding outcomes on most employment indicators, suggesting that this target population may be especially amenable to IPS interventions, though replication is needed. A subsequent multisite IPS study of clients with posttraumatic stress disorder is now nearing completion (Davis, 2011). While posttraumatic stress disorder is not usually classified as a serious mental illness, some researchers have argued that it should be, given its long-term nature and the disability it often engenders (Friedman & Rosenheck, 1996). As discussed in Chapter 8, the applicability of IPS to other diagnostic and disability groups is currently being explored by a number of research groups.

An unresolved question is whether noncompetitive employment outcomes are equivalent to competitive jobs with respect to their utility for clients, program managers, funders of rehabilitation services, and society at large. The IPS model is based on the argument that competitive jobs are greatly preferred over noncompetitive ones by clients themselves (Bedell, Draving, Parrish, Gervey, & Guastadisegni, 1998). In addition, a sustained period of competitive employment has been associated with better non-vocational outcomes in some studies (Bond, Resnick et al., 2001; Burns et al., 2009), whereas this has not been shown as clearly for noncompetitive jobs. We assume that the advantages of competitive jobs over noncompetitive ones are best evaluated in long-term studies (Penk et al., 2010). Nonetheless, several studies in this review found that control interventions were equally effective as IPS in achieving a range of paid employment outcomes when noncompetitive jobs were included. Finally, the costs associated with developing and maintaining noncompetitive job programs should also be considered; the costs are often enormous (Black, 1988). Moreover, the societal burden of developing and maintaining noncompetitive jobs is unsustainable on a large scale, in that costs are usually borne by governmental subsidies rather than by the private sector and clients typically do not pay taxes on noncompetitive jobs.

This review found low rates of early dropouts from IPS, in contrast to an early review noting high dropout rates among supported employment clients (Bond, Drake, Mueser, & Becker, 1997). Consistent with the assertive outreach component of the model, IPS programs have exceptionally low dropout rates, in most studies less than 10% in the first several months after program admission. Conversely, studies often report high dropout rates for control participants. The contrast in termination rates for IPS and control groups raises a different question, whether the superior employment outcomes for IPS can be attributed to attrition. In other words, what if the analyses reported in these studies (which compared the total samples enrolled in the IPS and the control groups, as required in an intent-to-treat design) were repeated with program dropouts removed? One study that has conducted this analysis found that IPS still had superior competitive employment outcomes to the control group in comparisons that excluded dropouts (Bond et al., 2007). Treatment exposure analyses were not reported, however, in the other randomized controlled trials. Perhaps control participants who dropped out did so because they viewed the control intervention as ineffective. Clearly, this question warrants further study.

Receipt of IPS services does not in itself improve non-vocational outcomes beyond services as usual. Improved non-vocational outcomes may only accrue for clients who work steadily over time in a competitive job (Bond, Resnick et al., 2001). As discussed in Chapter 6, these relationships need further exploration within longitudinal studies.

COMBINED RESULTS FROM FOUR RANDOMIZED CONTROLLED TRIALS

The preceding review makes a strong case for the effectiveness of IPS, yet like other reviews, it is hampered by the lack of standardization in competitive employment outcome measures used in the original studies. Consequently, reviewers have been tentative in drawing conclusions about the influence of IPS on many crucial dimensions of employment outcome. Specifically, while virtually all studies report outcomes for job acquisition—that is, whether a participant attained competitive employment at any time during the follow-up period—studies have been far less consistent in measuring job tenure, hours worked, and employment earnings. Consequently, cumulative knowledge about IPS outcomes has been limited with respect to these other dimensions of employment. This lack of standardization in employment measures has contributed to uncertainty regarding the scope of effectiveness of IPS. One widely held view is that IPS is effective in helping clients to *obtain* jobs, but not in helping them to *keep* jobs (Burton, 2009; Eack, Hogarty, Greenwald, Hogarty, & Keshavan, 2011; Mueser et al., 2005; Murphy, Mullen, & Spagnolo, 2005; Roberts & Pratt, 2007; Wallace, Tauber, & Wilde, 1999).

To address this gap in the literature, we compiled outcomes from four randomized controlled trials of IPS that had used a similar outcome battery (Bond, Campbell, & Drake, 2012). The combined sample of 681 study participants afforded a large-sample test of the effectiveness of IPS on job duration and other measures not consistently reported in the literature. In these analyses, IPS participants had significantly better outcomes than the control program participants on all eight competitive employment measures examined, with more than a threefold advantage for IPS with regard to percentage working 20 hours or more a week, total weeks worked, job tenure on longest-held job, total hours employed, and total wages.

LONG-TERM OUTCOMES

The goal of IPS is of course to help people find long-term, satisfying jobs rather than brief work experiences. People with mental illness, like everyone else, want employment that enhances income, that helps them to feel useful and socially connected, and that provides some long-term security. In other words, people want a career. Unfortunately, research grants usually last briefly, and the vast majority of studies include only a one-year or two-year follow-up at most. None of the completed randomized controlled trials of IPS have a follow-up period of more than 2.5 years from the point of enrollment in an IPS program. A critical question remains regarding the work patterns of people with psychiatric disabilities: what is their work like over many years?

Test (1995), using an early model of supported employment, reported that work outcomes gradually improved over seven years for young adults with schizophrenia. But she never published the details regarding long-term employment. Another early supported employment study also found positive competitive employment outcomes during the fourth year after study enrollment, when over half the clients surveyed were working (Bond, Dietzen, McGrew, & Miller, 1995).

Most IPS studies have followed clients from the point of admission to an IPS program, but one study, seeking to understand job tenure, enrolled clients in a longitudinal study at the point clients first started a competitive job (Bond & Kukla, 2011b). This research design resulted in a longer average follow-up period than most studies, because time to first job (which includes the process of engaging with an IPS program, searching for a job, and receiving a job offer) was not included in the follow-up interval. (As noted above, time to first job averages 19 weeks in randomized controlled trials of IPS.) The researchers followed a cohort of 82 consecutive admissions to four high-fidelity IPS programs over a two-year period. Overall, clients averaged 8.0 months job tenure in their initial job and 11.0 months of employment across all jobs. The authors concluded that among clients in high-fidelity IPS programs who obtain competitive jobs, job tenure was twice as long has been previously reported in the literature (Mueser et al., 2005), and about 40% become "steady workers," defined as employed continuously in at least 50% of months during follow-up.

We have followed several groups of IPS participants after their participation in short-term research studies. McHugo et al. (1998) followed participants from one randomized controlled trial for 3.5 years from program admission and found no statistical decrement in the proportion working, suggesting durability of the effects of IPS. Salyers et al. (2004) followed up a small group of IPS participants at 10 years after two day treatment programs converted to IPS and found that most had worked competitively. Approximately one-third of those interviewed had worked for at least 5 years, with the majority of jobs paying competitive wages. Few had transitioned to full-time employment with health benefits. Becker et al. (2007) re-interviewed 38 participants from two IPS studies 8–12 years after entering supported employment. All participants had worked at least one job in the intervening years. Most of the jobs (78%) were competitive and most of the study group (82%) had worked competitively. Study group participants averaged 3.39 competitive jobs and 3.55 jobs in total (i.e., competitive, set aside with competitive wage, volunteer, or sheltered). Study participants averaged 20 hours per week for the competitive jobs. The average total number of months worked on the longest competitive job was four years and seven months. At the 8–12-year interviews, 71% of the participants were working, and 71% reported working for more than half of the 8–12 year follow-up. Consistent with the principle of individualized job match, participants worked in a wide variety of jobs, with most in service, clerical, and sales categories. The great majority of participants continued to receive benefits at follow-up: 34 (90%) were receiving Social Security benefits, including 10 (26%) who received Supplemental Security Income and 28 (74%) who received Social Security Disability Insurance.

The long-term follow-up research must be considered as preliminary rather than definitive because of the small numbers of clients, studies, and locations. Nevertheless, two general findings are intriguing. First, about half the study participants in these studies became "steady workers" over the follow-up period. Recalling that the baseline employment rate in this population is less than 15%, a steady employment rate of 50% or more in these long-term follow-ups is far above the norm and suggests that increasing the overall rate of labor participation among people with psychiatric disabilities is possible. Second, the durability of employment outcomes in these studies contrasts with the attenuation effects found for many psychosocial interventions once the active intervention has been discontinued (e.g., Stein & Test, 1980). We speculate that once IPS clients begin working, the natural reinforcers in the workplace (a paycheck, making a meaningful contribution to society, social connectedness, a new identity) may provide incentives to continue working with modest supports from health professionals.

CHAPTER SUMMARY

This chapter summarizes the findings from a diverse group of IPS effectiveness studies. The evidence for superior competitive employment outcomes is strong and consistent. While longer-term follow-up studies are needed, the initial findings are promising. At present our working hypothesis is that approximately two-thirds of all clients entering IPS obtain competitive jobs, and of those who do, approximately half become steady workers.

6

NON-VOCATIONAL OUTCOMES

How does IPS affect non-vocational outcomes? This question is difficult to answer, requiring consideration of relevant participants, types and amounts of work, specific non-vocational outcomes, criteria for inferring causality, and timelines. We begin with two presuppositions. First, employment rather than vocational services per se may influence other outcomes. No theory posits that participating in supported employment by itself leads to improved non-vocational outcomes, and empirical research confirms the lack of relationship (Burns et al., 2009; Drake et al., 1999; Drake, McHugo, Becker, Anthony, & Clark, 1996; Gold et al., 2006; Kukla & Bond, submitted; Hoffmann et al. 2011; Latimer et al., 2006; Lehman et al., 2002; Mueser et al., 2004; Twamley, Narvaez, Becker, Bartels, & Jeste, 2008). All of the hypothesized gains pertain logically to employment rather than to pre-employment experiences. In other words, IPS serves as only a mediating variable that enables a higher percentage of people to obtain employment.

Second, because researchers cannot randomly assign people to competitive work versus joblessness, we must use nonexperimental approaches—e.g., correlational, quasiexperimental, and qualitative—to study the relationships between work and non-vocational outcomes. Without randomized controlled trials, how do we infer causality? One possibility is to rely on the well-known criteria that epidemiologist Bradford Hill (1965) developed to confirm the relationship between smoking and lung cancer: the association must be *strong* (substantial rather than weak correlations), *consistent* (relationships found in different groups), *specific* (work leads directly to the outcome), *temporal* (other outcomes follow employment), *on a gradient* (more work leads to better outcomes), *plausible* (a mechanism is clear), *coherent* (basic research supports the relationship), and *backed by evidence from analogous situations* (employment correlates with related outcomes).

THREE HYPOTHESES

Three common hypotheses involve non-vocational outcomes. First, work may improve people's incomes and enable them to escape from poverty. Second, work may enhance other psychosocial outcomes, such as self-esteem, social relationships, housing, or quality of life. Third, work may improve the course of mental illness and clinical indicators, such as severity of psychiatric symptoms and psychiatric hospitalizations.

How would employment improve these diverse outcomes? The income hypothesis is straightforward accounting: increased earnings from work sometimes displace disability or welfare payments but should still result in a net increase in total income. Is the net increase sufficient to help people escape from poverty? This is the critical question. For the second hypothesis, several possible mechanisms have been suggested. As a normal developmental and psychological process, work may enhance skills, increase perceptions of competence and mastery, and improve self-esteem and quality of life (Rosenfield, 1987). Work provides structure and social interactions in daily life, perhaps leading to an increased sense of well-being (Gahnstram-Strandqvist, Liukko, & Tham, 2003). Work is empowering because workers have a mainstream identity, status, and role (Dunn, Wewiorski, & Rogers, 2008). Socialization outside of the mental health system occurs with integration into the workplace and may promote friendships and social skills (Gates, Akabas, & Oran-Sabia, 1998; Mank, Cioffi, & Yovanoff, 1997; Rollins, Bond, Jones, Kukla, & Collins, 2012). Regarding the third hypothesis, work might enhance coping with mental illness by increasing motivation and confidence, decreasing stress, and enhancing social support—a complex series of connections. These theories are sensible and straightforward, but what does the research show? In this chapter we review the literature and examine longitudinal evidence from four randomized controlled trials of IPS.

Hypothesis 1: Work Improves Income and Reduces Poverty. How do people with mental illness fare financially when they work? The largest study addressing this question was the Employment Demonstration Project of the Substance Abuse and Mental Health Services Administration with 1773 participants (Cook, Leff et al., 2005). At the beginning of the study 74% were at or below poverty. Workers in this study earned, on average, $5786 per person over 24 months. To address the question of overall financial benefit, Cook (2008) determined the ratio of monthly income to expenses. Workers on Social Security Administration benefits had total income of 190% of their expenses versus 130% for non-workers. For those not on Social Security Administration benefits, the comparable figures were 160% versus 60%. The Employment Demonstration Project data fit with self-reports from a 16-year longitudinal study of clients with co-occurring mental illness and substance use disorder (Strickler, Whitley, Becker, & Drake, 2009). Steady workers reported that the extra income, although small in net dollars, made a big difference in quality of life, enabling them to pursue leisure activities as well as necessities. These figures are promising but do not answer the poverty question directly. The Social Security Administration's Mental Health Treatment Study (Frey et al., 2008; 2011) provides more complete economic findings, but the complete income analyses are still pending.

Hypothesis 2: Work Enhances Other Psychosocial Outcomes. Many cross-sectional correlational studies have shown that employment among people with serious mental illness is associated with psychological benefits such as quality of life (Fabian, 1989b, 1992) and self-esteem (Arns & Linney, 1993, 1995b; Matthews, 1980; Van Dongen, 1998). These correlations are, however, usually weak and are sometimes non-significant (Connell, King, & Crowe, 2011). The direction of causality is often uncertain.

Hypothesis 3: Work Improves Clinical Outcomes. Longitudinal studies of the course of schizophrenia have often found modest correlations between employment and symptoms (Cook & Razzano, 2000; Gaebel & Pietzcker, 1987; McGlashan, 1988; Möller, von Zerssen, & Wüschner-Stockheim, 1982; Strauss & Carpenter, 1977). Other studies have examined the relationship between vocational outcomes and symptoms with brief follow-up periods (Arns & Linney, 1993, 1995a; Brekke, Ansel, Long, Slade, & Weinstein, 1999; Brekke, Levin, Wolkon, Sobel, & Slade, 1993; Holzner, Kemmler, & Meise, 1998; Kemmler, Holzner, Neudorfer, Meise, & Hinterhuber, 1997; Scheid, 1993; Solinski, Jackson, & Bell, 1992). The relationships are usually weak, and the direction of association is again unclear. Psychiatric symptoms have predicted poorer employment outcomes for clients enrolled in vocational programs (Anthony, Rogers, Cohen, & Davies, 1995; Hoffmann & Kupper, 1997; Lysaker & Bell, 1995), and improvement in vocational functioning has been associated with improvement in symptoms (Anthony et al., 1995; Bell & Lysaker, 1997; Bell, Lysaker, & Milstein, 1996). Thus, researchers have sometimes concluded that lower clinical symptoms predict success in obtaining and holding a job and sometimes that employment leads to reduced symptoms.

Research on other clinical outcomes is sparse. Studies generally do not show that employment lowers rates of psychiatric hospitalizations (Bond, 1992; Bond, Drake, Mueser, & Becker, 1997; Crowther, Marshall, Bond, & Huxley, 2001). Research also generally shows no association between employment and alcohol and drug use (Sengupta, Drake, & McHugo, 1998). A recent longitudinal follow-up found, however, that employment preceded stable remission of co-occurring substance use disorders by several months (Xie et al., 2010). Little is known about the impact of employment on homelessness (Kirszner, McKay, & Tippett, 1991) or incarceration, although a general finding in the criminology literature is that employment is a key factor in preventing criminal recidivism (Andrews, 1995; Bushway & Reuter, 2002).

NON-VOCATIONAL OUTCOMES IN FOUR IPS STUDIES

Secondary analyses of four IPS controlled trials have examined the longitudinal impact of competitive employment on non-vocational outcomes (Bond, Resnick et al., 2001; Burns et al., 2009; Kukla, Bond, & Xie, 2012; Mueser et al., 1997). The secondary analyses from these studies used nonexperimental designs, but each sought to control for baseline differences (i.e., selection biases). In general, these studies suggest that, compared to no employment, a sustained period of time in competitive employment is associated with greater improvement over time in symptom control, quality of life, self-esteem, and social functioning.

The four studies used a similar research design. All were secondary analyses of randomized controlled trials of IPS (Bond et al., 2007; Burns et al., 2007; Drake et al., 1999; Drake et al., 1996). The major methodological features of these parent studies have already been summarized in Chapter 5 and will not be repeated here.

The four studies compared groups defined after the fact by employment outcomes. Two of the studies compared working to non-working clients during follow-up (Burns et al., 2009; Mueser et al., 1997), while two examined a subgroup of clients who worked a substantial amount of time during follow-up, defined by above-median earnings in one study (Bond, Resnick et al., 2001) and above-median weeks worked in the other (Kukla et al., 2012). We will refer to the group with substantial work as Steady Workers. In the Bond et al. (2001) study, the Steady Worker group was contrasted to the combined group of clients who did not work at all and those who worked minimally; those who worked in sheltered employment were excluded. In the Kukla et al. (2012) study, the Steady Worker group was compared to the group who did not work at all, with those who worked minimally or who worked in noncompetitive paid employment (e.g., agency-run businesses) excluded. The non-vocational measures varied considerably, but all studies examined psychiatric symptoms, psychiatric hospitalizations, and quality of life.

With regard to our three research hypotheses outlined above, the findings were modest. First, because income prior to study admission was not measured in detail in these studies, we could not address the first hypothesis. Second, with regard to subjective quality of life, two studies found modest differences between the working and nonworking groups, while two studies did not. Both studies examining self-esteem found an advantage for working clients over nonworking clients. Third, regarding course of illness, all four studies found some improvements in symptom control over time for working clients compared to nonworking clients. The improvement was a combination of worsening of symptoms for the nonworking group and improvement in symptoms for the working group. Improvements were not consistent across all symptom subscales. Two studies found that working clients were less likely to be hospitalized and two did not. In summary, the findings from these studies suggest a modest effect over an 18–24 month follow-up period of employment on psychological and illness management outcomes.

A recent secondary analysis of the Burns study included in the above review re-examined the question of the impact of work on non-vocational outcomes using a different analytic approach. Specifically, the research examined the time-lag effects of employment on non-vocational outcomes (Kilian et al., 2011). Using structural equation modeling, the authors concluded that "patients who received an IPS inter-vention spent more hours in competitive employment and, due to indirect positive effects of employment on clinical status, spent fewer days in psychiatric hospitals than patients who received conventional vocational training." Perhaps appropriate statistical models may detect improvements in non-vocational outcomes result-ing from steady employment that are not shown by statistical analyses using static groups defined after the fact, which was the primary methodological approach in earlier studies.

DO ADVERSE OUTCOMES OCCUR?

While acknowledging that employment is a valued client outcome, many profession-als, family members, clients, and the general public also fear adverse consequences of working. Put simply, many believe that work is too stressful. Furthermore, many assume that some clients are so fragile that working may upset their equilibrium and lead to relapse. Many psychiatrists, trained in the diathesis–stress model, are reluctant to encourage their patients to seek vocational help (West et al., 2005). Similarly, case managers fear that clients with serious mental illness are too ill to work (Braitman et al., 1995).

The demands of working of course are stressful, notably the demands of entry-level work (Ehrenreich, 2001), typical of jobs that people with serious mental ill-ness obtain in resuming their work lives. These clinical recommendations, how-ever, neglect the stresses of unemployment, poverty, and social isolation (Marrone & Golowka, 1999). In the general population, the effects of unemployment include increased substance abuse, physical problems, and psychiatric disorders, accom-panied by reduced self-esteem, loss of social contacts, alienation, and apathy (Blustein, 2008; Warr, 1987). Many of these outcomes, of course, are found in the psychiatric population. Some of the psychosocial sequelae attributed to serious mental illness are almost certainly related to the cumulative effects of living outside the mainstream of society, or social exclusion (Evans & Repper, 2000; Goodwin & Kennedy, 2005; Grove, Secker, & Seebohm, 2005; Huxley & Thornicroft, 2003). People with serious mental illness are among the most isolated and stigmatized in society (Huxley & Thornicroft, 2003), and those who are not working spend significantly more time sleeping and engaged in passive leisure (e.g., watching television)—an increase of more than four hours per day compared to the general working population (Hayes & Halford, 1996; Krupa, McLean, Eastabrook, Bonham, & Baksh, 2003).

In the early years of deinstitutionalization, several influential studies suggested deleterious effects of community programs with high expectations for people discharged after extended hospital stays (Goldberg, Schooler, Hogarty, & Roper, 1977). Studies directly assessing the potential adverse effects of IPS have, however, consistently failed to detect negative outcomes. For example, as reviewed in Chapter 5, studies testing the hypothesis that replacing supportive day treatment with more demanding IPS programs would be stressful and lead to negative outcomes have not found this to be true. Without exception, none has found increased rates of program dropouts, suicide attempts, hospitalizations, incarcerations, homelessness, or symptomatic relapses.

Another test of the hypothesis of the negative side effects of IPS comes from controlled trials (Bond, Drake, & Becker, 2008). In some studies, the control group participants worked in more protected work settings (e.g., agency-run businesses), supervised by mental health staff members, which theoretically would be less stressful. At the same time, the proportion of IPS participants who obtained competitive jobs far exceeded controls in every study. If working led to clinical problems, negative outcomes should have emerged for IPS participants. However, *none* of the IPS studies documented increased rates of psychiatric hospitalization for the IPS group compared to the control group.

CHAPTER SUMMARY

Several small studies show that employment is associated with better income, better psychosocial functioning, and better illness control. These relationships, however, show a mixed picture in relation to Hill's criteria. First, the associations are weak or moderate rather than strong. Second, some relationships are consistent across groups, such as increases in self-esteem, but others are not, such as decreases in symptoms. Third, many of the relationships are specific, for example, work leads to better income and self-esteem. Fourth, temporal relationships are generally clear: income and self-esteem increase after one becomes employed. Fifth, the evidence for a gradient is weak, although studies of steady workers versus minimal workers point in this direction. Sixth, the relationships are plausible; people should be more confident, feel better, and have more money when they are working. Seventh, the relationships are coherent because they accord with basic research in the general population. And, eighth, the relationships are backed by evidence from analogous situations in which people who are active in socially valued roles accrue other gains.

Thus, overall, support for our major hypotheses is consistent but weak, in part because studies have not been designed to test these relationships.

Future research could extend these finding in several directions. Studies should be prospective and longitudinal, should examine a variety of outcomes, should examine the gradient from occasional work to steady employment, and should consider the quality of jobs.

7

ECONOMIC OUTCOMES

Because of pressure to expand IPS capacity from clients and other stakeholders, several economists and policy experts have reviewed the economic research on IPS in the United States and elsewhere (Drake, Skinner, Bond, & Goldman, 2009; Karakus, Frey, Goldman, Fields, & Drake, 2011; Latimer, 2005; Sainsbury Centre, 2009; Salkever, 2011; Schneider, 2003). In this chapter, we discuss economic issues, some related to rehabilitation services in general and others specific to IPS.

NEED

People with psychiatric disabilities form the largest and fastest growing subgroup of the Social Security Administration's disability beneficiaries on Social Security Disability Insurance or Supplemental Security Income (Kouzis & Eaton, 2000; Mechanic, Bilder, & McAlpine, 2002). One reason for this growth may be an increasing number of people with psychiatric disorders applying for disability, based on a national survey that showed self-reported mental health disability increased from 2.0% in 1999 to 2.7% in 2009 (Mojtabai, 2011). During this same time, the rate was unchanged for self-reported disabilities from other conditions. Another reason given for the growth of the subgroup of beneficiaries with psychiatric disabilities has been that they generally are younger than other subgroups (Ferron, 1995; Kennedy & Manderscheid, 1992), which leads them to stay on disability rolls longer than other beneficiaries (McAlpine & Warner, 2000; Rupp & Scott, 1996). A 2005 report indicated that 28% of Social Security Disability Insurance (SSDI) beneficiaries and 35% of Supplemental Security Income (SSI) beneficiaries of working age were disabled by mental illness (Aron, Burt, & Wittenburg, 2005). By 2007, 2.13 million Americans, 40% of all SSI beneficiaries under 65, were disabled by mental illness (SAMHSA, 2010). Over 3 million people with psychiatric disabilities are SSDI and SSI beneficiaries. Other industrialized countries are also experiencing growth in the number of people with mental illness receiving disability benefits, partly attributable in some countries to changes in unemployment benefits (OECD, 2009).

Total Social Security spending for the group of SSDI and SSI beneficiaries with psychiatric disabilities exceeds $100 billion per year (SSA, 2010). Current disability policies provide critical support such as income and health insurance to many people but also entail major constraints (Bond, Xie, & Drake, 2007; Drake et al., 2009). Critics argue that the policies impose lifelong poverty and dependency and are antithetical to the goals of the Americans with Disabilities Act (Public Law 101–336). The majority of beneficiaries do live below the poverty level, and very few leave the programs for reasons other than death or aging out (.5% of beneficiaries on SSI or SSDI each year) (National Council on Disability, 2005; Rupp & Scott, 1998; SSA, 2010), although a recent analysis that followed a defined cohort of SSDI beneficiaries found an unexpectedly high rate of beneficiaries returning to work and terminating benefits (Liu & Stapleton, 2010). In addition, federal disability policies do not address prevention. Instead, people in the early phase of mental illness often find that they are pushed toward disability applications to pay for basic mental health care, acculturating them into the disabled role and consigning them to a life of poverty. If IPS were universally available, the nation could save $368 million annually in Medicaid, Social Security and other federal and state programs, according to one economic analysis, as shown in Table 7–1 (Drake et al., 2009).

COST

Two reviews of the costs of IPS services estimate that service costs for an individual client in the first and most intensive year of services, assuming full implementation according to IPS guidelines, to be approximately $4,000 in 2006 dollars (Latimer, Bush, Becker, Drake, & Bond, 2004; Salkever, 2011). Costs vary from site to site, and economies of scale may occur in larger agencies. Costs may also be higher during the process of implementation when extra training is required and before clinicians or teams are at full capacity. Cost estimates are very sensitive to caseload size, and vary according to cost of living.

COST-EFFECTIVENESS

Cost-effectiveness research compares the costs of two programs relative to the outcomes. Two kinds of cost-effectiveness studies have addressed IPS. In the first, a program shifts from facility-based services, such as rehabilitative day treatment, to IPS (Clark, 1998; Clark, Bush, Becker, & Drake, 1996). These studies find that

TABLE 7-1 COST SAVINGS FROM UNIVERSAL ACCESS TO IPS IN THE U.S.

Subgroup	Size of Population	Costs Associated with Providing Access to IPS	Net Savings to Social Security	Net Savings to Medicare/ Medicaid	Net Federal Government Saving (millions)
Working-age adults not enrolled in SSI/SSDI (includes young adults experiencing early psychosis)	173,000 new SSDI/SSI applicants annually	Recruitment costs of $100 per person and one-time cost of $4000 per IPS participant	Reduction in rate of new SSDI/SSI enrollees	Reduction in rate of new Medicaid/ Medicare recipients	$48
Working-age adults receiving SSDI or SSI	2.2 million SSDI and 1.6 million in SSI beneficiaries		Small savings to SSI among SSI beneficiaries who work	Large savings in subgroup who become steady workers	$320
Total					$368

All estimates annualized, expressed in 2006 $, and averaged over 5-year period. Summary of economic modeling estimates from Drake, Skinner et al. (2009)

IPS reduces costs and improves vocational outcomes and is therefore highly cost-effective. In a second type of study, IPS costs and outcomes are compared to those of another model of vocational services (Clark, Xie, Becker, & Drake, 1998; Dixon et al., 2002). In these studies, costs tend to be similar across the models, but vocational outcomes are two to three times greater for IPS participants. Thus, IPS again emerges as highly cost-effective.

Perspectives on earnings are more complex. Salkever (2011) recently reviewed earnings data from several IPS studies (Becker et al., 2001; Bond et al., 2007; Clark et al., 1998; Drake et al., 1999; Lehman et al., 2002; Mueser et al., 2004) and drew two conclusions. First, IPS consistently showed superiority over comparison conditions in terms of increased earnings from competitive employment. Second, differences between IPS and comparison groups in total earnings (for competitive and noncompetitive jobs) depended on the type of comparison vocational program. IPS was superior to day treatment and similar programs in both competitive and total earnings, but only in competitive earnings in relation to active outreach programs that placed people in sheltered settings. Third, research pertaining to IPS program impacts on non-earned income, including income from public sector benefit programs, was very limited. Such information could be combined with information on earnings impacts to measure more accurately the social costs of IPS programs.

COST OFFSETS

Cost offsets refer to potential reduced costs for non-vocational services, such as treatment expenditures by Medicare, Medicaid, and state and local public mental health agencies. Although modeling studies do indicate the possibility of cost offsets, particularly for young people (Drake et al., 2009), the evidence for cost offsets is minimal as of now (Salkever, 2011). Perhaps the strongest evidence in favor of cost offsets came from the European Union study (Burns et al., 2007), in which IPS participants across six European countries had fewer hospitalizations and days in hospital than those in other vocational programs.

Other indirect evidence suggests that the relationships between employment and treatment costs can inform us about the impacts of IPS on treatment costs. One study followed high-service use clients prospectively for 10 years to track services and costs (Bush, Drake, Xie, McHugo, & Haslett, 2009). Those who became steady workers used fewer and fewer mental health services over the years; by Year 10, annual costs had dropped from baseline levels of over $30,000 annually to $9732 for the steady worker group. Thus, assuming that IPS promotes employment, the strong negative relationship between employment and treatment costs could indicate expected treatment cost savings. Of course the correlational nature of these studies limits causal interpretations, as described earlier in the chapter on non-vocational outcomes.

FINANCING BARRIERS

The major obstacles to financing IPS are funding silos, discrimination, complexity, and resistance to change (Karakus et al., 2011). IPS prescribes integration of clinical and vocational services, but a variety of different agencies provide funding and control their finances carefully. At the federal level, the Centers for Medicare and Medicaid Services, the Department of Education (Vocational Rehabilitation), the Department of Labor, the Social Security Administration, the Department of Health and Human Services (Substance Abuse and Mental Health Services Administration), the Veterans Health Administration, and the Department of Housing and Urban Development provide funds for vocational and/or clinical services. Most of these agencies have multiple funding programs for vocational services. All have separate rules, regulations, and bureaucracies, many of which are difficult to understand. Mental health administrators often worry about Medicaid audits more than about providing ineffective services. At the state level, these programs are administrated differently in each state and combined with other funding sources such as state general funds and local foundations. At the local level even greater complexity (or chaos) arises by further organizational, funding, and even personal idiosyncrasies. For example, local providers often report that funding decisions by the federal–state vocational rehabilitation system vary from one counselor to the next.

The complexity of these various funding streams presents an overwhelming bureaucratic burden for local programs. The great majority of program leaders ignore evidence-based practices in favor of ineffective practices because financing is not aligned simply and straightforwardly (Goldman et al., 2001). Program leaders and financial officers of local programs do not have the time, expertise, and incentives to negotiate with multiple agencies and unclear rules.

Providers and agencies adopt new practices at a slow pace, even when the evidence is overwhelming that existing practices are ineffective or harmful (Drake, Skinner, & Goldman, 2008). Change is even more difficult in precarious economic times and when new practices are not reimbursed in a simple, straightforward fashion. Throughout the United States, billions of dollars each year are spent on ineffective rehabilitation programs, such as day treatment, sheltered workshops, training centers, and work enclaves (Salkever, 2011). Agencies, professional guilds, unions, providers, and advocates often resist transferring money to new services.

Financing Sources. The most common sources of funding for IPS are State Offices of Vocational Rehabilitation (Department of Education funds with some state match), the Community Mental Health Services Block Grant Program (Substance Abuse and Mental Health Service Administration), State Mental Health Authorities (general funds and grants), the Medicaid Rehabilitation Option or Case Management (Centers for Medicare and Medicaid Services with state match), One-Stop Centers (Department of Labor), work incentive programs such as Plans for Achieving Self Sufficiency, Impairment Related Work Expenses, and Trial Work Period (Social Security Administration), the Ticket to Work Program (Social Security Administration), the Veterans Health Administration, and various private donors, charitable organizations, and micro enterprise centers. Each of these sources is less than optimal (Karakus et al., 2011). State Departments of Mental Health and Vocational Rehabilitation have different cultures and find it difficult to collaborate. People with psychiatric disabilities are often excluded from Vocational Rehabilitation services. The Ticket to Work Program and most of the others do not align with evidence-based principles. The

One Stop Centers do not have the expertise to serve people with mental illness (Holcomb & Barnow, 2004). Different funding sources might be used to fund specific aspects of supported employment. Furthermore, states can request various waivers to depart from usual Medicaid regulations to fund supported employment. Each state has melded together its own mechanisms (Karakus et al., 2011). We discuss policy recommendations further below in the chapter on societal perspectives and public policy.

8

GENERALIZABILITY OF IPS

In this chapter we examine the generalizability of IPS across diverse populations, settings, communities, and nations. Unlike many psychosocial interventions, which were developed and evaluated within specialized settings and populations, IPS was developed and studied within real world settings, therefore mitigating the concerns about generalizability. Many psychosocial interventions do not transfer from university settings, which typically involve selected clients, clinicians, clinics, and conditions, to real world, or routine, service settings, which of course contain complicated clients with multiple comorbidities, routine workforce clinicians, underfunded treatment settings, and uncontrolled conditions. As we explained in Chapter 9, these differences constitute the distinction that researchers define between efficacy and effectiveness.

The crux of generalizing is this: does the intervention work with diverse users, in a variety of different settings, with routine practitioners, and without special conditions? To addresses these questions, we review the evidence from studies of subgroups, including historically underserved minorities, from implementations in routine settings, and from international studies.

GENERALIZING TO CLIENT SUBGROUPS

The question of generalizability of IPS to different subgroups can be divided into two questions. The first question concerns the effectiveness of IPS across the entire spectrum of clients with serious mental illness reflecting the heterogeneity of the population served by the public mental health system. In other words, *are there certain subgroups among clients with* serious mental illness *in the public mental health system who do not benefit from IPS?* For example, do older adults with serious mental illness benefit as much from IPS as younger clients? The second question concerns the applicability of IPS to new client populations clearly distinct from the original population for which the model was developed. In other words, *can the IPS model be adapted to new client groups beyond which the model was originally intended?* We will examine both these questions.

GENERALIZABILITY OF IPS TO CLIENT SUBGROUPS WITHIN THE PUBLIC MENTAL HEALTH SYSTEM

A huge empirical literature has been devoted to identifying client factors predicting employment outcomes, as summarized in numerous reviews (Bond & Drake, 2008; Christensen, 2007; Cook & Razzano, 2000; Marwaha & Johnson, 2004; McGurk & Mueser, 2004; Michon, van Weeghel, Kroon, & Schene, 2005; Tsang, Lam, Ng, & Leung, 2000; Tsang, Leung, Chung, Bell, & Cheung, 2010; Wewiorski & Fabian, 2004). In this chapter we provide only a selective summary of this literature.

Work History. Work history is consistently a robust predictor of future employment according to virtually all studies that have examined this factor, as summarized in an early paper by Anthony and Jansen (1984) and as noted in most subsequent reviews. The construct of work history is broad, however, and does not illuminate the key components accounting for superior employment outcome. Work history probably encompasses and combines many factors related to clients, their social supports, local professional services, local employers, local economy, and so forth.

Demographic and clinical factors. Aside from work history, reviewers have reached conflicting conclusions regarding which other client factors predict work outcomes. One review found negligible effect sizes for both demographic and clinical predictors (Wewiorski & Fabian, 2004), while a second concluded that social skills and social functioning were robust predictors of work outcome (Tsang et al., 2000). A third emphasized the predictive value of symptoms, social skill deficits, and cognitive impairments (Cook & Razzano, 2000); and a fourth identified work-related competencies and self-efficacy as the best predictors (Michon et al., 2005). Several recent reviewers have drawn attention to cognitive predictors of employment outcomes (Christensen, 2007; McGurk & Mueser, 2004).

One fundamental distinction often overlooked in the search for robust client predictors of outcome is between two subgroups: people receiving active vocational assistance versus general community samples, i.e., the general psychiatric population who are not receiving vocational assistance. The strong influence of cognitive functioning and symptoms on work found in general population samples is attenuated when analyses are limited to clients receiving IPS or other vocational assistance (Campbell, Bond, Drake, McHugo, & Xie, 2010; McGurk & Mueser, 2004). Presumably the support from the IPS team compensates for deficits that prevent clients from acquiring and keeping jobs.

One client characteristic deserving comment is co-occurring substance use disorder. Many professionals believe that active substance use precludes employment, routinely screening out such clients from vocational rehabilitation services. But most studies examining this factor have found no correlation with competitive employment outcomes (e.g., Mueser, Campbell, & Drake, 2011; Sengupta, Drake, & McHugo, 1998). A 10-year follow-up study of clients with co-occurring substance use disorders also found no association between active substance use and employment (Drake et al., 2006).

In contrast to substance use, two client characteristics that have not often been examined are criminal justice history and co-occurring physical health conditions. A large and growing proportion of clients with serious mental illness entering the public mental health system have a criminal justice history (Frounfelker, Glover, Teachout, Wilkniss, & Whitley, 2010). Criminal justice involvement is widely presumed to be a major barrier to employment because many employers now screen applicants using public data (Tschopp, Perkins, Hart-Katuin, Born, & Holt, 2007), but few studies have examined this directly. One study found that clients with serious mental illness and justice involvement had delayed entry into IPS services compared to those without justice involvement (Frounfelker et al., 2010). Once enrolled in IPS, however, clients with a criminal justice history had similar employment outcomes as those without this history (Frounfelker, Teachout, Bond, & Drake, 2011). Furthermore, a recent employer survey suggested that employers are more receptive to hiring people with a justice history than is widely believed (Swanson, Langfitt-Reese, & Bond, in press).

Clients with serious mental illness are at very high risk for a wide range of chronic physical illnesses and disabilities (Cimpean & Drake, 2011). Yet, like criminal justice involvement, this factor has been largely neglected in the vocational literature. Two exceptions were a multisite study of different employment models that found poorer competitive employment outcomes for individuals with co-occurring medical conditions (Cook et al., 2008) and a study of a community sample of individuals with schizophrenia-spectrum disorder that also found lower rates of employment for those with a co-occurring physical health condition (Waghorn, Lloyd, Abraham, Silvester, & Chant, 2008).

Race and ethnicity. The generalizability of IPS across ethnocultural groups can be summarized succinctly. Ethnocultural factors do not appear to influence competitive employment outcomes for clients enrolled in IPS programs. In numerous randomized controlled trials, African–American clients have achieved similar outcomes as Caucasian clients (Bond et al., 2007; Drake et al., 1999; Gold et al., 2006; Lehman et al., 2002; Mueser et al., 2004). Although the evidence is not as extensive, the same appears to hold true for Latino clients (Mueser et al., 2004). Of course, the applicability of IPS to many other ethnocultural groups has yet to be studied, so the more empirically grounded and precise conclusion would be that at present there are no known ethnocultural groups for whom IPS is inappropriate.

While the employment outcomes for different ethnocultural groups may be comparable, this does not mean that IPS services are delivered in an identical manner to all groups or that clients from different cultural backgrounds all experience and participate in IPS services in an identical way. Ethnographic studies have uncovered subtle modifications in IPS services to specific client subgroups (Alverson, Alverson, Drake, & Becker, 1998; Alverson, Carpenter, & Drake, 2006; Alverson & Vicente, 1998; Quimby, Drake, & Becker, 2001). Overall, the IPS model appears to be adaptable to different populations, with few if any substantive changes at the level of IPS principles.

Client attitudes. Expressed interest in working of course predicts employment outcomes because people who are actively looking for work are more likely to obtain employment than those who are not (Mueser et al., 2001). A core principle of the IPS model, based on respecting client choice, is that it should be offered to people who want to work. Conversely, enrolling clients who are not currently interested in working violates the principle of informed choice and is a poor use of resources. One study indirectly validated these assumptions by enrolling clients without regard to their interest in employment and subsequently achieving a low employment rate (Lehman et al., 2002).

For decades, researchers have sought to develop attitudinal scales that would precisely predict readiness (Allen, Hodgson, Marlow, & Lindsey, 1994; Cohen, Anthony, & Farkas, 1997; Gervey, 2010; Roberts & Pratt, 2010; Rogers et al., 2001). The conceptual frameworks have varied; they have included stage of change theory (Larson, Barr, Kuwabara, Boyle, & Glenn, 2007) and the theory of planned behavior (Corbière et al., 2011). For the most part, the predictive validity of scales derived from these attitude theories has been disappointing. Researchers have consistently found only weak correlations between attitudes and the distal outcome of successful employment. These findings, of course, mirror the general findings in the social psychological literature. The quest for paper-and-pencil tests that will identify good candidates for employment services has been mostly a fruitless venture, and simply asking clients if they want to work is probably as valid a predictor as an elaborate inventory.

IPS studies of targeted client subgroups. The applicability of IPS to targeted subgroups has not been studied extensively. A small number of studies examine specific target groups, such as Social Security Disability Insurance beneficiaries (Frey et al., 2011), young adults recently diagnosed with schizophrenia (Rinaldi et al., 2010), and middle-aged and older adults (Twamley, Narvaez, Becker, Bartels, & Jeste, 2008), but many important segments of the population of people with serious mental illness have not been targeted for services in specialized programs.

To overcome the problems of small and heterogeneous study groups, we combined data from four independent IPS studies (Bond et al., 2007; Drake et al., 1999; Drake, McHugo, Becker, Anthony, & Clark, 1996; Mueser et al., 2004), all randomized controlled trials of IPS versus other vocational services that included some degree of prevocational training, and used metaanalytic procedures to examine specific subgroups among the 681 total participants. These studies assessed three measures of competitive employment: *job acquisition* at any time during the 18-month follow-up, *total weeks worked* in any competitive job during follow-up, and *job tenure,* defined as total weeks worked on the longest-held competitive job during follow-up. The findings from these analyses are reported in Campbell et al. (2011).

As shown in Table 8–1, we defined subgroups based on work history, age, sex, ethnicity/race, education, marital status, Social Security status, and history of homelessness. The findings were similar across nearly all subgroups. In every instance, the effect sizes were positive and nearly all were moderate to large. In other words, for each subgroup, IPS participants had substantially better competitive employment outcomes than controls.

The side-by-side comparisons between subgroups categorized by a client characteristic (e.g., young versus old) revealed few instances in which one subgroup benefited far more from IPS than the other. For example, those with no prior work history benefited more from IPS for job acquisition while benefiting less for total weeks worked and job tenure. A few exceptions did emerge. For example, participants with more than a high school education benefited less than those with less education, and those who were divorced or separated fared relatively poorly.

Our metaanalysis thus showed that IPS outcomes generalize broadly to people with serious mental illness, with no clearly contraindicated subgroups. Every subgroup benefited more from IPS than from sheltered workshops, skills training, or other stepwise approaches. These findings are consonant with the zero exclusion principle.

GENERALIZABILITY OF IPS TO NEW POPULATIONS

IPS has been suggested as an appropriate program model for other groups besides clients with serious mental illness, including mothers receiving welfare benefits through the Temporary Assistance for Needy Families program, many of whom have undiagnosed or untreated mental illness (Chandler, 2011; Chandler, Meisel, Jordan, Rienzi, & Goodwin, 2005; Marrone, Foley, & Selleck, 2005; Timmons & Dreilinger, 2000), transition-aged youth with severe emotional disorders (National Council on Disability, 2008), and clients with addictive disorders (Rosenheck & Mares, 2007).

TABLE 8-1 MEAN EFFECT SIZES COMPARING OUTCOMES FOR IPS TO OTHER VOCATIONAL SERVICES WITHIN WORK HISTORY AND DEMOGRAPHIC SUBGROUPS

Independent Variable	Job Acquisition	p	Total Wks	p	Job Tenure	p	Mean Across 3 Outcome Areas
Work History:							
Paid Work in Community in 5 Years							
yes	1.06	.000	.83	.000	.78	.000	.89
no	1.25	.000	.63	.000	.60	.000	.83
Weeks on Paid Work in 5 Years							
< Median (17.3 weeks)	1.03	.000	.86	.000	.80	.000	.90
> Median (17.3 weeks)	1.22	.000	.66	.000	.65	.000	.84
Sociodemographic Characteristics							
Age							
<45 years	1.07	.000	.74	.000	.70	.000	.84
45 years or older	1.18	.000	.75	.000	.70	.000	.88
Sex							
male	1.16	.000	.84	.000	.84	.000	.95
female	.97	.000	.68	.000	.69	.000	.78
Race/Ethnicity							
Caucasian	1.04	.000	.72	.000	.66	.000	.81
African American	1.21	.000	.82	.000	.80	.000	.94
Latino	.84	.017	.83	.000	.84	.000	.84
Education Level							
< high school	1.42	.000	1.06	.000	.93	.000	1.14
= high school	1.26	.000	.83	.000	.78	.000	.96
> high school	.67	.000	.51	.000	.47	.000	.55
Marital Status							
never married	1.10	.000	.75	.001	.72	.003	.86
married/living together	1.13	.023	.94	.053	1.09	.029	1.05
other	.98	.000	.50	.055	.49	.061	.66
Disability Benefits							
SSI only	1.24	.000	.70	.000	.68	.000	.87
SSDI only	1.01	.000	.91	.000	.83	.000	.92
SSI & SSDI	1.24	.000	.89	.001	.82	.003	.98
No SS benefits	.84	.000	.89	.000	.82	.000	.85
Homelessness During Past Year							
yes	1.13	.000	.95	.000	.89	.000	.99
no	1.11	.000	.60	.000	.58	.000	.76

From Campbell, K., Bond, G. R., & Drake, R. E. (2011). Who benefits from supported employment: A meta-analytic study. *Schizophrenia Bulletin, 37*, 370–380. Reprinted with permission from Oxford University Press.

Another diagnostic group for which IPS may be appropriate is posttraumatic stress disorder; a recent randomized controlled trial found exceptionally good outcomes for clients with posttraumatic stress disorder receiving IPS compared with services as usual (Davis et al., 2012).

IPS has been piloted with a range of other disabilities, including patients with spinal cord injury (Ottomanelli et al., 2012) and traumatic brain injury. Finally, some observers have asked whether IPS is appropriate for people with less debilitating psychiatric conditions, such as anxiety disorders. In the case of workers who experience stress on the job, work place interventions provided by employers (Arends, van der Klink, & Bültmann, 2010) are more direct and practical than any set of interventions such as IPS provided outside the work site.

Overall, the research on IPS in nonpsychiatric populations is sparse, and thus our assumptions about its applicability to these other populations are speculative. We assume that that the more divergent the characteristics of a population from the original population for which the model was developed, the more cautious we should be in assuming generalizability. In other words, when transferring to new populations, IPS will need to be modified substantially to accommodate the psychosocial and medical aspects of the new population.

SUMMARY: GENERALIZABILITY OF IPS ACROSS CLIENT SUBGROUPS

Researchers continue to study client characteristics as predictors of employment. Prediction from these factors continues to be weak in general community samples. Client factors are even less influential among clients enrolled in IPS, probably because of the compensatory function of IPS services (McGurk & Mueser, 2004). Moreover, many client characteristics are relatively immutable. The concern is that this type of research can be used to limit access to services rather than to refine and individualize services. Research on client characteristics that may affect employment, such as co-occurring cognitive problems, medical disorders, or criminal justice involvement, needs to be tied directly to attempts to improve services.

IPS appears to be appropriate for most clients with serious mental illness regardless of specific background characteristics, including demographic, clinical, or work history. Nevertheless, critics continue to argue that some clients lack readiness and therefore need some form of prevocational training (Macias et al., 2008; Roberts & Pratt, 2007; Rogers, Anthony, Lyass, & Penk, 2006). One of the core principles of supported employment has always been inclusion based exclusively on client choice, that is, that no one who expresses a desire to work is excluded from receiving supported employment on the basis of personal characteristics (Wehman, 1988). This principle expresses a basic value, namely, that supported employment services should be accessible to all people with disabilities, irrespective of level of disability, symptoms, work history, or other factors assumed (or shown) to be predictors of better outcomes. But this value contravenes years of traditional vocational services that were based on the assumption that many clients were not ready for employment because of their vocational deficits (Roberts & Pratt, 2007). Such assertions are commonly made, for example, with regard to individuals with poor work histories or severe psychiatric symptoms.

GENERALIZING TO REAL WORLD SETTINGS

We address two different questions regarding the generalizability of IPS to real world settings. First, to what extent can the IPS model be adopted in different service environments? Second, to what extent can the findings from randomized controlled trials be extrapolated to routine service settings?

ADOPTION OF IPS IN DIFFERENT SERVICE ENVIRONMENTS

While the experiences from an IPS learning collaborative (described in Chapter 10) are the best evidence that IPS can be transported to usual care settings, many other examples of successful IPS programs in routine mental health care settings have been reported (Lucca, Henry, Banks, Simon, & Page, 2004; Oldman, Thomson, Calsaferri, Luke, & Bond, 2005; Rapp, Goscha, & Carlson, 2010; Resnick & Rosenheck, 2007; Rinaldi, Miller, & Perkins, 2010). As we review in Chapter 10, there are a growing number of successful initiatives to disseminate IPS throughout public mental health systems, not only in the United States, but elsewhere. The comparatively easy translation of IPS from randomized controlled trials to usual care is not a surprise to anyone familiar with the IPS literature because most IPS studies have been conducted in usual care settings.

Less extensively studied have been the types of organizations in which IPS can be located successfully. That is, can IPS be adapted to psychiatric rehabilitation centers, to freestanding comprehensive rehabilitation programs, to hospitals, to clubhouses, and to assertive community treatment teams? The answer seems to be mixed. In the case of hospital-based IPS programs, while there has been at least one successful implementation in Canada (Latimer et al., 2006), application in hospital settings may be more difficult because of institutional influences (Menear et al., 2011). In a study of implementation of IPS in six Veteran Affairs medical centers, paternalistic attitudes among staff, a lack of suitable organizational structure, and strong leadership undermined initial efforts to implement IPS (Pogoda, Cramer, Rosenheck, & Resnick, 2011). On the other hand, Maryland, which has a system of free-standing psychiatric rehabilitation agencies, has demonstrated considerable success in statewide adoption of IPS within these centers (Becker et al., 2007).

Other research has suggested that comprehensive rehabilitation agencies serving multiple disability groups have had less success in adopting IPS because of the challenges of integrating mental health treatment (Campbell et al., 2007). The adoption of IPS within clubhouse programs probably has been inhibited by the clash in some of the tenets of the respective models, but examples of clubhouse-based IPS programs have been reported in the literature. Regarding employment outcomes for assertive community treatment teams, the evidence has been mixed (Kirsh & Cockburn, 2007). Discussions about the integration of IPS with ACT often focus on the conflict between the assertive community treatment model principle that all team members provide clinical services and the IPS model principle that employment specialists focus exclusively on employment services. But one study has shown that IPS and ACT can be combined successfully (Gold et al., 2006).

EXTRAPOLATING THE FINDINGS FROM RANDOMIZED CONTROLLED TRIALS TO ROUTINE SERVICE SETTINGS

Most randomized controlled trials of IPS have been conducted in real world settings, so in this sense the findings from controlled trials are directly applicable to such service environments. But controlled trials of IPS provide limited information for establishing employment *benchmarks* in routine mental health settings for several reasons. First, the timeframes are different. In routine practice, agencies evaluate outcomes monthly or quarterly, rather than over follow-up periods of 12 months or more, as in controlled trials. Second, controlled trials report findings from intent-to-treat samples (i.e., everyone is followed), whereas routine program evaluation data include only active clients (i.e., clients who drop out are not followed). Third, randomized controlled trials often include carefully selected clients, clinicians, training, or other conditions that make them different from real world programs. One recent study found that quarterly employment outcomes for three supported employment programs were less than half what they had been while the same programs were participating in randomized trials (Gold, Macias, Barreira, Tepper, & Frey, 2010).

To address this aspect of generalizability, we examined employment outcomes from 151 programs participating in a national IPS learning collaborative between 2002 and 2010 (Becker, Drake, & Bond, 2011). These outcomes provided the best available benchmarks for real world employment. In Chapter 10 we describe the method used to develop benchmarks, which indicated that an IPS program attaining 41% quarterly competitive employment rate attained "good performance." This method gives a yardstick for assessing whether an IPS program is achieving expected outcomes. The many programs in routine practice achieving this benchmark are testimony to the generalizability of the IPS model.

GENERALIZING TO OTHER COUNTRIES

IPS is just beginning to be broadly adopted in other countries. For example, in the United Kingdom, several first-episode psychosis teams provide supported employment (Brabban & Kelly, 2008). Wide dissemination of early psychosis teams sometimes staffed with a supported employment specialist is occurring in Canada, Norway, Sweden, the Netherlands, and Italy. In the meantime, IPS programs for clients with serious mental illness are being implemented in Canada, in many parts of Europe, including the United Kingdom (Rinaldi, Miller, & Perkins, 2010), the Netherlands (van Erp et al., 2007), Denmark, Spain, Italy, Switzerland (Hoffmann, Jäckel, Glauser, & Kupper, 2011), Sweden (Bejerholm, Larsson, & Hofgren, 2011), Norway, Australia (Waghorn, Collister, Killackey, & Sherring, 2007), New Zealand (Browne, Wright, Waghorn, & Stephenson, 2009), and in a few Asian cities, including the Hong Kong area of China (Wong et al., 2008) and a suburb of Tokyo, Japan (Oshima, 2011).

Worldwide interest in the IPS model is also suggested by the increased frequency of IPS studies conducted outside the United States reported since 2007. Of the 16 controlled trials of IPS reviewed in the Chapter 5, 7 were conducted outside the United States (in Canada, Australia, China, and Europe). Overall, the results were strong and positive in countries outside the United States, suggesting that IPS could be effective in other settings with extremely different healthcare, disability, economic, and workforce systems. However, we also found outcomes differences between the U.S. and non-U.S. studies. Combining samples across studies, 374 (62.1%) of 602 IPS clients from the 9 U.S. studies obtained competitive employment, compared with 245 (48.3%) of 507 IPS clients from the 7 non-U.S. studies, χ^2 (1) = 21.3, $p < .001$ (See Bond, Drake, & Becker, 2012).

In particular, the European and Canadian studies had poorer outcomes than the U.S. studies, while the outcomes from the Hong Kong and Australian studies were comparable to those in the United States. Understanding the reasons for these differences will be important for policy planners and service providers as IPS continues to be disseminated internationally. Diminished effectiveness for IPS, particularly in Europe, has typically been attributed to labor and disability policies that can impede returns to work (Burns et al., 2007). In Sweden, bureaucratic inertia and attitudinal barriers within the welfare system have impeded the development of effective IPS services (Bejerholm, Larsson, & Hofgren, 2011; Hasson, Andersson, & Bejerholm, 2011). A Dutch study has also described the challenges in implementing IPS (van Erp et al., 2007). Systems barriers are formidable and to some extent represent challenges not found in the United States. IPS leaders in several other countries have pursued strategies to overcome these barriers (Boyce, Secker, Floyd, Schneider, & Slade, 2008; Rinaldi, Miller, & Perkins, 2010; Waghorn et al., 2007). Further international studies are needed to examine the nature and strength of these policy factors and to determine what adaptations are needed. At present, too few international randomized controlled trials have been conducted to draw strong conclusions about the influence of policy and of economic, cultural, and societal factors.

An alternative explanation for the poorer employment outcomes in some IPS studies conducted outside the United States is that they have often had inadequate technical assistance and training for staff, leading to substandard implementation. Without adequate fidelity, the effectiveness of a program is attenuated (Bond, Becker, & Drake, 2011). While all of the published U.S. studies were either conducted by, or received consultation from, the developers of the IPS, only two of the six non-U.S. studies (Burns et al., 2007; Latimer et al., 2006) received direct input from the model developers. Geographic distance is likely a factor for this difference. The quality of implementation of the non-U.S. studies is generally difficult to evaluate because of the lack of process details contained in their published reports. Two non-U.S. multisite studies have reported substandard fidelity at some study sites (Burns et al., 2007; Michon, van Vugt, & van Busschbach, 2011).

ROLE OF ENVIRONMENTAL FACTORS

Under the rubric of environmental factors, we include a diverse range of exogenous variables, including societal and cultural influences, access to supported employment, financing, regulatory factors, community size, and local economy. While most observers readily acknowledge the importance of these factors, they are not well studied. We briefly review some the existing research on the role of these factors.

Societal and Cultural Influences. Customs, cultural norms, history, and economics profoundly affect the prospects for employment in different nations (Drake et al., 2011; Thornicroft, Brohan, Rose, Sartorius, & Leese, 2009). One consideration is the well-known finding of better outcomes for schizophrenia in developing countries, attributed to greater tolerance for deviance (Isaac, Chand, & Murthy, 2007; Krishnadas, Moore, Nayak, & Patel, 2007). Stigma and discrimination regarding serious mental illness has been hypothesized to vary cross-culturally, although the research is unclear (Ozawa & Yaeda, 2007; Priebe, Warner, Hubschmid, & Eckle, 1998; Tsang et al., 2007). Ethnographic studies confirm that ethnic groups differ in their beliefs about work (Alverson & Vicente, 1998; Quimby, Drake, & Becker, 2001) a finding that has implications for the design of employment services.

Access to Supported Employment. One huge barrier to competitive employment is lack of access to high-quality services. The extent of this lack of access is not well documented, but a national survey conducted in the U.S. reported that 2.1% of clients receiving community mental health services were enrolled in supported employment (SAMHSA, 2009). Lack of access can be explained to some extent by practitioner attitudes (Braitman et al., 1995) and absence of referrals (Casper & Carloni, 2007). But the fundamental barrier is failure to align healthcare funding with evidence-based practices (Goldman et al., 2001; Karakus, Frey, Goldman, Fields, & Drake, 2011).

Financing. Several different financing mechanisms have been advanced to promote better employment outcomes for people with serious mental illness. In healthcare, one financing model that received attention is called pay-for-performance (P4P) (Rosenthal, Frank, Li, & Epstein, 2005). In the vocational rehabilitation field, the performance-based approach to funding has been associated with the "milestone approach" in which vocational programs are paid according to the achievement of specific goals, such as job placement or holding the job for a specific period of time. One controlled study found that incentivizing employment programs in this fashion significantly improved outcomes (McGrew, Johannesen, Griss, Born, & Katuin, 2005). Another demonstration of the utility of performance-based funding was a statewide demonstration in which small incentives on a center-wide basis had incremental effects (Rapp, Huff, & Hansen, 2003). The Ticket to Work program is one example of a federal program adopting the performance-based funding model. The Ticket to Work program has demonstrated one pitfall of the performance-based approach: If the incentive schedule is unrealistic, it will not be adopted (Salkever, 2003). Another fundamental weakness of performance-based financing is the danger of selection, in which programs enroll clients who are more likely to achieve employment and avoid enrolling those who are more disabled.

One alternative to performance-based financing is *fidelity-based* financing. Currently three states (Maryland, Oregon, and Kansas) are reimbursing agencies with employment programs that achieve high fidelity on the IPS Fidelity Scale (Bond, Becker, & Drake, 2011). The reasoning is that higher fidelity leads to better outcomes, as the research summarized in Chapter 4 suggests. Moreover, fidelity-based financing does not incentivize selection. One of the states pursuing this financing model has produced evidence that this assumption has held up in an annual statewide evaluation (Hepburn & Burns, 2007).

Regulatory Factors. Health and disability regulations and labor laws probably overwhelm other factors in determining employment outcomes for people with serious mental illness. The regulations of the disability system exert a profound disincentive on seeking work throughout the world (Bond, Xie, & Drake, 2007; Burns et al., 2007; Cook, 2006; GAO, 2007; Livermore, Goodman, & Wright, 2007; van Erp et al., 2007). Although much has been written about social, employer, and economic factors, health and disability policies are the major barriers to competitive employment for people with serious mental illness, at least in the United States. Most people with schizophrenia must enter the federal disability system (Social Security) in order to obtain income assistance and insurance (Medicaid or Medicare). Once on disability and federal insurance, they have strong incentives to remain unemployed. Only a small minority of those receiving disability benefits accept offers for employment services, according to a recent study (Frey et al., 2011), and few ever leave the disability roles (Livermore, Goodman, & Wright, 2007; Rupp & Scott, 1996). For clients receiving Social Security Disability Insurance (SDDI), earning above the "Substantial Gainful Activity" (SGA) level in nine different months can trigger a review of benefits and possible ineligibility. In a recent study of over 2,000 SSDI beneficiaries, only about 8% of beneficiaries enrolled in IPS exceeded the Substantial Gainful Activity level during the last month of follow-up (Frey et al., 2011).

Outside the United States, health insurance is not tied to disability, but employment and disability policies still create barriers to competitive employment (Burns et al., 2007; Menear et al., 2011; van Erp et al., 2007; Waghorn et al., 2007). In a study conducted in six European nations, Burns et al. (2007) defined *benefits trap* by asking the IPS worker at each site "whether they considered their client group to be at risk of having their income reduced if they took a job" (p. 1149). London and Groningen were rated as high-risk sites, Ulm and Zürich as low-risk, and Rimini and Sofia as no-risk. Degree of risk was associated with effect size of the difference between the IPS group and controls at each site.

Community Size. Although it is widely assumed that IPS services are more difficult to deliver in rural areas than in cities, evidence does not support this belief (Drake et al., 1998; Haslett, Bond, Drake, Becker, & McHugo, 2011). The demands of employment services (job development and job support) differ based on community size (Carlson, 2009). Compared to rural communities, large cities have more employers and greater anonymity, and the job search process is more formal. Mental health services in rural communities rely more on natural supports than those in urban programs (Rapp & Goscha, 2011). Travel time is a factor in rural communities, although in large congested cities, travel time is also a challenge. Despite many differences, fidelity of IPS implementation is not affected by rural location (Becker, Xie, McHugo, Halliday, & Martinez, 2006).

Local Economy. During the recession beginning in 2008, persons with disabilities were more deeply affected by job loss and underemployment than were people without disabilities (Fogg, Harrington, & McMahon, 2010). Several studies have examined the impact of the local unemployment rate on job placement rates for employment programs. Three studies have found significant associations (Becker et al., 2006; Burns et al., 2007; Cook et al., 2006) and a fourth found weak associations (Salkever et al., 2007). Restriction in range in general unemployment rates may account for the lack of statistical association in studies with nonsignificant findings. Overall, the evidence is growing that local economies affect employment rates for people with serious mental illness. That being said, the impact of the local economy should not be overstated. In the IPS learning collaborative described above, the overall employment rate for IPS programs did decline during the recent recession, but the decline was only a few percentage points (Becker et al., 2011).

CHAPTER SUMMARY

In this chapter we reviewed the generalizability of IPS to different client subgroups, to different countries, to different communities and to different environmental conditions. Researchers continue to focus on factors that are relatively easy to study rather than those that are powerful and meaningful from a public health perspective. The field continues to produce studies of factors that are immutable or that affect tiny portions of the variance in meaningful outcomes. For example, our review suggests a much smaller role for client factors than is accorded by most researchers. Specifically, we have estimated that client factors account for less than 10% of the variance in competitive employment outcomes for clients enrolled in IPS (Bond & Drake, 2008).

Although the current evidence is mostly anecdotal, many environmental factors, such as labor and disability laws, appear to influence both the success of IPS and the extent to which it is modified when it is adopted. The benefits trap is the best-documented example of an environmental influence on IPS success. The local economy, i.e., the unemployment rate, does appear to have an influence, but possibly not as great as commonly believed, at least when that rate is in single digits. Surprisingly, community size has not been shown to influence the effectiveness of IPS.

The question of IPS transportability outside the United States remains unanswered. While the published studies suggest that the labor and disability laws in some European countries may make a direct replication of IPS difficult, there are also indications that IPS transports well to other countries, such as Australia and the Hong Kong region of China. Finally, before concluding that the IPS must undergo radical adaptations in another nation, IPS programs should receive sufficient training and guidance to implement the model with high fidelity.

In this chapter we have omitted any discussion of program and model features as factors influencing IPS outcomes and hence the generalizability of IPS. The program characteristics related to the program itself—its implementation, program fidelity, and staffing, and service intensity—were discussed in Chapter 4. Our research has led us to hypothesize that program factors account for 25%–50% of the variance in client outcomes (Bond & Drake, 2008). Unlike client factors, program and staffing factors are malleable, suggesting reason for optimism in terms of attaining good competitive employments through a process of continuous quality improvement.

9

METHODOLOGICAL
CONSIDERATIONS

In this chapter we consider several methodological topics, some for the sake of clarifying the approaches we have described in previous chapters and some because they represent areas needing further research. Research on real world problems is complex and proceeds on the basis of serendipity, the vagaries of research funding, and a host of other nonscientific considerations.

This chapter is divided into two main sections. The first section, *Developing an Evidence-based Practice*, outlines the steps in establishing a program of research and clarifying some choices made in IPS research. The second section, *Common Methodological Issues*, examines many critical details in the planning and execution of research.

DEVELOPING AN EVIDENCE-BASED PRACTICE

Developing an evidence-based practice involves a stepwise approach. Rounsaville, Carroll, and Onken (2001) described a three-stage approach: 1) feasibility and pilot testing, 2) randomized controlled trials, and 3) studies to demonstrate generalizability and implementation (Onken, Blaine, & Battjes, 1997). Interventions that have passed the first two stages are considered evidence-based practices. Our group has used the following four-step process (Mueser & Drake, 2005, 2011).

Step 1. Articulating the Problem. All interventions begin with a problem for which an effective treatment is needed. The problem area should be regarded as meaningful (e.g., a need for meaningful activity). The problem should be defined and measured in a reliable and valid way (Nunnally, 1978). Reliable measurement involves reproducibility: inter-rater reliability (i.e., different observers see the same thing), internal reliability (e.g., different items on a scale are related to one-another), and test–retest reliability (i.e., showing stability of the measure over relatively brief periods of time in the absence of intervention). Valid measurement includes correlations with related measures or behavioral indices. Measures also should be sensitive to change. Developing an effective intervention requires reliable and valid measures of important outcomes.

Some interventions have broad goals (e.g., improving quality of life), while others have narrow goals (e.g., independent living skills). Broad outcomes are often difficult to assess, whereas a narrow behavioral target is often assessed more easily and reliably.

Defining the target population broadly has the advantage of maximizing the number of clients who may potentially benefit from an intervention, but most interventions apply only to subgroups (e.g., IPS is for people who want a job). Intervention development includes specifying the individuals who might benefit. Research often starts narrowly and expands to more general populations.

Step 2. Identifying Possible Treatments. New interventions are developed by several different approaches: for example, using theories regarding the problem area, using theories of behavior change, adapting successful interventions used with other populations, adapting successful interventions used for other problems, or discovering interventions serendipitously.

Psychotherapy based on relational frame theory exemplifies the first approach (Hayes, Barnes-Holmes, & Roche, 2001). According to this theory, humans' capacity for language and thought enables them to interpret and respond to their thoughts as though they were real world experiences rather than symbolic representations. Based on this theory, Acceptance and Commitment Therapy (Hayes, Strosahl, & Wilson, 1999) teaches clients to accept rather than trying to control unpleasant thoughts and feelings, which are largely beyond their control and have limited basis in reality.

Extending social skills training based on social learning theory (Bandura, 1969) to a wide range of social problems (Liberman, DeRisi, & Mueser, 1989) and using motivational interviewing based on the stages of change concept (Prochaska & DiClemente, 1984) to addictive disorders (Miller & Rollnick, 2002) illustrate the second approach. The crux of social learning theory is that people learn from observing others' behavior, as well as from the consequences of their behavior. Social skills training involves the systematic teaching of social behaviors through a combination of modeling skills, role-playing, receiving positive and corrective feedback, and practicing skills in natural situations. Based on the observation that changes toward healthier behavior tend to occur through a sequence of distinct stages (precontemplation, contemplation, preparation, behavior change, and maintenance), motivational interviewing helps people articulate their personal goals and explore the steps and barriers to achieving those goals, thereby enhancing the client's own motivation to address substance abuse.

The IPS model represents the third approach (Becker & Drake, 2003). IPS was adapted from promising supported employment approaches for individuals with developmental disabilities (Wehman & Moon, 1988). Employment specialists work collaboratively with mental health treatment teams to help clients find and succeed in competitive jobs that match their personal preferences.

Adaptations of assertive community treatment (Stein & Santos, 1998; Stein & Test, 1980) follow the fourth approach. Originally developed to address the problem of frequent hospitalizations, assertive community treatment has been used for several other problems, such as homelessness (Lehman, Dixon, Kernan, & DeForge, 1997), substance abuse (Drake et al., 1998), and involvement in the criminal justice system (Morrissey, Meyer, & Cuddeback, 2007).

Finally, serendipity has been the dominant model for developing pharmacological interventions for mental illness. Although this seems less likely to occur for complex psychosocial interventions, many rehabilitation interventions stem from observing techniques that clients have discovered themselves. For example, the teaching of coping skills to manage persistent psychotic symptoms (Tarrier et al., 1993) was initially based on naturalistic studies that demonstrated that clients with schizophrenia often develop their own strategies for coping with distressing symptoms (Alverson, Becker, & Drake, 1995; Falloon & Talbot, 1981).

Step 3. Pilot Testing the Intervention. Pilot testing an intervention establishes feasibility and potential. Secondary goals include standardizing the intervention and developing a measure of fidelity. Pilot testing typically involves providing the intervention to a small number of clients and observing the targeted outcomes. Prior to formal pilot testing, researchers try the intervention with a few clients to examine suitability, mode of delivery, intensity, and need for modifications. Once these aspects are clear, researchers must establish feasibility.

Feasibility includes acceptability and retention. Acceptability refers to willingness to participate in an intervention, while retention involves staying in treatment long enough to achieve benefits. Interventions can only be effective if clients are willing to join and participate. As a general rule, dropout rates of less than 20% are good, in the 20–30% range are acceptable, and over 30% are problematic.

Pilot studies also examine whether or not the intervention has potential to improve the targeted outcomes. Researchers disagree about the need for a control group during pilot testing. Those who use a pre-post-follow-up design without a control group must interpret improvements in selected outcomes as meaningful compared to expectations. If functioning in targeted problem areas is relatively stable without treatment, improvements following the intervention can be attributed to the intervention. But most psychiatric problems fluctuate over time, so improvements could be due to natural history. Controlled research designs that include a comparison group, such as randomized controlled trials or quasiexperimental studies, provide stronger evidence, but often lack sufficient statistical power to detect significant differences. Researchers should therefore state from the outset that the pilot study aims to show that some clients benefit and to estimate the likely magnitude of the change (called the effect size), not to show statistical significance. However, researchers should also be cautioned that effect sizes based on relatively small pilot studies are often inaccurate and may lead to the premature rejection of a potentially effective intervention (Kraemer, Mintz, Noda, Tinklenberg, & Yesavage, 2006).

The pilot study is usually based on an outline of the intervention program or a draft of the manual. Because valuable experience delivering the intervention is gained during the pilot study, a formal treatment manual can readily be written based on the pilot. When a draft of a manual exists prior to the pilot study, some modifications are usually made after the study is completed based on the additional clinical experience. The specificity of manuals varies greatly from one project to another, and depends partly on the nature of the intervention. Most treatment manuals include information to orient clinicians to the nature of the problem, as well as some conceptual foundations to the intervention. Specific guidelines are provided regarding the logistics of the intervention, identification of clients for whom the intervention is designed, curriculum, teaching skills, and guidance for handling common problems. Manuals often provide clinical vignettes to illustrate treatment principles and incorporate specific instruments for assessment and monitoring clinical outcomes. The length of treatment manuals varies from 20 pages to 200 pages.

During pilot testing, researchers also need to establish methods to verify that an intervention is delivered in a manner consistent with the treatment model. Such verification is crucial to conducting a rigorous assessment of the intervention. Researchers must first establish that the intervention has been implemented as intended before determining its effects. Expert judgments are often used to establish fidelity. In this method, a recognized expert on the intervention obtains information regarding the implementation (e.g., by observing therapy sessions, reviewing case notes, conducting interviews) and provides feedback regarding the degree of adherence to the model. Alternatively, specific behavioral anchor points for rating adherence can be used to train raters and make fidelity ratings. Objective fidelity ratings avoid the expense and potential bias of expert ratings. Fidelity scales have become the standard in the field (Bond et al., 2000), because they provide specific information to address implementation problems and to explore the relationship between fidelity and outcome.

Step 4. Evaluating the Intervention in Randomized Controlled Trials. Rigorous evaluation is the sine qua non of evidence-based interventions. In this section, we briefly address several of the most crucial aspects of randomized controlled trials, including the experimental design, the selection of a control group, inclusion/exclusion criteria for the target population, the setting for the trial, and the choice of outcome measures.

The randomized controlled trial is considered superior to other research designs because it controls for group equivalence. Many important variables are unknown or unobserved, and quasiexperimental designs almost inevitably compare nonequivalent groups. For interventions delivered at the level of the treatment team or mental health agency, randomizing organizational units and not study participants may be the only option. When treatment teams or mental health centers are randomly assigned to receive the experimental intervention or the control intervention, the true unit of analysis is the mental health treatment team or agency rather than the individual. Statistical techniques exist to deal with the clustering of individuals within groups. In practice, researchers often compare the outcomes of individual clients treated on different teams or in different mental health centers. This design is not considered a pure randomized controlled trial because each client does not have an independent and equal chance of being in either intervention. Nevertheless, this design has advantages over many other approaches because the agencies or mental health centers are assigned by randomization and are therefore likely to be equivalent.

In selecting the comparison group for a randomized controlled trial, the common options are an equally intensive intervention, a less intensive intervention, treatment as usual, placebo treatment, or no treatment (e.g., a waiting list). Each option has advantages and disadvantages. In practice, the selection reflects pragmatic considerations as well as the specific research question.

Pilot work should guide selection of the inclusion and exclusion criteria for the randomized controlled trial. These criteria inevitably involve a trade-off between efficacy and effectiveness. Efficacy studies use narrowly defined criteria to maximize the chance of finding significant differences, whereas effectiveness studies use broad criteria to maximize real-world applicability, or generalizability.

Similar considerations influence site selection because location will affect transferability to other settings. Clinical trials conducted in routine mental health centers rather than in university clinics (i.e., the effectiveness design) maximize the potential for applicability to the kinds of settings in which most people receive treatment. By contrast, efficacy studies are conducted in highly controlled settings, with specially trained clinicians, and other constrained conditions, for the sake of isolating and controlling the treatment intervention. Traditionally, interventions have been tested first in efficacy trials and then in effectiveness trials. Recently, however, some interventions are developed and tested under effectiveness conditions to ensure generalizability from the outset. Needless to say, recruitment, training, high-fidelity implementation, retention, and assessment challenge researchers in multifarious ways.

Measurement should address outcomes, implementation/process, and theory. Outcome measures assess the goals of the intervention (e.g., work, quality of social relationships, symptom severity, relapses, and hospitalization), as identified and measured since the earliest steps of developing an evidence-based practice. Primary outcomes reflect the most important targets, while secondary outcomes include areas that may be improved by changes in the primary outcomes. For example, the primary outcome of supported employment is working, measured by percentage of clients who are employed, number of hours they are working, wages, and length of employment. Employment may also affect secondary outcomes such as self-esteem, symptoms, and life satisfaction.

Implementation and process measures assess whether the interventions were provided as intended and whether clients received the interventions. These measures can be broadly divided into those that evaluate fidelity to the treatment model and those that record clients' exposure to treatment. Treatment exposure measures include information such as the number, duration, and time of treatment contacts.

Randomized controlled trials can also provide valuable information regarding how an intervention works, how theoretical constructs interact with functional outcomes, and how different outcomes are related. Theory testing and development can guide the refinement of an intervention to enhance effectiveness.

COMMON METHODOLOGICAL ISSUES IN IPS RESEARCH

In the first section of this chapter we examined broad strategies for conducting a program of research starting from the nascent stages of development of any novel psychosocial intervention to the mature stages of evaluation and dissemination. In this second section we discuss specific methodological issues that have been especially salient in IPS research.

Design. Two overarching topics are the efficacy vs. effectiveness distinction and the choice of basic research designs. Efficacy and effectiveness are extremes on a continuum (Wells, 1999). In general, efficacy studies aim to examine the effect of the intervention in ideal, highly controlled circumstances, whereas effectiveness studies attempt to examine interventions under more typical practice conditions, often referred to as "routine" or "real world" settings. In efficacy research, the participants, interventions, monitoring conditions, clinicians, settings, measures, and so on are carefully selected. The difficulty with efficacy research is that results from studies of this type often do not generalize to real world conditions, for a variety of reasons. For instance, the participants have more complicated problems or are difficult to engage, the clinicians have less time or are unable to learn the intervention, the mental health agency has difficulty paying for the intervention, and so forth.

In effectiveness research, investigators attempt to use real world conditions: all potential participants are eligible, the setting is a routine clinic or mental health center rather than a university clinic, the clinicians are part of the regular workforce, the intensity of the intervention is realistic, and other conditions represent usual practice as closely as possible. The research methods may also be less rigorous. One central finding in effectiveness research is that efficacious interventions may show much smaller effects or no effect at all, for a wide variety of reasons (Weisz & Jensen, 1999). Researchers therefore need to be scrupulous, often relying upon mixed methods, to discern the reasons.

Research on intervention development often proceeds in stages from pilot study to efficacy to effectiveness to cost-effectiveness (Mueser & Drake, 2011; Rounsaville, Carroll, & Onken, 2001). As an alternative, a compromise solution melds efficacy and effectiveness methods. For example, the intervention is designed, piloted, and tested under more real world conditions from the beginning, bypassing the stage of testing the model in highly controlled settings. The initial phases may be complicated in this approach, but the intervention is highly likely to generalize because of the developmental circumstances. As described in Chapter 1, the melding strategy has been our preference in IPS studies. Virtually all IPS studies have been conducted under real world conditions, progressing from quasiexperimental designs to randomized controlled trials, and more recently to an emphasis on large-scale implementation studies.

The main trade-off of testing a program model in real world settings is that that these conditions introduce a host of confounding variables that a controlled setting seeks to avoid. For example, in a classic efficacy trial, the sample inclusion criteria may exclude any participant with a co-occurring condition, such as substance abuse. Another common restriction is to limit participants to a specific diagnosis, such as schizophrenia. A third example of an exclusion criterion is screening out anyone who has any prior exposure to vocational services. While the primary motivation behind such exclusions is to reduce noise in the statistical analysis, these restrictions limit generalizability.

The best, and possibly only, exemplar of an IPS efficacy trial was done by Nuechterlein and his colleagues (2008). Conducted at a teaching hospital, this study required participants to have a period of stabilization before formally entering the IPS program, which is itself a compromise of a core IPS principle. Although this study is important in establishing the generalizability of IPS to clients experiencing a first-episode psychosis, it needs replication in the public mental heath system before it will be fully vetted.

One other research design deserves mention, namely, the cluster randomized controlled trial (Campbell, Mollison, Steen, Grimshaw, & Eccles, 2000).

In this design, sites, rather than individuals, are randomized. This design is currently being used in a large NIMH contract evaluating IPS and other services for young adults experiencing a first episode of psychosis (Kane, work in progress). The main advantage of this approach is that it greatly reduces the problem of treatment contamination when practitioners at a site observe others offering an alternative program model. The main disadvantage is that while statistical methods are used to compensate for the confounding effects of site differences, this design cannot obviate that influence. This problem is greatest when the number of study sites is small (e.g., Salyers et al., 2010). Another application of cluster randomization is random assignment of practitioners to receive special training and evaluating the impact on their clients. Interpretive difficulties arise with this design as well.

Multisite evaluations in which participants are randomized to experimental and control conditions are exceptionally daunting, especially as the number of sites grows. A very common finding in such studies is site variability in the quality of implementation resulting in variable site-level outcomes. As described in Chapter 10, over 85% of sites in a complicated 23-site randomized trial successfully achieved high fidelity to the IPS model (Frey et al., 2011), demonstrating that large multisite randomized controlled trials of IPS are feasible.

Participants. Who are the appropriate participants in IPS studies and in IPS services? Following the previous discussion, our preference has been to include all volunteers without exclusions based on symptoms, poor work history, or any other measure of work readiness. Zero exclusion is an essential principle of IPS because professionals have historically screened many people out of vocational services, despite little empirical validity for these decisions. Zero exclusion accords with client preferences and social justice.

Some observers have criticized IPS for its lack of outreach to individuals who do not have competitive employment goals, as well as the exclusion of clients without vocational goals from IPS evaluations (Macias, DeCarlo, Wang, Frey, & Barreira, 2001; Macias et al., 2009; Roberts & Pratt, 2007). This criticism ignores ethical principles such as respect for the individual and autonomy. All clients with serious mental illness should be encouraged to pursue work and should be informed about supported employment, and case managers and other members of the treatment team should strive to create a culture in which work is valued (Gowdy, Carlson, & Rapp, 2004). At the same time, however, respect for the individual's legal right to informed decision making and the pragmatic perspective of shared decision making (O'Connor et al., 2007) dictate that the decision to enter supported employment should be the participant's active choice based on a clear understanding of what the decision means. A decision aid to educate clients about IPS and to encourage their engagement has recently been developed and pilot tested with promising results (Haslett, 2011).

Research information groups. One of the innovations in study design pioneered by Dartmouth researchers is the *research information group* (Bebout, Becker, & Drake, 1998; Drake, Becker, & Anthony, 1994). Used routinely in all Dartmouth randomized controlled studies of IPS, the research information group provides an introduction to prospective study participants regarding the requirements and benefits for study participation, including a careful description of the programs to which they could be assigned. To participate in a study, a person is required to attend a minimum number of information group meetings (typically at least two), on the assumption that repeated exposure to the material not only increases participant understanding and commitment to the research and but also helps ensure true informed consent. Participants in IPS studies have generally appreciated the informational group.

The criticism that research information groups introduce a selection bias that skews the sample enrolling in IPS studies may be overstated to the extent that most people choose to enroll in a research study if they attend one or two informational groups. For example, in a study enrolling new admissions to a psychiatric rehabilitation agency identified 400 clients who were potentially eligible for the study. Of these, 296 (74%) attended at least one informational group. Of these, 200 enrolled in the study—over 2/3 of those attending an information group and 50% of the original client pool (Bond et al., 2007). The most common reasons for not joining the study were reluctance to attend the rehabilitation agency and a lack of vocational goals, both valid reasons for exclusion from a practical as well as scientific standpoint. The perils of enrolling clients without regard to vocational goals was vividly demonstrated in a study that ignored this factor, resulting in a low study retention rate and poor outcomes (Lehman et al., 2002).

The research information group was particularly critical in a study of Social Security Disability Insurance beneficiaries who were identified and contacted using rosters generated from Social Security records (Frey et al., 2011). The overall study recruitment rate from this unsolicited invitation was 14%. However, among eligible beneficiaries attending an informational group 59% agreed to join the study. In summary, the information group is a valuable innovation for ethical, scientific, and practical reasons and is congruent with a shared decision making philosophy.

Interventions. Supported employment has a broad range of definitions and representations. Not all of these are evidence-based, not all are called IPS, and not all that call themselves IPS actually embody the basic features. Defining and measuring psychosocial models has been a ubiquitous problem (Brekke, 1988). So what is really IPS? The development of the IPS fidelity scale was described in Chapter 3. The central role of fidelity and fidelity measurement in the scientific evaluation of IPS has been stressed throughout this book. It is one of the hallmarks of this intervention. We suggest that evaluations of the effectiveness of IPS include a systematic assessment of IPS fidelity conducted by qualified evaluators. Without this evaluation it is difficult to understand anomalous findings. Some examples illustrate this point. A large multisite evaluation of what was purported to be IPS yielded low employment outcomes (Rosenheck & Mares, 2007). In studying these results, the most plausible explanation is that the dissemination effort did not ensure high fidelity to the IPS model (Bond, 2007). The implementation issues in the Howard et al. (2010) study have been well documented (Campbell, 2010; Latimer, 2010). IPS augmentation studies have been beset by fidelity problems as well; two such studies allocated set-aside jobs to one or more of their experimental conditions, thereby confounding their interpretation (Bell, Greig, Zito, & Wexler, 2007; Tsang, Fung, Leung, Li, & Cheung, 2010).

Another use of fidelity assessments in multisite studies is to provide a way of interpreting poorer outcomes if some sites have substandard performance (e.g., Burns et al., 2007). This use is especially important as the number of sites grows.

In summary, assessment of fidelity is crucial for IPS research, perhaps especially given the fact that these studies are almost always conducted in real world settings. But even if they were conducted in controlled settings, fidelity assessment would be crucial. Although the examples given above are in the service of detecting failures to implement at high fidelity as a means to understanding study findings, the more important and more powerful use of fidelity scales in IPS research is to guide implementation as the study is being conducted. Several successful IPS trials were in jeopardy of collapse in early stages but were rescued through fidelity reviews and subsequent improvements in program implementation (Bond et al., 2007; Gold et al., 2006). The recently completed Mental Health Treatment Study achieved high fidelity in over 85% of the sites through the effort of three quality management project directors who supervised the implementation and maintenance of fidelity (Frey et al., 2011).

Comparison conditions. As part of the American Recovery and Reinvestment Act of 2009, Congress allocated funds for comparative effectiveness research, defined as "the generation and synthesis of evidence that compares the benefits and harms of alternative methods to prevent, diagnose, treat and monitor a clinical condition, or to improve the delivery of care" (Sox & Greenfield, 2009, p. 203). While this legislation concerned health care, its relevance to IPS is that it framed the question of effectiveness as one in which an experimental intervention is evaluated against a standard treatment. The Food and Drug Administration similarly requires successful completion of comparative effectiveness studies with positive results as one condition before approving a new medical treatment (Leff, 2005).

In the case of vocational services for people with serious mental illness, the existing vocational approaches available at the time IPS came to the scene generally had weak or nonexistent evidence bases (Bond, 1992; Bond, Drake, Becker, & Mueser, 1999). To a large extent, this remains true today. The control groups used in the IPS studies reviewed earlier have been variable, but in some of these studies, the comparator was a program model regarded at the time as being state of the art.

In summary, the comparison conditions in IPS studies have been heterogeneous. Remarkably, despite this diversity, the IPS findings have been quite robust. In some instances, highly regarded alternative models have performed poorly.

Settings. Interventions are often developed and tested in university clinics or laboratories, which permit researchers to exert maximal control and monitoring. Yet the setting, clinicians, and situation may be so artificial that the study includes unusual participants, provides unusually intensive services, and produces results that are not reproducible in usual care settings. For example, vocational research in Veteran Affairs medical centers, in which researchers are the job supervisors, clients are unpaid, and everyone does the same job, might be considered efficacy research. Settings such as these permit testing of very specific factors, but may not generalize to real world settings.

In IPS research, we have chosen to do everything in real world settings, thus maximizing the potential for generalizing. But such settings preclude certain kinds of studies. For example, our ability to interview and study employers and job demands has been constrained because many employers do not even know their employees have disabilities. Inviting employers to be research participants in evaluation of the IPS model is not practical because it compromises the employer role. Not only would this violate the informed choice about disclosure among IPS participants, but it would also introduce numerous confounds to the hiring process and supervision of employees.

Environmental measures. As discussed earlier, environmental variables, such as local unemployment rate, state and local regulations, and other contextual variables, are rarely reported in detail in research studies, even though these may exert major influences on outcomes. Future research should systematically address these shortcomings through assessing environmental factors.

Process measures. As suggested above, measuring fidelity is essential for any IPS study. Our recommendation is to use the Supported Employment Fidelity Scale, following the procedures outlined in the fidelity manual (Becker, Swanson, Bond, & Merrens, 2008). Another critical variable that has not been standardized in IPS studies is the measurement of engagement in IPS and in other services at the site. Precise dates of terminating from IPS services should be sought, although by its nature, dropping out is often not signaled by a specific event. Dropout status should not depend solely on agency records, which may be dictated by vagaries of administrative policies and financial incentives. Another variable that is related but not identical to IPS termination is discontinuation of all services from the study site. The research team should also zealously seek to obtain precise information about program termination. Finally, a third type of discontinuation is termination, defined as a formal withdrawal from the study or, more frequently, loss to follow-up. *Program* dropouts (i.e., clients who terminate from IPS or for the service agency) are of course not identical to *study* dropouts. Following the logic of intent-to-treat designs, we obtain as much information as possible from program dropouts over the follow-up period (Lachin, 2000). Even if a full outcome battery cannot be obtained, partial information on employment status at follow-up greatly enhances the completeness of the data.

Another domain of interest in IPS studies is service utilization. When the study site routinely collects service contacts, for example, for Medicaid billing purposes, it is sometimes possible to retrieve and use to study associations between service intensity and employment outcomes (e.g., McGuire, Bond, Clendenning, & Kukla, 2011). As information technology improves and electronic data bases are more common, the prospects for collecting service data for research purposes continue to improve.

Outcome measures. Important measurement issues include *content of measures, frequency, data sources, data collection methods,* and *data entry.* Regarding measurement content, we divide the discussion into vocational and non-vocational measures.

Content of employment measures. We endorse the recent call for the creation of a core employment outcome battery to which all IPS researchers subscribe (Drebing, Bell, Campinell, & Fraser, 2012). The first step is to develop a shared vocabulary for key terms, such as *competitive employment, casual labor, employment rate,* and *job tenure.* While the terminology used in the literature has been fairly consistent, there has been some confusion, especially regarding the concept of job tenure. Recently, Bond and Kukla (2011b) replaced the term job tenure with the concept of job *duration,* measuring it in terms of all jobs, first job, and longest-held job. Another terminological ambiguity involves the variety of paid employment, especially when jobs are subsidized, set-aside, or make-work positions. We recommend that studies carefully classify all jobs according to the typology developed by Bond et al. (2007).

One unfortunate development prominent in the early psychosis literature has been the collapsing of employment and education outcomes into a single measure of "vocational outcome." We understand the rationale for giving equal weight to both goals, especially in light of the primacy of client choice. But the issue here is not individualization of goals; the issue is precision of measurement. When educational outcomes are prominent, the measurement strategy should be to report educational and employment outcomes separately, in addition to a composite measure of both, as Rinaldi et al. (2010) have done in their review.

After establishing a shared vocabulary, a core set of measures that all studies include or at least aspire to include is critical. The absence of a standard battery has resulted in inconsistent reporting of key outcomes in major studies (Bond, Drake, & Becker, 2008; Kinoshita et al., 2010). For example, many studies have not reported total earnings from employment, despite the utility of this measure for understanding clients' personal economies. With respect to job satisfaction, this measure has not been routinely collected, nor have investigators used the same instrument. Probably the most commonly used job satisfaction tool is the Indiana Job Satisfaction Scale (Resnick & Bond, 2001), though it has not been established as superior to alternatives.

Measuring job tenure in randomized controlled trials has been problematic because many participants are employed at the end of follow-up (i.e., many job tenures are right-censored). Thus, the literature consistently underestimates job tenure. In studies with fixed follow-up periods, the time between study enrollment and first day employed also reduces the possible period to accrue time in employment because participants often spend the first few months of the study involved in engagement, job development, interviewing, and other activities. The optimal solution, of course, is to conduct long-term follow-up studies. In the absence of long-term follow-up, we propose weeks worked during follow-up as the single most valid measure of job duration (Bond & Kukla, 2011b). Weeks worked ignores the issue of number of jobs held, consistent with the IPS principle of helping clients obtain a new job if an initial job is unsatisfactory or ends for any reason. For primary studies, metaanalyses, or narrative reviews in which participants are followed for variable periods of time, a standardized measure of job duration is *percentage* of time worked during a follow-up period (i.e., weeks worked/total weeks of follow-up).

We recently proposed a conceptual framework for classifying objective employment measures into four semi-independent domains: *job acquisition, job duration, workweek,* and *total hours/wages* (Bond, Campbell, & Drake, 2012). Job acquisition includes *percentage of clients working at any time* and *time to first job.* Job duration includes *percentage of time worked, total weeks worked,* and *job tenure in longest-held job.* Workweek measures include *number of hours worked per week* and *percentage working full-time and working 20 hours or more.* Total hours/ wages includes *total hours* and *total earnings.* This framework is just a beginning; a comprehensive framework would include many other domains. In addition, within each domain are many useful indicators that could be captured as part of a standard outcome battery. The Rehabilitation Services Administration defines "successful closure" for clients within its system using a measure that fits in the duration domain (Fraser et al., 2008). Another important measure of duration found in the IPS literature is the "steady worker" concept, defined as working at least 50% of the follow-up period (Bond & Kukla, 2011b; Goldberg & Harrow, 2004). Vocational researchers would benefit by incorporating economic concepts related to productivity, which includes both quantity and quality of work, but also components of lost productivity, such as absenteeism and presenteeism (Zhang, Bansback, & Anis, 2011). Vocational research should also routinely track clients working above substantial gainful activity, as defined by the Social Security Administration (GAO, 2002).

Type of occupation, as measured by the Standard Occupational Classification System can also be examined (http://www.bls.gov/soc/). The literature has almost completely neglected the measurement of job quality (Butterworth et al., 2011) and work stress (Dewa, Lin, Kooehoorn, & Goldner, 2007). Simple and valid measures of job quality are needed to complement the many measures of work quantity outlined above. We also recommend assessing reasons for job endings (Becker et al., 1998).

Ideally, a unified conceptual framework encompassing employment measures as used in diverse fields of inquiry, including vocational rehabilitation, occupational therapy, longitudinal research, and economics, as well as measures used by federal agencies such as the Department of Labor, the Rehabilitation Services Administration, and the Social Security Administration, would provide a common vocabulary and an opportunity to make meaningful comparisons of studies across disciplines.

Content of non-vocational outcomes. The choice of an optimal set of non-vocational measures is far less clear-cut than for employment measures, in terms of both conceptualization and measurement. Regarding what domains to measure, many studies have included psychiatric hospitalizations, symptoms, self-esteem, and quality of life. Some researchers have included measures of social network (either at the work place or outside the job) (Rollins, Bond, Jones, Kukla, & Collins, 2011; Rollins, Mueser, Bond, & Becker, 2002), and a few have examined social functioning. Surprisingly, vocational studies that include measures of recovery are rare (Connell, King, & Crowe, 2011). We do not know of any randomized controlled trial that has included short-term or long-term measures of recovery.

In summary, recommendations in the non-vocational domain are far less obvious because IPS research has consistently failed to show any effects for non-vocational outcomes. We do not have specific recommendations for domains to measure, nor do we recommend specific instruments, given the lack of hard evidence. Perhaps the essential point here is that we continue to investigate the long-term impacts of working on non-vocational outcomes.

Data sources. The principle of triangulation applies to the compilation of employment outcome measures. We strongly recommend multiple data sources, which typically include participant interviews, case records, and interviews with employment specialists. Once these data are compiled, the data are cross-checked and discrepancies often require returning to different data sources. Research assistants often have good insights into the best resolution of reporting discrepancies.

Optimally, data collection methods should be comparable between study conditions. In the Mental Health Treatment Study, which had a usual-treatment control group, the employment data were much richer for the IPS condition, but we were bound to draw solely on self-report obtained for both conditions (Frey et al., 2011).

Level of precision of measurement. The question of recommended level of precision to use in measurement depends on the criticality of the measure in question, the ease of obtaining precise measures, and the utility of more precise measurement. A concrete example illustrates our point. Specific dates (including day of month) are crucial for measuring job starts and job endings. In one study, only month and year were recorded; this lack of precision made estimation of job tenure imprecise.

Frequency of data collection. We distinguish between two types of outcome data: summary reviews of one's status at a fixed point in time, and timeline data. The first kind of data refers to assessment of phenomena such as symptom status or quality of life. Of course symptoms fluctuate over time, but the convention of assessing at fixed intervals is deeply engrained in mental health services research. For these variables, a fixed interview schedule, typically annually or semiannually, is appropriate.

Regarding timeline data, the goal is to develop a full accounting of the employment status during the follow-up period. In essence, we are interested in constructing a complete diary of employment during this period, showing changes in all variables outlined above. Because the degree of unreliability of retrospective reporting is associated with the latency of the reporting period, frequent contact (e.g., monthly) with respondents regarding the main employment outcome variables is critical. Depending on the length of follow-up period, accuracy of client self-report can be improved using the time-line follow-back methodology (Tsemberis, McHugo, Williams, Hanrahan, & Stefancic, 2007). Fortunately, employment status is relatively static over time for most respondents most of the time. A participant who is employed or unemployed for six months continuously should be able to report this accurately.

The issue of missed interviews looms large in IPS studies. The goal in IPS studies is to compile a complete timeline for the follow-up period. Consequently, if an interview does not occur at its scheduled time, we recommend completing it off schedule, even if it is late. The goal for the employment outcome portion of the measurement is to construct a complete calendar over the follow-up period; consequently, the interview questions should be adjusted accordingly if there are missing interviews.

Data collection methods. Virtually all of the employment measures we recommend are objective measures. These measures lend themselves to close-ended questions. These in turn can be automated in computerized data collection procedures that can be completed by study participants on laptops and mobile devices, with coaching from research assistants. Data collection from other sources (e.g., charts) can also be automated through electronic records.

Clinical significance. A final comment concerns the meaning, or clinical significance, of outcomes. Psychotherapy researchers often include information on normative comparisons of their outcomes (Jacobson, Roberts, Berns, & McGlinchey, 1999; Kendall, Marrs-Garcia, Nath, & Sheldrick, 1999). The psychiatric rehabilitation field has lagged behind psychotherapy research in thinking through the issue of clinical significance. Given the nonlinear course of psychiatric illnesses, cutoff scores based on general population norms (when they are available) might very well represent a misapplication of the concept of clinical significance. Further complicating the picture, a clinically significant change may sometimes occur even when there has been no change in symptoms (Kazdin, 1999). In fact, people with mental illness often value functional outcomes and quality of life more than clinical outcomes (Deegan & Drake, 2006). In psychiatric rehabilitation, personal preferences are valued more strongly than clinical outcomes. To illustrate this point, consider the relatively common situation in which antipsychotic medications control symptoms but create drowsiness, motor impairments, or cognitive slowing that prevent working. Many people prefer to live with some symptoms so that they can feel alert and competent enough to work.

Long-term follow-up. The single largest gap in the IPS outcome literature has been the relative lack of long-term follow-up studies, as reviewed in Chapter 5. Research grants generally permit only short-term follow-ups. The great majority of vocational research covers brief periods of 12 – 24 months, insufficient to understand a person's vocational career and long-term recovery. Especially early in the process of becoming a worker, people with minimal work experience may want to try different jobs, may have some failures, and may want to take time out for more education to prepare for a better job. Thus we have tried to extend the follow-up periods of research grants, trying to discern longer-term employment trajectories.

CHAPTER SUMMARY

Evidence-based practices are scientifically validated interventions that help people with mental illnesses to achieve improvements in meaningful areas of their lives. Developing and establishing an evidence-based practice requires attention to scientific detail, considerable time, and multiple steps. We have described the major steps as: 1) articulation of the problem area, 2) identification of possible treatments, 3) pilot testing the intervention, and 4) controlled evaluation of the intervention.

The planning and execution of a successful study requires creativity, attention to detail, and persistence. We have described some of the strategic choices in designs, control groups, sampling, measures, and data collection procedures that are prominent in the research we have conducted. These methodological issues are in addition to the general issues common to all mental health services research, as extensively described in textbooks and handbooks on research methods.

III

IMPLEMENTATION, LIMITATIONS, FUTURE DIRECTIONS, AND CONCLUSIONS

Having discussed the background, development, evolution, and research on IPS, we now turn to the future. Chapter 10 examines the research on implementation and sustainability of IPS. Research over 20 years has clarified the components and strengths of IPS, and in Chapter 11 we review the limits of IPS and discuss future research. Finally, in Chapter 12 we discuss policy recommendations that could benefit hundreds of thousands of people with serious mental illnesses in the United States and around the world.

10

IMPLEMENTING IPS

The Institute of Medicine (2006) described the enormous gap between existing services and evidence-based practices as a chasm. One significant aspect of the problem is that agencies do not implement evidence-based programs with high fidelity. Instead they leave out or modify crucial aspects of the model, thereby almost certainly reducing effectiveness. With regard specifically to IPS, the finding that fidelity predicts employment outcomes is firmly established (Bond, Becker, & Drake, 2011). Yet many programs do not offer high-fidelity IPS.

Implementation is a complex and poorly understood process, especially when it involves two disciplines and service systems that have been separate for many years. Leadership, funding, structures, processes, training, and many other factors are critical to achieve high-fidelity implementation. In this chapter, we review what is known about successful implementation of IPS.

CONCEPTUAL FRAMEWORK

The field of research known as implementation science is in a nascent state, with expert opinions and anecdotes far exceeding the number of hard facts (Fixsen, Naoom, Blase, Friedman, & Wallace, 2005). Implementation has been at the heart of IPS field research from early on. In the National Evidence-Based Practices Project (Drake et al., 2001), Dartmouth researchers began developing a conceptual model. We present a provisional conceptual model in Figure 10–1, based largely on this project (Torrey, Bond, McHugo, & Swain, 2011; Torrey et al., 2001).

The investigators for the National Evidence-Based Practices Project classified implementation factors as either positive or negative. Positive factors included

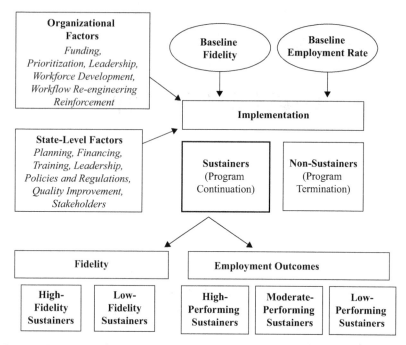

FIGURE 10-1 Factors Influencing Successful Implementation

facilitators (such as organizational characteristics promoting change) and *strategies* (specific activities to promote the practice, such as training). Negative implementation factors were considered *barriers*. Five implementation factor content domains were defined: *Prioritization* (expressing positive attitudes and attending to implementation above other competing demands), *Leadership* (inspiring, setting goals, planning, and managing the implementation), *Workforce development* (selecting an effective workforce and training and supervising them), *Workflow re-engineering* (devoting time and resources to redesigning program structures and policies), and *Reinforcement* (using data, such as fidelity and outcomes, to improve services).

Prioritization entails agency administrators attending to the implementation above other competing demands (Aarons, 2004). Effective leadership can inspire, drive, and manage change (Kimberly & Cook, 2008; Wang, Hyun, Harrison, Shortell, & Fraser, 2006). Successful implementation requires development of a workforce with the knowledge, attitudes, and skills to do the job (Hoge, Huey, & O'Connell, 2004; Hoge et al., 2005; Schoenwald, Hoagwood, Atkins, Evans, & Ringeisen, 2010). Continuous quality improvement studies stress the domain of workflow re-engineering, seeking to understand how the system (including technology) can support desired practices (Bodenheimer, 1999; Shortell, Bennett, & Byck, 1998).

Finally, studies of practice reinforcement look at the role of data and feedback in shaping results (Jamtvedt, Young, Kristoffersen, O'Brien, & Oxman, 2006).

THE NATIONAL EVIDENCE-BASED PRACTICES PROJECT

The National Evidence-Based Practices Project evaluated the implementation of five evidence-based practices across 53 sites in eight states over a two-year period (McHugo et al., 2007). Nine sites in three states implemented IPS (Bond, McHugo, Becker, Rapp, & Whitley, 2008; Marshall, Rapp, Becker, & Bond, 2008). The implementation model, based on a literature review, practical experience of services researchers, and focus groups with stakeholders, included two main components. The first was an implementation resource kit ("toolkit"), which contained such materials as videos illustrating the practice, a practitioner workbook, brochures for different stakeholders, and quality improvement tools. The second component was a consultant/trainer, usually located in a state technical assistance center, who provided assistance according to guidelines developed for the project (Torrey, Lynde, & Gorman, 2005). The training included a kickoff session to introduce the practice to all stakeholders and skills-based modules for practitioners, followed by need-based training and on-going clinical supervision to the program leaders and practitioners. Consultation was provided to the leadership of the agency concerning concomitant organizational changes.

An independent researcher in each site documented training and implementation activities through regular interviews with trainers and program leaders, reviews of clinical records, and monthly site visits for observation. Interviews, recorded and transcribed verbatim, and observations recorded as field notes, were entered into a qualitative database and coded along 26 dimensions of implementation activity (Torrey et al., 2011). After two years of data collection, implementation monitors compiled detailed summary reports for each site following a systematic protocol. We examined these reports to identify common factors reported to be influential in improving fidelity, as measured by the 15-item IPS fidelity scale (Bond, Becker, & Drake, 2011; Bond, Becker, Drake, & Vogler, 1997).

At baseline, all sites were in the low fidelity range, meaning that none were close to adhering to IPS principles. Yet by six months 50% attained high fidelity, and all sites did so by 12 months. At 2-year follow-up, 89% of sites maintained high fidelity. What factors, then, accounted for attaining high fidelity?

In the course of implementing IPS, all sites had to overcome adversity, including funding cuts, staff resistance, and staff turnover. The qualitative data contained in the site summaries suggested two barriers to high fidelity and four strategies used to overcome these barriers. The two common barriers were the existence of baseline vocational services that were in direct conflict with the principles of IPS and staff resistance. Each site developed its own strategies for overcoming these barriers and achieving fidelity. The qualitative interviews identified four common themes:

1. *Discontinuing nonevidence-based vocational services.* Sites initially provided vocational services that conflicted with IPS. All nine sites took prompt action to transform existing vocational services. For example, three centers discontinued prevocational programs, one site phased out a sheltered enclave, and the mental health authority in one state ended reimbursement for placement of clients in mental health agency jobs.

2. *Making rapid structural changes through administrative action.* A key element in the implementation model is the provision of periodic fidelity feedback to sites, with specific recommendations for change. These reports provided concrete suggestions for each of the items on the scale that indicated low fidelity.

Within 6–12 months, the supported employment programs showed dramatic improvements on 12 (80%) of the fidelity items. The common denominator was that most or all of these were structural changes. These fidelity items reflected specific and measurable standards that could be instituted by administrative fiat and easily enforced. For example, all sites moved toward adopting the IPS standard of a maximum caseload ratio per employment specialist, which in some cases was at variance with state standards as well as the perceived financial break-even point. Similarly, all sites adopted the standard of focusing on competitive employment, even those previously invested in providing protected jobs.

Structural changes leading to higher fidelity usually required freeing up resources for the supported employment program or aligning agency policies and procedures to be consistent with the program model. In most instances, structural changes were instituted at the direction of, or with the approval of, the center director. Examples of administrative actions included: creating or protecting supported employment staff positions (even in the face of budgetary pressures and downsizing within the agency), reclassifying vocational specialist role descriptions (which were previously limited to day treatment settings) to include delivery of services in the community, assigning employment specialists to mental health treatment teams, modifying productivity standards to be consistent with supported employment program requirements, and changing documentation to incorporate supported employment progress notes.

3. *Using quality improvement techniques.* In the quality improvement literature, measurement is the precursor to making changes: a familiar slogan is, "What gets measured gets done" (Shannon, Robson, & Sale, 2001). Tracking performance is not enough, of course, practitioners also must be held accountable. Following this philosophy, several employment team leaders pinpointed areas needing improvement.

They then defined and tracked simple performance indicators in these areas. In a program identifying poor communication with the treatment team as an area needing improvement, the employment team leader asked each employment specialist to count the number of treatment teams to which her clients were assigned and to calculate the percentage of clients on each team. These data were used to make the caseload distribution more efficient by reducing the number of teams with which each employment specialist worked. Other indicators included the number of employer contacts/week for each employment specialist, percentage of time in the community, and time between admission and first employer contact.

4. Gradually improving integration of employment team with clinical services. Integration of supported employment and clinical services is critical for achieving competitive employment outcomes (Cook, Lehman et al., 2005; Drake, Becker, Bond, & Mueser, 2003). Yet even in well-managed agencies, supported employment programs find it challenging to achieve full integration with the treatment teams, and this area of program operation is typically the last to achieve high fidelity. Case managers are often skeptical about supported employment until an IPS program starts showing success in helping participants gain employment. Integration was especially difficult to achieve at the one site in which clinical services were provided by another agency.

Unlike most components of fidelity, integration was not easily achieved through administrative fiat, although assigning employment specialists to specific mental health teams helped in some cases. Assigning clients from a limited number of treatment teams to each employment specialist was another administrative strategy. In a few cases, resignations by resistant case managers improved collaboration. Impressionistically, the supervisory roles for both the employment team and the treatment team appear critical for attaining integration.

Sustaining IPS. Two years following the implementation phase of the National Evidence-Based Practices Project, the research team conducted telephone interviews to determine which sites were still operating (Swain, Whitley, McHugo, & Drake, 2009), finding that seven (78%) of the nine IPS sites had been sustained. Program administrators in sites that discontinued IPS reported financing problems and staff turnover; those that sustained the practices reported state support, training and supervision, and evaluative feedback on fidelity and outcomes as facilitators.

Summary. Given the evidence that people with psychiatric disabilities infrequently receive effective services (Drake & Essock, 2009; Lehman, Steinwachs, & PORT Co-Investigators, 1998; Tashjian, Hayward, Stoddard, & Kraus, 1989; U.S. Department of Health and Human Services, 1999; West et al., 2005), the findings that eight of the nine supported employment sites achieved high fidelity at the 2-year conclusion of the project is impressive. We concluded that *it is feasible to implement IPS with high fidelity within 1 year from start-up of a new program.* This conclusion has been reinforced in subsequent work and is one critical feature of IPS—that it is possible to implement IPS well within a relatively brief period of time—shorter than the 4-year start-up period suggested in some reviews (Fixsen et al., 2005).

Successful implementation, however, depends on the presence of predisposing factors—leadership, adequate funding, and systematic attention to fidelity. This level of success in the National Evidence-Based Practices Project underscored the critical role of top-level agency administrators who were most responsible for making the rapid structural changes and taking the difficult and often unpopular steps to abandon long-standing vocational programs contraindicated by the evidence base. Many of these structural changes focused on the supported employment team. Fidelity items that involved a broader cross-section of the agency, like integration with clinical services, were slower to improve.

Many questions remain, however. For example, the agencies involved in the project volunteered, i.e., they were "early adopters" (Rogers, 2003). Their top-level administrators were committed to implementing IPS. Attempts to implement IPS in nonvolunteering sites face different dynamics that will undoubtedly slow or prevent achievement of high fidelity. Furthermore, the consultant/trainers involved in the project were exceptional professionals with much experience in supported employment and in providing consultation. Would the level of success achieved by these sites have been less with less qualified consultant/trainers? These questions must await future research.

MENTAL HEALTH TREATMENT STUDY

The Mental Health Treatment Study was a large-scale field study to evaluate whether access to IPS and systematic medication management, coupled with the removal of programmatic disincentives, could enable Social Security Disability Insurance (SSDI) beneficiaries with schizophrenia or affective disorder to return to work. Conducted over a 5-year period (2006–2010), this multisite randomized controlled trial enrolled over 2200 SSDI beneficiaries in 23 demonstration sites in the United States (Frey et al., 2011). While the main focus of the study was on the effectiveness of the package of services on client outcomes, one critical element in ensuring a fair test of the study hypotheses was ensuring full implementation of the IPS model at each of the study sites. In this chapter we examine implementation in this study to illustrate the challenges of implementing and maintaining of high fidelity over time in a large-scale multisite project.

Implementation in this project differed in three ways from the National Evidence-Based Practices Project. First, the Mental Health Treatment Study examined the implementation and maintenance process in sites that mostly had already established IPS programs or employment programs resembling IPS. Second, one new challenge was *engaging SSDI beneficiaries who had not been previously enrolled in mental health treatment at the study site.* Historically IPS has most frequently been implemented in agencies already providing mental health services to clients who then were offered IPS. Third, the quality management process was quite different from the earlier project, as described below.

Site selection in the Mental Health Treatment Study was based on three criteria. First, with just a few exceptions, the research team purposively selected sites that were already assumed to be providing IPS or a close approximation. The judgment that a site was already providing IPS or IPS-like services followed several steps. Specifically, the research team drew on the pool of sites from the IPS Learning Collaborative (described below) and other professional contacts (e.g., sites that had previously participated in IPS research studies). As a further quality control step, Drake and Becker made site visits to each of the prospective sites prior to final selection. (Only two sites were excluded based on this visit.) Second, the sites were selected to represent a geographic spread across the United States. Because several regions of the country (i.e., much of the West, South, and Southwest) had no exemplars of IPS, some centers were recruited that had no existing IPS services, and implementation in these sites more closely resembled the new program start-up found in the National Evidence-Based Practices Project. The final site selection criterion was that all sites voluntarily agreed to participate in the project (Frey et al., 2008).

We used several strategies to help ensure fidelity to the IPS model in the Mental Health Treatment Study, including the work of three experienced clinicians and program leaders with expertise in IPS who served as "quality management project directors." Responsibility for consultation to the 23 sites was divided among the three quality management project directors, who made weekly phone calls to the sites to offer technical assistance in implementing IPS and treatment services. The quality management project directors also made annual visits to their assigned sites to conduct fidelity reviews.

The primary focus of the weekly phone contact was reviewing the progress of each beneficiary, and helping a nurse care coordinator assigned to assist clients enrolled in the study to develop good employment and clinical intervention plans. Consultations also included discussions about implementation of the IPS model to ensure fidelity. The quality management project directors also reviewed employment-related updates (i.e., any new jobs obtained, follow-along supports provided, barriers to gaining employment, and reasons for job terminations).

Future articles will describe the implementation findings in detail. Overall, the Mental Health Treatment Study achieved many program areas of excellent implementation as well as areas where implementation fell short of high fidelity. The most important finding was that a large majority of the sites achieved and sustained high fidelity across the entire study period. The few exceptions to successful implementation related to unresponsive leadership, finances, and unavailability of specific mental health interventions.

Given many instances in the literature in which multisite projects have failed because of inadequate implementation (Bond, 2007; Brekke, 1988; Drake, Essock, & Bond, 2009; Michie, Fixsen, Grimshaw, & Eccles, 2009), the high quality of implementation *and* documentation of that implementation with a well-validated fidelity scale is a noteworthy achievement. We attribute overall successful IPS implementation to judicious site selection and careful monitoring and fidelity reviews provided by skilled consultants.

LEARNING COLLABORATIVE STRATEGIES FOR ENHANCING SUSTAINABILITY

While an empirically based literature on implementation is starting to emerge from the National Evidence-Based Practices Project and other studies (Fixsen et al., 2005; McGovern, 2011; McGovern, Lambert-Harris, McHugo, Giard, & Mangrum, 2010; Proctor et al., 2009), the literature on sustainability is inchoate and inconclusive (Aarons, Hurlburt, & Horwitz, 2011; Greenhalgh, Robert, MacFarlane, Bate, & Kyriakidou, 2004; Wiltsey Stirman, Kimberly, Cook, Calloway, Castro, & Charns, 2012). We need to identify methods to sustain practices that do not require the intensive labor employed during the implementation phase.

One method for sustaining and improving a practice is known as the *learning collaborative* model. As described in the healthcare literature, learning collaboratives involve multidisciplinary teams from a network of hospitals or clinics that meet with researchers to discuss their processes of care and desired improvements. Teams select targets for change, establish a strategy to achieve benchmarks, visit and support each other, and collect data to monitor key outcomes (Mold & Peterson, 2005). In 1995, the Institute for Healthcare Improvement formalized the strategies of learning collaboratives in the Breakthrough Series (Kilo, 1988). The learning collaborative approach relies upon *transparency* (sites share process and outcome data), *examination of natural variation* (site variation in outcomes), *peer support* (participants from low-performing sites learn from those from high-performing sites), and *expert assistance* from researchers.

Several programs using the learning collaborative approach have demonstrated long-term improvements in quality of care. A recent systematic review of research on the learning collaborative model found positive outcomes across nine controlled studies (Schouten, Hulscher, van Everdingen, Huijsman, & Grol, 2008). Although few national learning collaboratives in mental health have thus far developed, the National Institute of Mental Health used this approach to disseminate the community support program in the 1970s (Tessler & Goldman, 1982).

THE IPS LEARNING COLLABORATIVE

In 2001, the Dartmouth Psychiatric Research Center, with philanthropic support from the Johnson & Johnson Office of Corporate Contributions, created a program to advance implementation and dissemination of IPS in the United States (Drake, Becker, Goldman, & Martinez, 2006). We refer to this program as the IPS Learning Collaborative.

During an initial pilot project, the Dartmouth team collaborated with state mental health and vocational rehabilitation authorities in Connecticut, South Carolina, and Vermont. Subsequently, the program gradually expanded to 12 states (Connecticut, Illinois, Kansas, Kentucky, Maryland, Minnesota, Missouri, Ohio, Oregon, South Carolina, Vermont, Wisconsin) and the District of Columbia, with over 130 sites currently providing IPS as part of the program.

The IPS Learning Collaborative uses a two-stage implementation strategy, as shown in Figure 10–2. States receive seed money over four years to launch their statewide IPS implementation. The Dartmouth team meets directly with trainers, mental health authorities, and state vocational rehabilitation leaders to help plan and implement IPS. The state liaisons select local sites and provide training and technical assistance. Once the initial sites achieve good fidelity to the model, the state team disseminates the IPS model more broadly and expands the number of sites.

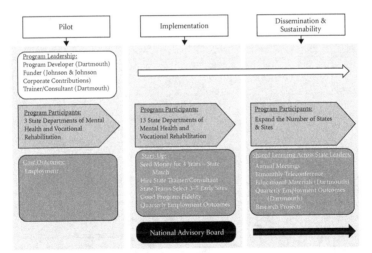

FIGURE 10–2 Evolution of a Mental Health Learning Collaborative on Supported Employment: Johnson & Johnson–Dartmouth Community Mental Health Program. From Becker, D. R., Drake, R. E., Bond, G. R., Nawaz, S., Haslett, W. R., & Martinez, R. A. (2011). A national mental health learning collaborative on supported employment. *Psychiatric Services, 62*, 7.704-706. Reprinted with permission from the American Psychiatric Association.

As part of their application process, state collaborators from mental health and vocational rehabilitation specify their plans to choose initial sites, provide training and technical assistance, establish funding, and expand implementation statewide in a sustainable way. State leaders develop consensus within both systems for the implementation of IPS; create a statewide supported employment leadership team to oversee the implementation, monitoring, and sustaining of IPS; and hire a full-time consultant and trainer to provide regular on-site technical assistance to participating agencies.

In the first year, the state team addresses mental health and vocational rehabilitation funding mechanisms, policies, and procedures to facilitate the adoption of IPS. They use a competitive site selection process to identify initial sites. The trainer consults with agency leaders regarding structures to support the implementation of IPS. The trainer meets with the employment staff and demonstrates ways to build relationships with employers, and shadows employment specialists to help them develop skills. The trainer also attends multidisciplinary treatment team meetings to help them focus on employment goals.

In the subsequent years, the state team assists sites in implementing the critical components of IPS using the updated 25-item IPS Fidelity Scale (Becker et al., 2008; see Appendix). Over time, states have also expanded the number of sites providing IPS. Dartmouth has collated quarterly employment data from state reports and distributes summaries, as shown in Figure 10–3. Over a 9-year period, the annual average number of clients served each quarter in IPS has grown from 792 to 10,075, while the annual average number employed each quarter has increased from 299 to 4,001. Outcomes denote clients who have worked a competitive job at any time during the quarter.

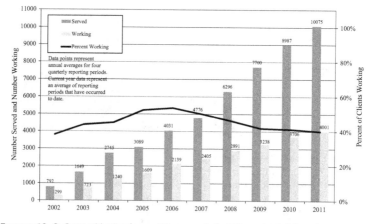

FIGURE 10–3 Competitive Employment Outcomes in the IPS Learning Collaborative 2002–2010

From the beginning, the IPS Learning Collaborative has emphasized increasing the availability of high-quality IPS services in member states. Over time, several patterns have emerged. First, all states have continued to participate after their 4-year grants have ended. State and local participants value the group learning process and other opportunities to exchange information with colleagues across the country. Second, representatives from all participating states have continued to attend an annual 2-day meeting to share information, ideas, and data. Third, state liaisons and program leaders have welcomed opportunities to participate in research.

Members of the learning collaborative agreed to make decisions regarding meetings, data collection, and projects by consensus. Research proposals are discussed on the group's email list and bimonthly teleconferences. Some proposals impact all the states, for example, changes in data collection, while participation in other projects is voluntary.

Recently, we developed a set of benchmarks, setting goals for individual programs to attain (Becker, Drake, & Bond, 2011). Benchmarks are standard levels by which others can be measured. Benchmarks should be attainable, should represent a level of excellence determined by data rather than theory (Kiefe et al., 1998), and should improve the quality of care (Kiefe et al., 2001). Benchmarks can also indicate a minimal standard. Therefore, to provide a range of benchmarks, we used outcome data collected between 2002 and 2010 by 151 programs participating in the IPS learning collaborative. We defined benchmarks a priori using the statistical definitions for the 25th, 50th, and 75th percentiles (Tukey, 1977).

The outcome measure we used for these benchmarks was the quarterly competitive employment rate. As shown in Figure 10–4, the values are 31%, 41%, and 50%, respectively for the 25th, 50th, and 75th percentiles. We interpret these as follows: IPS programs meeting or exceeding a 31% quarterly competitive employment rate meet a *minimal* benchmark, those reaching or exceeding a 41% rate meet a *good performance* benchmark, and those reaching or exceeding a 50% rate meet a *high performance* benchmark.

In other words, a benchmark of 31% competitive employment is minimal. Any program under this mark should be in a start-up mode or should receive technical assistance. A high-performance benchmark of 50% quarterly employment should be a realistic goal for mature programs that want to be excellent. Even at the minimal standard, the performance of the IPS Learning Collaborative sites compare favorably to the 26%–30% rate for supported employment reported in the literature (Gold, Macias, Barreira, Tepper, & Frey, 2010). Based on the research on goal-setting (Clarke, Crowe, Oades, & Deane, 2009; Latham & Locke, 2007) and on the learning collaborative literature (Kiefe et al., 2001), providing agencies with realistic benchmarks should enhance performance.

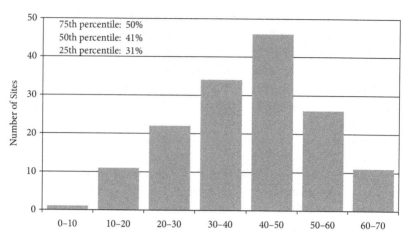

FIGURE 10–4 Histogram of Mean Site-Level Employment Rates in IPS Learning Collaborative (2002-2010)".

Sustaining IPS services has become a central concern of the collaborative. Under the pressures of the national recession and state budget cuts, public mental health services have continued to erode. Members of the collaborative have shared information about how to sustain services in this difficult environment. The growth of the IPS Learning Collaborative has continued despite a period of high unemployment across the United States (Fogg, Harrington, & McMahon, 2010). State leaders, providers, families, and clients recognize the centrality of employment to recovery and want evidence-based supported employment.

One unusual feature of this collaborative is its two-tiered nature. National activities generally involve the Dartmouth team and state-level liaisons, while leaders within each state organize trainings, data sharing, and other activities for local site participants. State teams share responsibility with sites for helping them to achieve good fidelity and benchmarks for employment outcomes.

Several factors challenge the operation of this learning collaborative. Changes in leadership at the state level endanger the continuity of state support. As a way to address turnover in state leadership, the Dartmouth team routinely provides new state mental health and vocational rehabilitation leaders with information about the national program, invites new state IPS trainers and mental health and vocational rehabilitation coordinators to a 3-day training at Dartmouth, and offers assistance. The dire state of public mental health in the U.S. is another threat. As states continue to cut budgets, mental health is a likely target. The learning collaborative helps to organize advocates.

Summary. The evolution of the IPS Learning Collaborative exemplifies the best practices process. Despite enormous pressures on community mental health programs that have generally eroded psychosocial services, members of the collaborative have been able to expand services, improve quality, and achieve good outcomes through a process of sharing goals, outcome data, regular communication, and research.

11

LIMITATIONS AND FUTURE RESEARCH

By improving vocational outcomes for many people, enhancing recoveries from serious mental illness, and perhaps preventing some amount of disability, IPS has inspired optimism in many parts of the world. Of course IPS does not benefit everyone with mental illness (Drake & Bond, 2008), and in this chapter we enumerate several limitations of IPS and discuss potential solutions.

LIMITATIONS

Not all persons with psychiatric disabilities are motivated to pursue work (Mueser, Salyers, & Mueser, 2001; Rogers, Walsh, Masotta, & Danley, 1991). Some have adopted meaningful roles other than competitive employment, but others avoid work because they fear losing benefits (MacDonald-Wilson, Rogers, Ellison, & Lyass, 2003), lack confidence (Westermeyer & Harrow, 1987), receive little encouragement from their counselors and psychiatrists (West et al., 2005), or cannot access appropriate help (Drake & Essock, 2009; Hall, Graf, Fitzpatrick, Lane, & Birkel, 2003). Perhaps changes in societal stigma, insurance and health care regulations, and the culture of mental health care may help many people to increase their aspirations and try employment rather than accept a life of poverty and disability. As we discuss below, researchers are studying efforts to put more information and decision-making in the hands of clients.

Approximately one-third of those who enter IPS are unsuccessful in finding a competitive job (Bond, Drake, & Becker, 2008). Some of these individuals decide not to pursue work when they receive benefits counseling and understand fully the potential loss of benefits, but others encounter difficulties related to psychiatric illnesses, cognitive deficits, medical problems, inadequate services, and other barriers (Frey et al., 2011). As described below, researchers are attempting to address these specific barriers.

Some of the people who obtain competitive employment have limited success, such as short-tenured jobs or negative job endings (Becker et al., 1998; Mueser et al., 2005). Fears of losing insurance, performance problems, episodes of illness, cognitive difficulties, and other barriers impede their efforts to work (Johannesen, McGrew, Griss, & Born, 2007). Many clients nevertheless go on to succeed in subsequent jobs, but researchers are attempting to address the specific barriers that underlie their difficulties.

Among those clients who become steady workers, few leave the disability system entirely (Becker, Whitley, Bailey, & Drake, 2007; Salyers, Becker, Drake, Torrey, & Wyzik, 2004). Their movements toward independence may be constrained by disability and insurance regulations, but many people report that working part-time is optimal for a variety of reasons (Strickler, Whitley, Becker, & Drake, 2009). Researchers are attempting to understand the types, amounts, and environments of employment that constitute optimal fits. All clients should be able to increase their incomes above poverty levels by working.

Another open question is whether IPS can be used to help other populations. Research to date has focused almost entirely on people with severe and persistent mental illnesses. But many other populations, such as people with primary substance use disorders or traumatic brain injuries, are in need of vocational services. Can IPS, perhaps with appropriate adjustments, help any of these other groups?

Finally, as a result of the well-recognized science-to-service gap in the U.S. health care system, the adoption of evidence-based supported employment across the country is progressing slowly (Institute of Medicine, 2006; NAMI, 2006; New Freedom Commission on Mental Health, 2003). The 15% employment figure for people with serious mental illness is unlikely to improve significantly until a larger portion of people have access to high-quality IPS (Drake, Skinner, Bond, & Goldman, 2009). We discuss these policy issues in Chapter 12.

FUTURE RESEARCH

The future of IPS depends, in part, on continued research. As we have emphasized throughout, the IPS model is not intended to be static. We consider several near-term possibilities next.

Client-centeredness. The crux of recovery-oriented services is client-centeredness: honoring the aspirations, goals, and journeys of people with mental illnesses (Davidson, Drake, Schmutte, Dinzeo, & Andres-Hyman, 2009; Slade, 2009). The voices of mental health system users have determined the development of IPS from the beginning, and IPS prescribes careful individualization based on informed choices by users (Swanson & Becker, 2010). As recovery enters the lay literature, people's recovery stories continue to emphasize the importance of mainstream employment (e.g., Carter, Golant, & Cade, 2010). By contrast, some professionals continue to emphasize that many people cannot work and need to be protected in sheltered settings (Hoffmann & Kupper, 2003; Warner & Mandiberg, 2006; Watzke, Galvao, & Brieger, 2008). These latter beliefs recapitulate arguments for long-term institutionalization in the 1970s and, like those previous positions, may diminish over time as more people are in recovery and as public attitudes change.

In the meantime, several lines of current research emphasizing mental health service users' perspectives are emerging. Some of the most promising approaches involve empowering mental health clients to demand effective services by creating client-directed service accounts, incorporating IPS training within peer-run organizations, providing electronic decision support systems to enhance knowledge and shared decision making, and employing peers as employment specialists. A few examples illustrate the possibilities. Andrews, Drake, Haslett, and Munusamy (2010) are developing web-based applications that clients and families can use to access accurate information about IPS and other vocational services, to have greater input into planning their own vocational services, and to participate actively in documenting their needs and progress. Swarbrick and colleagues (2009) have been developing employment services that incorporate IPS training within peer-run programs. Swendsen, Ben-Zeev, and Granholm (2012) and many other investigators are developing mobile applications that can be used to enhance functioning throughout the day, including on jobs. Ongoing research in each of these areas is likely to enhance client-centeredness.

Families. For years, families have understandably advocated for long-term supports and economic security for their relatives. More recently, they have embraced the crucial role of regular employment in the recovery process and have begun advocating for employment services. Family organizations in several states are leading the advocacy for IPS programs (Swanson et al., 2011).

Research on families and employment is meager. In one study of IPS, families of Latino clients were successfully involved in making vocational decisions, illustrating adaptation of the model for cultural reasons (Alverson & Vicente, 1998). Another study of supported employment recruited families to aid in developing jobs, but family involvement did not improve vocational outcomes (McFarlane, 2002). Nevertheless, families are often involved in creating expectations, in arranging informal employment, and in making decisions regarding work and disability. More research on their involvement is clearly needed.

Workforce. Few professionals learn IPS skills in graduate school because few universities offer training in IPS. Training the existing workforce has therefore been critical for dissemination, implementation, and sustainability (Becker et al., 2011). Several states, including Kansas, Maryland, Ohio, Oregon, New York, and Vermont, have established technical assistance centers on IPS

(Rapp, Goscha, & Carlson, 2010). These centers provide various combinations of training, technical assistance, and fidelity reviews; Dartmouth backs them up with educational resources, train-the-trainer seminars, and on-line courses (Becker et al., 2011).

Beyond formal coursework, current approaches to improving IPS skills include field mentoring, outcome-based supervision, and collaborative learning groups (Becker et al., 2011). Each of these needs systematic study to determine the optimal means to achieving an effective workforce. One current research strategy is to identify what successful employment specialists do in hopes that these skills can be codified and taught to others (Glover & Frounfelker, 2011a, 2011b; Kostick, Whitley, & Bush, 2010; Taylor & Bond, submitted).

State vocational rehabilitation counselors are essential partners in the development and maintenance of IPS services. Research on the role of these counselors emphasizes the importance of a collaborative relationship with IPS employment specialists (Oulvey, Carpenter-Song, & Swanson, submitted). Working as a team, they can provide a wide range of material resources as well as practical and emotional supports. Operating principles emanating from the Rehabilitation Act and its amendments are sometimes interpreted as conflicting with IPS principles, but many Departments of Vocational Rehabilitation and individual counselors have become IPS champions, as described by Swanson and colleagues (2011).

Progress in offering recovery-oriented care generally and IPS in particular also depends on changing the attitudes and training of mental health professionals (Slade, 2009). IPS requires a team approach (Swanson & Becker, 2010), and clients often report that they went to work because their doctor told them that they could (Becker et al., 2007). In general, mental health professionals of all disciplines need to emphasize strengths, functional behaviors, and optimism (Rapp & Goscha, 2011).

Process. Within the IPS model, many clinical issues warrant further study. What are the best techniques for activating clients, for developing jobs, for supporting people in jobs, and for helping them to make transitions from one job to another? How should clients handle disclosure? How should job applicants approach the issue of involvement with the justice system? Each of these topics needs more research (Glover & Frounfelker, 2011a; Jones, 2011; Swanson, Langfitt-Reese, & Bond, in press).

One future goal for IPS is to move toward individualizing services based on specific client characteristics—what is now termed personalized medicine (Drake, Cimpean, & Torrey, 2009). For example, specific cognitive strategies might be tailored for people with problems maintaining attention, for people with residual psychotic symptoms, or for people with social anxiety. Other strategies might be optimal for people who want to pursue school before employment, for those with physical health limitations, and for those with other social problems.

Employers. Improving employment opportunities for people with disabilities involves employers as well as employees. The optimal techniques for motivating employers to hire people with disabilities are, however, unclear. Should this be done through general antidiscrimination campaigns (Thornicroft, Brohan, Rose, Sartorius, & Leese, 2009)? Should it involve reaching out to employer organizations and having employers share their experiences with other employers? Are special tax incentives or other financial strategies effective?

One first step may be a better understanding of the perspectives of employers, a largely neglected area of research (Biggs, Hovey, Tyson, & MacDonald, 2010). For example, some large companies have a set policy of not hiring people with a justice system record (Rodriguez & Emsellem, 2011), while others are flexible in their willingness to hire people with both mental illness and a justice history, provided they are convinced that applicants can perform the work and have made amends for crimes (Swanson, Langfitt-Reese, & Bond, in press). Effective employment specialists often develop jobs by learning the needs and conditions of individual employers, one business at a time, but technology may enable greater efficiency.

Communities. How the characteristics of local communities influence employment of people with psychiatric disabilities is also poorly understood. In the absence of systematic research, expert opinion prevails but is often wrong. For example, many experts believe that jobs are harder to obtain in rural communities, but this belief has not been supported empirically (Haslett, Bond, Drake, Becker, & McHugo, 2011). Similarly, the local unemployment rate is assumed to affect IPS employment outcomes (Bond & Drake, 2008), but the size of the association is often overestimated. Other community factors, such as the diversity and flexibility of jobs, free bus service, community action programs to hire people with disabilities, and business leadership, deserve study.

Programs and Systems. At the program level, many administrative issues are pertinent: organization, financing, implementation, clinical records, fidelity, and sustainability, to name a few. One essential issue is developing strategies for integrating rehabilitation with clinical services. Research robustly supports integration (Cook et al., 2005), but the mechanisms for achieving this are unclear. Maryland developed a unique approach that involves paying providers directly for integrating mental health and rehabilitation services (Becker et al., 2007). Helping programs to achieve fidelity is another critical issue. IPS fidelity strongly predicts outcomes (Bond, Becker, & Drake, 2011), but fidelity visits by experts and related technical assistance strategies are expensive. How to monitor and enhance fidelity on a large scale is unclear. One proposed strategy is to bypass fidelity assessments for sites with exemplary employment outcomes, using benchmarks developed in a large longitudinal data base of IPS programs (Becker, Drake, & Bond, 2011).

Connecting with Mainstream Vocational Research. To some degree, vocational research on people with psychiatric disabilities has developed independently from vocational research on the general public, often emphasizing counseling, skills training, and mental health deficits. Large issues in mainstream vocational research, such as the role of employee assistance programs, concerns regarding absenteeism and presenteeism, workplace morale, and the quality of specific jobs, have been relatively ignored in the research on psychiatric rehabilitation. Now that people with mental illnesses have established clearly that most want to work and can do so, these parallels with the mainstream workforce need to be studied.

Improving IPS. Efforts to amplify and expand IPS, both for new populations and for clients who have not succeeded IPS programs, are in progress. We first consider new populations, for whom the IPS model may need modifications.

Two recent randomized controlled trials have shown that adding supported education to IPS is effective for people experiencing a first or early episode of psychosis, because many young clients have educational goals as well as vocational goals (Killackey, Jackson, & McGorry, 2008; Nuechterlein et al., 2008). This adaptation to create IPS supported education/employment represents another example of listening carefully to mental health service users. Another recent randomized controlled trial demonstrated that IPS helped military veterans diagnosed with posttraumatic stress disorder to obtain competitive employment (Davis et al., 2012). Still another randomized controlled trial underway is designed for people who have justice system records as well as serious mental illness (Bond, work in progress). Researchers are studying IPS with other populations, including people with less severe mental disorders, primary substance use disorders, traumatic brain injuries, or spinal cord injuries.

What about the clients with serious mental illness who do not currently benefit from IPS? As we reviewed earlier, IPS employment outcomes have been robust across different subgroups of people with serious mental illness, such as those with co-occurring substance use disorders and people from minority backgrounds (Campbell, Bond, & Drake, 2011). But in most studies at least one-third of the participants do not achieve vocational success. One approach to enhance outcomes for potential nonresponders has been to supplement services for nonresponders with specific enhancements. Examples include adding motivational interviewing, social skills training, cognitive training, or other cognitive strategies to IPS. Adding motivational interviewing has thus far not enhanced success (Drebing, Rosenheck, Drake, Penk, & Rose, 2009). Similarly, adding social skills training has been tried with mixed outcomes (Mueser et al., 2005). On the other hand, a variety of approaches to enhancing cognition have shown some success (McGurk & Wykes, 2008). Cognitive enhancements typically include several components: educating employment specialists to be aware of such problems and to look for appropriate job matches, emphasizing compensatory strategies on the job, and practicing cognitive tasks to improve performance. Whether these improvements are due to attention, building cognitive skills, or compensating for deficits remains unclear, but this is an active area of research.

Other barriers warrant similar attention. For example, the recent Mental Health Treatment Study included many clients with comorbid medical illnesses that affected employment outcomes (Frey et al., 2011). IPS specialists in this study often struggled to coordinate with medical specialists and to develop jobs for some clients with very limited mobility. Similar issues involve justice system involvement, symptoms of posttraumatic stress disorder, limited education, and so on.

The goal of continued IPS research is clear: to ensure that every client with mental illness who wants to work has access to effective services and has opportunities to work in appropriate settings at appropriate amounts. To a large extent, success will require policy changes, which we discuss next.

12

POLICY RECOMMENDATIONS

The increasing number of people disabled by psychiatric disorders has emerged as an economic, workforce, and recovery issue in high-income countries around the world (OECD, 2009). A large proportion of people with disabilities in these countries want to work, and current research on IPS, reviewed earlier, shows that the majority could become steady part-time workers. Employment improves their lives in several ways: finances, self-esteem, quality of life, and perhaps even the course of their mental health. Employment of people with psychiatric disabilities also benefits society by including them in the financial and social mainstream, by reducing mental health expenditures, and by addressing stigma.

Two major barriers prevent people with psychiatric disabilities from becoming employed: (1) disincentives within the health care and social insurance systems and (2) lack of access to IPS. Overcoming these barriers will require major policy changes.

Countries differ in the extent to which their policies related to employment, insurance, and disability reinforce or impede social recovery (Burns et al., 2007). In the United States, rights to employment and accommodations are protected by legislation through the Americans with Disabilities Act. Moreover, the U.S. employment market allows for a flexible range of full-time, part-time, permanent, and nonpermanent jobs; employers receive small tax incentives for hiring people with disabilities; and employers can hire people with disabilities without suffering huge penalties if the employee becomes unable to work. These factors offer significant advantages over more rigid employment systems in many other countries. At the same time, however, people with disabilities in the United States can lose their modest benefits and health insurance, sometimes suddenly and completely, by working above specified limits. Furthermore, the rules are sufficiently complicated that, without benefits counseling, few clients can understand how employment would affect their package. Nonetheless, virtually every client knows that obtaining Social Security benefits is difficult, that one can lose these benefits by earning too much income, and that health insurance (Medicaid and/ or Medicare) is tied to the benefits. Thus, clients often cite fear of losing benefits as a major barrier to employment (MacDonald-Wilson, Rogers, Ellison, & Lyass, 2003; O'Day & Killeen, 2002).

Even more significant than the benefits and insurance barrier is the paucity of IPS programs in the United States: only a very small minority of people in need currently access IPS (SAMHSA, 2009). Few programs can offer IPS because the fragmented system of federal, state, and local funding sources is not aligned with evidence-based practices. Many states provide millions of dollars for hospital-based rehabilitation, day center rehabilitation, sheltered workshops, training programs, and other ineffective programs, but not IPS, because Medicaid pays for the ineffective programs. Community mental health programs struggle to obtain reimbursement for IPS services by cobbling together payments from Medicaid, the state vocational rehabilitation agency, the Ticket-to-Work program, state general funds, federal block grants, foundation grants, and other sources. Federal agencies are actively discussing and experimenting with new regulations, but a simple funding stream is not yet available (Karakas et al., 2011). Instead, agencies, guilds, and programs act to protect their boundaries and finances, thereby preventing rational solutions.

Given these policy dilemmas in the United States, what can be done? We suggest several principles for policy makers. First, for long-term illnesses, consider a life span perspective, including primary, secondary, and tertiary prevention to minimize disability. Second, unlink health insurance and disability status. Third, make certain that disability regulations reinforce recovery rather than continued disability. Fourth, fund evidence-based recovery services rather than ineffective segregated services. Fifth, reduce societal stigma by increasing incentives for schools to educate people with disabilities and for employers to hire them.

1. *The life span perspective.* Because serious mental illnesses often persist for years, health and disability policies need to consider the entire trajectory of impairment, from the earliest stages to the potential for disabling outcomes. Policies need to address prevention, treatment, and rehabilitation. Because childhood behavioral and familial characteristics can affect later employment difficulties (Caspi, Wright, Moffitt, & Silva, 1998), we must invest in early childhood programs, parenting interventions, and other family-oriented prevention programs that are based on rigorous research evidence (Sawhill & Baron, 2010).

For individuals early in the course of illness, policies should emphasize preserving functional roles and community connections rather than asylum and segregation (Killackey, Jackson, & McGorry, 2008; Killeen & O'Day, 2004; Nuechterlein et al., 2008). The goal should be to reconnect people to school, work, and social networks as rapidly as possible by providing needed supports in order to prevent disability.

For those experiencing mental illness and disability status over years, policies need to encourage part-time employment as a form of treatment to promote recovery. Initiatives must recognize that many people with psychiatric disabilities want to work, that they are often able to work when provided with appropriate services, and that work, even part-time employment, is highly therapeutic and advantageous for them.

2. *Unlink health insurance from disability.* No one should have to apply for long-term disability in order to obtain health insurance, and no one should fear losing needed health insurance by going to work. The United States is the only wealthy country in the world that sets up these perverse incentives by linking health insurance to disability status. People with a long-term illness such as schizophrenia need lifetime insurance coverage to prevent adverse outcomes to themselves, their families, their communities, and society. Perhaps the Affordable Healthcare Act will accomplish this goal. If not, other policy initiatives should address this issue. Health insurance and high-quality care are prerequisites for preventing and minimizing the multifarious costs of disability.

3. *Reinforce recovery rather than disability.* Disability policies must balance the need for income and supports with the wishes of individuals to participate in the workforce. Thus, eligibility for disability must weigh concerns about avoiding poverty and burdensome application processes against concerns about "moral hazard" associated with too lenient criteria for disability benefits creating dependency and a disincentive to work (Danziger, Frank, & Meara, 2009). Those who are relatively early in the course of illness and applying for disability status need to be encouraged to pursue functional recovery rather than to maintain the disabled role while they are applying for benefits (Social Security Advisory Board, 2006). For example, a diagnosis of schizophrenia, which includes the criteria of at least two years duration and disability in several domains, may, by itself, be sufficient to qualify for benefits, without the individual having to spend months or years proving that he or she is substantially or permanently disabled (Burkhauser, Butler, & Weathers, 2002). Nearly everyone with schizophrenia has a serious impairment and needs help, not barriers, to preserve functional status. Policies should provide immediate help but also encourage a return to school and work as soon as possible.

For those with disability benefits, more gradual disability payment reductions would encourage beneficiaries to try working and to experience steady employment for some years before reductions begin. For example, because Supplemental

Security Income is so meager in the United States, permitting people with psychiatric disabilities to work part-time and retain benefits would enable them to escape extreme poverty and would still reduce the healthcare budget as they pursue functional roles.

Another practical measure would be to allow those who have already qualified for disability benefits to have much greater flexibility in having those benefits restored quickly and in full if a period of employment ends. The expectation of complex re-application procedures should be eliminated as a substantial disincentive. In other words, policies at every step should encourage rather than discourage functioning.

4. *Fund evidence-based supported employment.* Policies need to strengthen incentives for providers as well as clients (Burt & Aron, 2003; Cook, Leff et al., 2006; Flynn, 1999; MacDonald-Wilson et al., 2003; Prince et al., 2007; Social Security Advisory Board, 2006; Thornicroft, 2006). IPS and other evidence-based practices need strong leadership at the national and local governmental levels in order to develop financing mechanisms that incentivize high-fidelity implementation and functional outcomes (Finnerty et al., 2009). Current funding policies encourage providers to operate hospitals, day centers, training programs, and other services that are ineffective approaches to rehabilitation. Meanwhile, only 2% of clients in the U.S. public mental health system have access to supported employment, and the availability of other evidence-based practices is similarly inadequate (SAMHSA, 2009). This severe misalignment of financing mechanisms and effective services results in waste and prolongs disability.

Mental health providers need to be reimbursed for providing appropriate amounts of evidence-based services and for outcomes, not for providing large amounts of services. For people with psychiatric disability, appropriate evidence-based services include interdisciplinary, team-based collaboration rather than large amounts of uncoordinated services from separate providers (Cook, Lehman et al., 2005; Drake, Becker, Bond, & Mueser, 2003; Frey et al., 2008). In particular, mental health services need to be carefully coordinated with vocational, physical health, substance abuse, supported housing, social care, and criminal justice services because many individuals have needs in all of these areas. Accountability means that reimbursements should be based on realistic benchmarks regarding functional outcomes, adjusted for needs and exogenous circumstances. Service area data can be used to generate risk-adjusted, realistic benchmarks for independent housing, formal education, and competitive employment—outcomes that users of the mental health system desire and that are worthy of prospective payments. Assessing fidelity of evidence-based practices in addition to outcomes can discourage programs from selecting against clients with severe or multiple difficulties.

Two basic approaches to funding IPS are possible. One is to increase the efficiency of current mechanisms and make sure that the regulations are clear for all providers. This approach continues to rely on a combination of different funding mechanisms, but encourages providers to be more efficient in accessing existing options for Medicaid and the state vocational rehabilitation agency (Karakas et al., 2011). A second possibility would be more radical: Funds from several federal agencies could be combined and administered at the state level. For example, if funds from several federal agencies that have responsibilities for workforce, disability, and health issues could be combined and administered by one state agency to fund evidence-based employment services on the basis of capitation and outcomes, the dearth of effective services would begin to change immediately.

To modify the disability benefits culture, a variety of strategies needs to be tried, coupled with systematic evaluation of their success. A few pilot studies have been launched, some successfully. In the United States, the Mental Health Treatment Study represents one such pilot endeavor, incorporating adequate financing and integrated services with high-quality supported employment (Frey et al., 2011). Another promising approach is to pay supported employment providers on the basis of client outcomes (McGrew, Johannesen, Griss, Born, & Katuin, 2005). In fact, a wide range of measures has been tried across the world from which lessons can and should be drawn (Adam, Emmerson, Payne, & Goodman, 2007).

Finally, service users could be given more choice, influence, and control to select services and to control resources intended to improve their quality of life. Self-directed support arrangements—such as personal budgets or direct payments—would likely shift demand toward recovery-oriented services such as IPS.

5. *Reinforce schools and employers.* Employers and school officials also need realistic incentives for helping people with psychiatric disabilities maintain their connections to these institutions and to return to functioning as soon as possible if they have incurred a prolonged period of separation. This will require strengthening illness management and return-to-work programs. Tax incentives and health insurance policies could be used to reward schools and employers for encouraging supported education and supported employment services and for hiring people with disabilities part-time. Whether disability rights legislation, as opposed to economic incentives, can facilitate changing employer behavior remains uncertain.

Overall, these changes in disability policy will require deemphasizing the biomedical model of disability and recognizing that disability status is determined largely by psychological, social, economic, and environmental factors. Psychiatric symptoms are minimally correlated with functional outcomes. Treatment is necessary but not sufficient to help people maintain or establish functional status.

Disability policies must recognize these realities, emphasize psychosocial services and supports, and minimize the adverse effects of existing policies.

In sum, people with severe and persistent mental illnesses need individualized, evidence-based services as well as policy changes to reverse the trend toward increased rates of disability. These changes could benefit the affected individuals, their families, and society.

FINAL NOTE

After 20 years of clinical development enhanced by outcomes research, IPS has enhanced the mental health system's movement toward a recovery orientation and has clearly emerged as an evidence-based practice. IPS has also become the most researched of all models in the vocational rehabilitation field (Drebing et al., 2012). Progress has occurred in part because IPS helps users of mental health services directly with what they say they want and provides them with choices and control at every decision point, in part because IPS is direct and pragmatic, and in part because IPS integrates services within one team. But the critical leap forward has been a commitment to empiricism. Theories about vocational rehabilitation have abounded for years, but some turned out to be wrong just as some proved to be correct. The only way to tell the difference was to measure outcomes. Consider a few examples. The theory that people needed months of counseling to make a realistic job selection was incorrect, while the theory that paying attention to their job choices would result in better job matches was correct. The theory that separating rehabilitation and clinical services was helpful proved incorrect, while the theory that people needed professional benefits counseling was right.

Many challenges remain, however, and the field needs to continue to push the frontiers. We have reviewed our work over two decades and suggested several research avenues. Others will undoubtedly have better ideas. We look forward to these developments. Preserving a static IPS model has never been our goal—helping more people with mental illness to achieve the employment outcomes they value is the goal.

APPENDIX

SUPPORTED EMPLOYMENT FIDELITY SCALE*

1/7/08

Rater: **Site:**   **Date:**   **Total Score:**

Directions: Circle one anchor number for each criterion.

Criterion	Data Source**	Anchor
Staffing		
1. Caseload size: Employment specialists have individual employment caseloads. The maximum caseload for any full-time employment specialist is 20 or fewer clients.	MIS, DOC, INT	1= Ratio of 41 or more clients per employment specialist. 2= Ratio of 31-40 clients per employment specialist. 3= Ratio of 26-30 clients per employment specialist. 4= Ratio of 21-25 clients per employment specialist. 5= Ratio of 20 or fewer clients per employment specialist.
2. Employment services staff: Employment specialists provide only employment services.	MIS, DOC INT	1= Employment specialists provide employment services less than 60% of the time. 2= Employment specialists provide employment services 60 - 74% of the time. 3= Employment specialists provide employment services 75 - 89% of the time. 4= Employment specialists provide employment services 90 - 95% of the time. 5= Employment specialists provide employment services 96% or more of the time.

*Formerly called IPS Model Fidelity Scale
**See end of document for key

SUPPORTED EMPLOYMENT FIDELITY SCALE   1

3. **Vocational generalists:** Each employment specialist carries out all phases of employment service, including intake, engagement, assessment, job placement, job coaching, and follow-along supports before step down to less intensive employment support from another MH practitioner. (Note: It is not expected that each employment specialist will provide benefits counseling to their clients. Referrals to a highly trained benefits counselor are in keeping with high fidelity, see Item # 1 in "Services".)

MIS, DOC, INT, OBS

1= Employment specialist only provides vocational referral service to vendors and other programs.

2= Employment specialist maintains caseload but refers clients to other programs for vocational services.

3= Employment specialist provides one to four phases of the employment service (e.g. intake, engagement, assessment, job development, job placement, job coaching, and follow along supports).

4= Employment specialist provides five phases of employment service but not the entire service.

5= Employment specialist carries out all six phases of employment service (e.g. program intake, engagement, assessment, job development/job placement, job coaching, and follow-along supports).

ORGANIZATION

1. **Integration of rehabilitation with mental health treatment thru team assignment:** Employment specialists are part of up to 2 mental health treatment teams from which at least 90% of the employment specialist's caseload is comprised.

MIS, DOC, INT, OBS

1= Employment specialists are part of a vocational program that functions separately from the mental health treatment.

2= Employment specialists are attached to three or more mental health treatment teams. OR Clients are served by individual mental health practitioners who are not organized into teams. OR Employment specialists are attached to one or two teams from which less than 50% of the employment specialist's caseload is comprised.

3= Employment specialists are attached to one or two mental health treatment teams, from which at least 50 - 74% of the employment specialist's caseload is comprised.

4= Employment specialists are attached to one or two mental health treatment teams, from which at least 75 - 89% of the employment specialist's caseload is comprised.

5= Employment specialists are attached to one or two mental health treatment teams, from which 90 - 100% of the employment specialist's caseload is comprised.

---

*Formerly called IPS Model Fidelity Scale
**See end of document for key

SUPPORTED EMPLOYMENT FIDELITY SCALE

2. Integration of rehabilitation with mental health treatment thru frequent team member contact: Employment specialists actively participate in weekly mental health treatment team meetings (not replaced by administrative meetings) that discuss individual clients and their employment goals with shared decision-making. Employment specialist's office is in close proximity to (or shared with) their mental health treatment team members. Documentation of mental health treatment and employment services is integrated in a single client chart. Employment specialists help the team think about employment for people who haven't yet been referred to supported employment services.

MIS, DOC INT, OBS

1= One or none is present.

2= Two are present

3= Three are present.

4= Four are present.

5= Five are present.

All five key components are present.

• Employment specialist attends weekly mental health treatment team meetings.

• Employment specialist participates actively in treatment team meetings with shared decision-making.

• Employment services documentation (i.e., vocational assessment/profile, employment plan, progress notes) is integrated into client's mental health treatment record.

• Employment specialist's office is in close proximity to (or shared with) their mental health treatment team members.

• Employment specialist helps the team think about employment for people who haven't yet been referred to supported employment services.

3. Collaboration between employment specialists and Vocational Rehabilitation counselors: The employment specialists and VR counselors have frequent contact for the purpose of discussing shared clients and identifying potential referrals.

DOC, INT OBS, ISP

1= Employment specialists and VR counselors have client-related contacts (phone, e-mail, in person) less than quarterly to discuss shared clients and referrals. OR Employment specialists and VR counselors do not communicate.

2= Employment specialists and VR counselors have client-related contacts (phone, e-mail, in person) at least quarterly to discuss shared clients and referrals.

3= Employment specialists and VR counselors have client-related contacts (phone, e-mail, in-person) monthly to discuss shared clients and referrals.

4= Employment specialists and VR counselors have scheduled, face-to-face

*Formerly called IPS Model Fidelity Scale
**See end of document for key

meetings at least quarterly, OR have client-related contacts (phone, e-mail, in person) weekly to discuss shared clients and referrals.

5= Employment specialists and VR counselors have scheduled, face-to-face meetings at least monthly and have client-related contacts (phone, e-mail, in person) weekly to discuss shared clients and referrals.

1= Employment specialists are not part of a vocational unit.

2= Employment specialists have the same supervisor but do not meet as a group. They do not provide back-up services for each other's caseload.

3= Employment specialists have the same supervisor and discuss clients between each other on a weekly basis. They provide back-up services for each other's caseloads as needed. OR, If a program is in a rural area where employment specialists are geographically separate with one employment specialist at each site, the employment specialists meet 2-3 times monthly with their supervisor by teleconference.

4= At least 2 employment specialists and a team leader form an employment unit with 2-3 regularly scheduled meetings per month for client-based group supervision in which strategies are identified and job leads are shared and discuss clients between each other. They provide coverage for each other's caseloads when needed. OR, If a program is in a rural area where employment specialists are geographically separate with one employment specialist at each site, the employment specialists meet 2-3 times per month with their supervisor in person or by teleconference and mental health practitioners are available to help the employment specialist with activities such as taking someone to work or picking up job applications.

5= At least 2 full-time employment specialists and a team leader form an employment unit with weekly client-based group supervision based on the supported employment model in which strategies are identified and job leads are shared. They provide coverage for each other's caseloads when needed.

4. Vocational unit: At least 2 full-time employment specialists and a team leader comprise the employment unit. They have weekly client-based group supervision following the supported employment model in which strategies are identified and job leads are shared. They provide coverage for each other's caseload when needed.

MIS, INT, OBS

*Formerly called IPS Model Fidelity Scale
**See end of document for key

5. Role of employment supervisor: Supported employment unit is led by a supported employment team leader. Employment specialists' skills are developed and improved through outcome-based supervision. All five key roles of the employment supervisor are present.

MIS, INT, DOC, OBS

1= One or none is present.

2= Two are present.

3= Three are present.

4= Four are present.

5= Five are present.

Five key roles of the employment supervisor:

• One full-time equivalent (FTE) supervisor is responsible for no more than 10 employment specialists. The supervisor does not have other supervisory responsibilities. (Program leaders supervising fewer than ten employment specialists may spend a percentage of time on other supervisory activities on a prorated basis. For example, an employment supervisor responsible for 4 employment specialists may be devoted to SE supervision half time.)

• Supervisor conducts weekly supported employment supervision designed to review client situations and identify new strategies and ideas to help clients in their work lives.

• Supervisor communicates with mental health treatment team leaders to ensure that services are integrated, to problem solve programmatic issues (such as referral process, or transfer of follow-along to mental health workers) and to be a champion for the value of work. Attends a meeting for each mental health treatment team on a quarterly basis.

• Supervisor accompanies employment specialists, who are new or having difficulty with job development, in the field monthly to improve skills by observing, modeling, and giving feedback on skills, e.g., meeting employers for job development.

• Supervisor reviews current client outcomes with employment specialists and sets goals to improve program performance at least quarterly.

SUPPORTED EMPLOYMENT FIDELITY SCALE

*Formerly called IPS Model Fidelity Scale
**See end of document for key

6. Zero exclusion criteria: All clients interested in working have access to supported employment services regardless of job readiness factors, substance abuse, symptoms, history of violent behavior, cognition impairments, treatment non-adherence, and personal presentation. These apply during supported employment services too. Employment specialists offer to help with another job when one has ended, regardless of the reason that the job ended or number of jobs held. If VR has screening criteria, the mental health agency does not use them to exclude anybody. Clients are not screened out formally or informally.

DOC, INT
OBS

1= There is a formal policy to exclude clients due to lack of job readiness (e.g., substance abuse, history of violence, low level of functioning, etc.) by employment staff, case managers, or other practitioners.

2= Most clients are unable to access supported employment services due to perceived lack of job readiness (e.g., substance abuse, history of violence, low level of functioning, etc.).

3= Some clients are unable to access supported employment services due to perceived lack of job readiness (e.g., substance abuse, history of violence, low level of functioning, etc.).

4= No evidence of exclusion, formal or informal. Referrals are not solicited by a wide variety of sources. Employment specialists offer to help with another job when one has ended, regardless of the reason that the job ended or number of jobs held.

5= All clients interested in working have access to supported employment services. Mental health practitioners encourage clients to consider employment, and referrals for supported employment are solicited by many sources. Employment specialists offer to help with another job when one has ended, regardless of the reason that the job ended or number of jobs held.

7. Agency focus on competitive employment: Agency promotes competitive work through multiple strategies. Agency intake includes questions about interest in employment. Agency displays written postings (e.g., brochures, bulletin boards, posters) about employment and supported employment services. The focus should be with the agency programs that provide services to adults with severe mental illness. Agency supports ways for clients to share work stories with other clients and staff. Agency measures rate of competitive employment and shares this information with agency leadership and staff.

DOC, INT,
OBS

1= One or none is present.

2= Two are present.

3= Three are present.

4= Four are present.

5= Five are present.

Agency promotes competitive work through multiple strategies:

• Agency intake includes questions about interest in employment.

• Agency includes questions about interest in employment on all annual (or semi-annual) assessment or treatment plan reviews.

SUPPORTED EMPLOYMENT FIDELITY SCALE

6

*Formerly called IPS Model Fidelity Scale
**See end of document for key

- Agency displays written postings (e.g., brochures, bulletin boards, posters) about working and supported employment services, in lobby and other waiting areas.

- Agency supports ways for clients to share work stories with other clients and staff (e.g., agency-wide employment recognition events, in-service training, peer support groups, agency newsletter articles, invited speakers at client treatment groups, etc.) at least twice a year.

- Agency measures rate of competitive employment on at least a quarterly basis and shares outcomes with agency leadership and staff.

8. Executive team support for SE: Agency executive team members (e.g., CEO/Executive Director, Chief Operating Officer, QA Director, Chief Financial Officer, Clinical Director, Medical Director, Human Resource Director) assist with supported employment implementation and sustainability. All five key components of executive team support are present.	DOC, INT, OBS

1= One is present.

2= Two are present.

3= Three are present.

4= Four are present.

5= Five are present.

- Executive Director and Clinical Director demonstrate knowledge regarding the principles of evidence-based supported employment.

- Agency QA process includes an explicit review of the SE program, or components of the program, at least every 6 months through the use of the Supported Employment Fidelity Scale or until achieving high fidelity, and at least yearly thereafter. Agency QA process uses the results of the fidelity assessment to improve SE implementation and sustainability.

- At least one member of the executive team actively participates at SE leadership team meetings (steering committee meetings) that occur at least every six months for high fidelity programs and at least quarterly for programs that have not yet achieved high fidelity. Steering committee is defined as a diverse group of stakeholders charged with reviewing fidelity, program implementation, and the service delivery system. Committee develops written action plans aimed at developing or sustaining high fidelity services.

SUPPORTED EMPLOYMENT FIDELITY SCALE

7

- The agency CEO/Executive Director communicates how SE services support the mission of the agency and articulates clear and specific goals for SE and/or competitive employment to all agency staff during the first six months and at least annually (i.e., SE kickoff, all-agency meetings, agency newsletters, etc.). This item is not delegated to another administrator.

- SE program leader shares information about EBP barriers and facilitators with the executive team (including the CEO) at least twice each year. The executive team helps the program leader identify and implement solutions to barriers.

SERVICES

1. Work incentives planning: All clients are offered assistance in obtaining comprehensive, individualized work incentives planning before starting a new job and assistance accessing work incentives planning thereafter when making decisions about changes in work hours and pay. Work incentives planning includes SSA benefits, medical benefits, medication subsidies, housing subsidies, food stamps, spouse and dependent children benefits, past job retirement benefits and any other source of income. Clients are provided information and assistance about reporting earnings to SSA, housing programs, VA programs, etc., depending on the person's benefits.

DOC, INT
OBS, ISP

1= Work incentives planning is not readily available or easily accessible to most clients served by the agency.

2= Employment specialist gives client contact information about where to access information about work incentives planning.

3= Employment specialist discusses with each client changes in benefits based on work status.

4= Employment specialist or other MH practitioner offer clients assistance in obtaining comprehensive, individualized work incentives planning by a person trained in work incentives planning prior to client starting a job.

5= Employment specialist or other MH practitioner offer clients assistance in obtaining comprehensive, individualized work incentives planning by a specially trained work incentives planner prior to starting a job. They also facilitate access to work incentives planning when clients need to make decisions about changes in work hours and pay. Clients are provided information and assistance about reporting earnings to SSA, housing programs, etc., depending on the person's benefits.

*Formerly called IPS Model Fidelity Scale
**See end of document for key

2. Disclosure: Employment specialists provide clients with accurate information and assist with evaluating their choices to make an informed decision regarding what is revealed to the employer about having a disability.

DOC, INT OBS

1= None is present.

2= One is present.

3= Two are present.

4= Three are present.

5= Four are present.

• Employment specialists do not require all clients to disclose their psychiatric disability at the work site in order to receive services.

• Employment specialists offer to discuss with clients the possible costs and benefits (pros and cons) of disclosure at the work site in advance of clients disclosing at the work site. Employment specialists describe how disclosure relates to requesting accommodations and the employment specialist's role communicating with the employer.

• Employment specialists discuss specific information to be disclosed (e.g., disclose receiving mental health treatment, or presence of a psychiatric disability, or difficulty with anxiety, or unemployed for a period of time, etc.) and offers examples of what could be said to employers.

• Employment specialists discuss disclosure on more than one occasion (e.g., if clients have not found employment after two months or if clients report difficulties on the job.)

3. Ongoing, work-based vocational assessment: Initial vocational assessment occurs over 2-3 sessions and is updated with information from work experiences in competitive jobs. A vocational profile form that includes information about preferences, experiences, skills, current adjustment, strengths, personal contacts, etc. is updated with each new job experience. Aims at problem solving using environmental assessments and consideration of reasonable accommodations. Sources of information include the client, treatment team, clinical records, and with

DOC, INT, OBS, ISP

1= Vocational evaluation is conducted prior to job placement with emphasis on office-based assessments, standardized tests, intelligence tests, work samples.

2= Vocational assessment may occur through a stepwise approach that includes: prevocational work experiences (e.g. work units in a day program), volunteer jobs, or set aside jobs (e.g., NISH jobs agency-run businesses, sheltered workshop jobs, affirmative businesses, enclaves).

3= Employment specialists assist clients in finding competitive jobs directly without systematically reviewing interests, experiences, strengths,

*Formerly called IPS Model Fidelity Scale
**See end of document for key

the client's permission, from family members and previous employers.

etc. and do not routinely analyze job loss (or job problems) for lessons learned.

4= Initial vocational assessment occurs over 2-3 sessions in which interests and strengths are explored. Employment specialists help clients learn from each job experience and also work with the treatment team to analyze job loss, job problems and job successes. They do not document these lessons learned in the vocational profile, OR The vocational profile is not updated on a regular basis.

5= Initial vocational assessment occurs over 2-3 sessions and information is documented on a vocational profile form that includes preferences, experiences, skills, current adjustment, strengths, personal contacts, etc. The vocational profile form is used to identify job types and work environments. It is updated with each new job experience. Aims at problem solving using environmental assessments and consideration of reasonable accommodations. Sources of information include the client, treatment team, clinical records, and with the client's permission, from family members and previous employers. Employment specialists help clients learn from each job experience and also work with the treatment team to analyze job loss, job problems and job successes.

4. Rapid job search for competitive job: Initial employment assessment and first face-to-face employer contact by the client or the employment specialist about a competitive job occurs within 30 days (one month) after program entry.

DOC, INT, OBS, ISP

1= First face-to-face contact with an employer by the client or the employment specialist about a competitive job is on average 271 days or more (> 9 mos.) after program entry.

2= First face-to-face contact with an employer by the client or the employment specialist about a competitive job is on average between 151 and 270 days (5-9 mos.) after program entry.

3= First face-to-face contact with an employer by the client or the employment specialist about a competitive job is on average between 61 and 150 days (2-5 mos.) after program entry.

4= First face-to-face contact with an employer by the client or the employment specialist about a competitive job is on average between 31 and 60 days (1-2 mos.) after program entry.

5= The program tracks employer contacts and the first face-to-face contact with an employer by the client or the employment specialist about a competitive job is on average within 30 days (one month) after program entry.

SUPPORTED EMPLOYMENT FIDELITY SCALE

10

5. Individualized job search: Employment specialists make employer contacts aimed at making a good job match based on clients' preferences (relating to what each person enjoys and their personal goals) and needs (including experience, ability, symptomatology, health, etc.) rather than the job market (i.e., those jobs that are readily available). An individualized job search plan is developed and updated with information from the vocational assessment/profile form and new job/educational experiences.

DOC, INT OBS, ISP

1= Less than 25% of employer contacts by the employment specialist are based on job choices which reflect client's preferences, strengths, symptoms, etc. rather than the job market.

2= 25-49% of employer contacts by the employment specialist are based on job choices which reflect client's preferences, strengths, symptoms, etc., rather than the job market.

3= 50-74% of employer contacts by the employment specialist are based on job choices which reflect client's preferences, strengths, symptoms, etc., rather than the job market.

4= 75-89% of employer contacts by the employment specialist are based on job choices which reflect client's preferences, strengths, symptoms, etc., rather than the job market and are consistent with the current employment plan.

5= Employment specialist makes employer contacts based on job choices which reflect client's preferences, strengths, symptoms, lessons learned from previous jobs etc., 90-100% of the time rather than the job market and are consistent with the current employment/job search plan. When clients have limited work experience, employment specialists provide information about a range of job options in the community.

6. Job development - Frequent employer contact: Each employment specialist makes at least 6 face to-face employer contacts per week on behalf of clients looking for work. (Rate for each then calculate average and use the closest scale point.) An employer contact is counted even when an employment specialist meets the same employer more than one time in a week, and when the client is present or not present. Client-specific and generic contacts are included. Employment specialists use a weekly tracking form to document employer contacts.

DOC, INT

1= Employment specialist makes less than 2 face-to-face employer contacts that are client-specific per week.

2= Employment specialist makes 2 face-to-face employer contacts per week that are client-specific, OR Does not have a process for tracking.

3= Employment specialist makes 4 face-to-face employer contacts per week that are client-specific, and uses a tracking form that is reviewed by the SE supervisor on a monthly basis.

4= Employment specialist makes 5 face-to-face employer contacts per week that are client-specific, and uses a tracking form that is reviewed by the SE supervisor on a weekly basis.

SUPPORTED EMPLOYMENT FIDELITY SCALE

11

*Formerly called IPS Model Fidelity Scale
**See end of document for key

5= Employment specialist makes 6 or more face-to-face employer contacts per week that are client specific, or 2 employer contacts times the number of people looking for work when there are less than 3 people looking for work on their caseload (e.g., new program). In addition, employment specialist uses a tracking form that is reviewed by the SE supervisor on a weekly basis.

7. Job development - Quality of employer contact: Employment specialists build relationships with employers through multiple visits in person that are planned to learn the needs of the employer, describe what the SE program offers to the employer, convey client strengths that are a good match for the employer. (Rate for each employment specialist, then calculate average and use the closest scale point.)

DOC, INT, OBS

1= Employment specialist meets employer when helping client to turn in job applications, OR Employment specialist rarely makes employer contacts.

2= Employment specialist contacts employers to ask about job openings and then shares these "leads" with clients.

3= Employment specialist follows up on advertised job openings by introducing self, describing program, and asking employer to interview client.

4= Employment specialist meets with employers in person whether or not there is a job opening, advocates for clients by describing strengths and asks employers to interview clients.

5= Employment specialist builds relationships with employers through multiple visits in person that are planned to learn the needs of the employer, convey what the SE program offers to the employer, describe client strengths that are a good match for the employer.

8. Diversity of job types: Employment specialists assist clients in obtaining different types of jobs.

DOC, INT, OBS, ISP

1= Employment specialists assist clients obtain different types of jobs less than 50% of the time.

2= Employment specialists assist clients obtain different types of jobs 50-59% of the time.

3= Employment specialists assist clients obtain different types of jobs 60-69% of the time.

4= Employment specialists assist clients obtain different types of jobs 70-84% of the time.

*Formerly called IPS Model Fidelity Scale
**See end of document for key

5= Employment specialists assist clients obtain different types of jobs 85-100% of the time.

9. Diversity of employers: Employment specialists assist clients in obtaining jobs with different employers.

DOC, INT, OBS, ISP

1= Employment specialists assist clients obtain jobs with the different employers less than 50% of the time.

2= Employment specialists assist clients obtain jobs with the same employers 50-59% of the time.

3= Employment specialists assist clients obtain jobs with different employers 60-69% of the time.

4= Employment specialists assist clients obtain jobs with different employers 70-84% of the time.

5= Employment specialists assist clients obtain jobs with different employers 85-100% of the time.

10. Competitive jobs: Employment specialists provide competitive job options that have permanent status rather than temporary or time-limited status, e.g., TE (transitional employment positions). Competitive jobs pay at least minimum wage, are jobs that anyone can apply for and are not set aside for people with disabilities. (Seasonal jobs and jobs from temporary agencies that other community members use are counted as competitive jobs.)

DOC, INT, OBS, ISP

1= Employment specialists provide options for permanent, competitive jobs less than 64% of the time, OR There are fewer than 10 current jobs.

2= Employment specialists provide options for permanent, competitive jobs about 65- 74% of the time.

3= Employment specialists provide options for permanent competitive jobs about 75-84% of the time.

4= Employment specialists provide options for permanent competitive jobs about 85-94% of the time.

5= 95% or more competitive jobs held by clients are permanent.

SUPPORTED EMPLOYMENT FIDELITY SCALE

*Formerly called IPS Model Fidelity Scale
**See end of document for key

11. Individualized follow-along supports:
Clients receive different types of support for working a job that are based on the job, client preferences, work history, needs, etc. Supports are provided by a variety of people, including treatment team members (e.g., medication changes, social skills training, encouragement), family, friends, co-workers (i.e., natural supports), and employment specialist. Employment specialist also provides employer support (e.g., educational information, job accommodations) at client's request. Employment specialist offers help with career development, i.e., assistance with education, a more desirable job, or more preferred job duties.

DOC, INT, OBS, ISP

1= Most clients do not receive supports after starting a job.

2= About half of the working clients receive a narrow range of supports provided primarily by the employment specialist.

3= Most working clients receive a narrow range of supports that are provided primarily by the employment specialist.

4= Clients receive different types of support for working a job that are based on the job, client preferences, work history, needs, etc. Employment specialists provide employer supports at the client's request.

5= Clients receive different types of support for working a job that are based on the job, client preferences, work history, needs, etc. Employment specialist also provides employer support (e.g., educational information, job accommodations) at client's request. The employment specialist helps people move onto more preferable jobs and also helps people with school or certified training programs. The site provides examples of different types of support including enhanced supports by treatment team members.

12. Time-unlimited follow-along supports:
Employment specialists have face-to-face contact within 1 week before starting a job, within 3 days after starting a job, weekly for the first month, and at least monthly for a year or more, on average, after working steadily, and desired by clients. Clients are transitioned to step down job supports from a mental health worker following steady employment. Employment specialists contact clients within 3 days of learning about the job loss.

DOC, INT, OBS, ISP

1= Employment specialist does not meet face-to-face with the client after the first month of starting a job.

2= Employment specialist has face-to-face contact with less than half of the working clients for at least 4 months after starting a job.

3= Employment specialist has face-to-face contact with at least half of the working clients for at least 4 months after starting a job.

4= Employment specialist has face-to-face contact with working clients weekly for the first month after starting a job, and at least monthly for a year or more, on average, after working steadily, and desired by clients.

5= Employment specialist has face-to-face contact within 1 week before starting a job, within 3 days after starting a job, weekly for the first month, and at least monthly for a year or more, on average, after working steadily and desired by clients. Clients are transitioned to step down job supports, from a mental health worker following steady employment clients. Clients are transitioned to step down job supports from a mental health worker following steady employment.

SUPPORTED EMPLOYMENT FIDELITY SCALE

14

*Formerly called IPS Model Fidelity Scale
**See end of document for key

Employment specialist contacts clients within 3 days of hearing about the job loss.

13. Community-based services: Employment services such as engagement, job finding and follow-along supports are provided in natural community settings by all employment specialists. (Rate each employment specialist based upon their total weekly scheduled work hours, then calculate the average and use the closest scale point.)

DOC, INT
OBS

1= Employment specialist spends 30% time or less in the scheduled work hours in the community.

2= Employment specialist spends 30 - 39% time of total scheduled work hours in the community.

3= Employment specialist spends 40 -49% of total scheduled work hours in the then community.

4= Employment specialist spends 50 - 64% of total scheduled work hours in the community.

5= Employment specialist spends 65% or more of total scheduled work hours in the community.

14. Assertive engagement and outreach by integrated treatment team: Service termination is not based on missed appointments or fixed time limits. Systematic documentation of outreach attempts. Engagement and outreach attempts made by integrated team members. Multiple home/community visits. Coordinated visits by employment specialist with integrated team member. Connect with family, when applicable. Once it is clear that the client no longer wants to work or continue SE services, the team stops outreach.

MIS, DOC,
INT, OBS

1= Evidence that 2 or less strategies for engagement and outreach are used.

2= Evidence that 3 strategies for engagement and outreach are used.

3= Evidence that 4 strategies for engagement and outreach are used.

4= Evidence that 5 strategies for engagement and outreach are used.

5= Evidence that all 6 strategies for engagement and outreach are used: i) Service termination is not based on missed appointments or fixed time limits. ii) Systematic documentation of outreach attempts. iii) Engagement and outreach attempts made by integrated team members. iv) Multiple home/community visits. v) Coordinated visits by employment specialist with integrated team member. vi) Connect with family, when applicable.

SUPPORTED EMPLOYMENT FIDELITY SCALE

*Formerly called IPS Model Fidelity Scale
**See end of document for key

*Data sources:

MIS   Management Information System
DOC   Document review: clinical records, agency policy and procedures
INT   Interviews with clients, employment specialists, mental health staff,
       VR counselors, families, employers
OBS   Observation (e.g., team meeting, shadowing employment specialists)
ISP   Individualized Service Plan

2/14/96
6/20/01, Updated
1/7/08, Revised

*Formerly called IPS Model Fidelity Scale
**See end of document for key

Supported Employment Fidelity Scale Score Sheet

Staffing		
1.	Caseload size	Score:
2.	Employment services staff	Score:
3.	Vocational generalists	Score:
Organization		
1.	Integration of rehabilitation with mental health thru team assignment	Score:
2.	Integration of rehabilitation with mental health thru frequent team member contact	Score:
3.	Collaboration between employment specialists and Vocational Rehabilitation counselors	Score:
4.	Vocational unit	Score:
5.	Role of employment supervisor	Score:
6.	Zero exclusion criteria	Score:
7.	Agency focus on competitive employment	Score:
8.	Executive team support for SE	Score:
Services		
1.	Work incentives planning	Score:
2.	Disclosure	Score:
3.	Ongoing, work-based vocational assessment	Score:
4.	Rapid search for competitive job	Score:
5.	Individualized job search	Score:
6.	Job development—Frequent employer contact	Score:
7.	Job development—Quality of employer contact	Score:
8.	Diversity of job types	Score:
9.	Diversity of employers	Score:
10.	Competitive jobs	Score:
11.	Individualized follow-along supports	Score:
12.	Time-unlimited follow-along supports	Score:
13.	Community-based services	Score:
14.	Assertive engagement and outreach by integrated treatment team	Score:
		Total:

115 – 125	= Exemplary Fidelity
100 - 114	= Good Fidelity
74 – 99	= Fair Fidelity
73 and below	= Not Supported Employment

*Formerly called IPS Model Fidelity Scale
**See end of document for key

SUPPORTED EMPLOYMENT FIDELITY SCALE

REFERENCES

Aarons, G. A. (2004). Mental health provider attitudes toward adoption of evidence-based practice: The Evidence-Based Practice Attitude Scale (EBPAS). *Mental Health Services Research, 6,* 61–74.

Aarons, G. A., Hurlburt, M., & Horwitz, S. M. (2011). Advancing a conceptual model of evidence-based practice implementation in public service sectors. *Administration and Policy in Mental Health and Mental Health Services Research, 38,* 4–23.

Abrams, K., DonAroma, P., & Karan, O. C. (1997). Consumer choice as a predictor of job satisfaction and supervisor ratings for people with disabilities. *Journal of Vocational Rehabilitation, 9,* 205–215.

Adam, S., Emmerson, C., Payne, C., & Goodman, A. (2007). Early quantitative evidence on the impact of the Pathways to Work pilots (Research Report 354) (http://research.dwp.gov.uk/asd/asd5/rports2005-2006/rrep354.pdf). Retrieved January 18, 2010.

Adams, J. R., & Drake, R. E. (2006). Shared decision-making and evidence-based practice. *Community Mental Health Journal, 42,* 87–105.

Addis, M. E., Wade, W. A., & Hatgis, C. (1999). Barriers to dissemination of evidence-based practices: Addressing practitioners' concerns about manual-based psychotherapies. *Clinical Psychology: Science and Practice, 6,* 430–441.

Allen, B. A., Hodgson, W. P., Marlow, V. L., & Lindsey, J. K. (1994). A practical model for a vocational readiness program in a day treatment setting. *Hospital and Community Psychiatry, 45,* 374–376.

Allness, D. J., & Knoedler, W. H. (2003). *The PACT model of community-based treatment for persons with severe and persistent mental illness: A manual for PACT start-up* (2nd ed.). Arlington, VA: NAMI.

Alverson, H. S., Alverson, M., Drake, R. E., & Becker, D. R. (1998). Social correlates of competitive employment among people with severe mental illness. *Psychiatric Rehabilitation Journal, 22*(1), 34–40.

Alverson, H. S., Carpenter, E., & Drake, R. E. (2006). An ethnographic study of job seeking among people with severe mental illness. *Psychiatric Rehabilitation Journal, 30,* 15–22.

Alverson, H. S., & Vicente, E. (1998). An ethnographic study of vocational rehabilitation for Puerto Rican Americans with severe mental illness. *Psychiatric Rehabilitation Journal, 22*(1), 69–72.

Alverson, M., Becker, D. R., & Drake, R. E. (1995). An ethnographic study of coping strategies used by people with severe mental illness participating in supported employment. *Psychosocial Rehabilitation Journal, 18*(4), 115–128.

Americans with Disabilities Act of 1990. Public Law 101–336.

Anderson, P. R. (1999). Open employment services for people with disabilities in Australia, 1995 to 1997. *Journal of Vocational Rehabilitation, 13*, 79–94.

Andlin-Sobocki, P., Jönsson, B., Wittchen, H.-U., & Olesen, J. (2005). Costs of disorders of the brain in Europe. *European Journal of Neurology, 12*(Supplement 1), 1–27.

Andrews, D. A. (1995). The psychology of criminal conduct and effective treatment. In L. McGuire (Ed.), *What works: Reducing reoffending. Guidelines from research and practice* (pp. 35–62). Sussex, England: John Wiley.

Andrews, H., Barker, J., Pittman, J., Mars, L., Struening, E., & LaRocca, N. (1992). National trends in vocational rehabilitation: A comparison of individuals with physical disabilities and individuals with psychiatric disabilities. *Journal of Rehabilitation, 58*, 7–16.

Andrews, S. A., Drake, T., Haslett, W., & Munusamy, R. (2010). Developing web-based online support tools: The Dartmouth decision support software. *Psychiatric Rehabilitation Journal, 34*, 37–41.

Anthony, W. A., & Blanch, A. (1987). Supported employment for persons who are psychiatrically disabled: An historical and conceptual perspective. *Psychosocial Rehabilitation Journal, 11*(2), 5–23.

Anthony, W. A., Cohen, M., Farkas, M. D., & Gagne, C. (2002). *Psychiatric rehabilitation* (2nd ed.). Boston: Center for Psychiatric Rehabilitation.

Anthony, W. A., & Jansen, M. A. (1984). Predicting the vocational capacity of the chronically mentally ill: Research and implications. *American Psychologist, 39*, 537–544.

Anthony, W. A., Rogers, E. S., Cohen, M., & Davies, R. R. (1995). Relationships between psychiatric symptomatology, work skills, and future vocational performance. *Psychiatric Services, 46*, 353–358.

Arends, I., van der Klink, J. J., & Bültmann, U. (2010). Prevention of recurrent sickness absence among employees with common mental disorders: design of a cluster-randomised controlled trial with cost-benefit and effectiveness evaluation. *BMC Public Health, 10*, 132 (http://www.biomedcentral.com/1471-2458/10/132).

Arns, P. G., & Linney, J. A. (1993). Work, self, and life satisfaction for persons with severe and persistent mental disorders. *Psychosocial Rehabilitation Journal, 17*(2), 63–79.

Arns, P. G., & Linney, J. A. (1995a). Relating functional skills of severely mentally ill clients to subjective and societal benefits. *Psychiatric Services, 46*, 260–265.

Arns, P. G., & Linney, J. A. (1995b). The relationship of service individualization to client functioning in programs for severely mentally ill persons. *Community Mental Health Journal, 31*, 127–137.

Aron, L., Burt, M., & Wittenburg, D. (2005). *Recommendations to the Social Security Administration on the design of the Mental Health Treatment Study*. Washington, DC: Urban Institute.

Azrin, N. H., & Philip, R. A. (1979). The job club method for the job handicapped: A comparative outcome study. *Rehabilitation Counseling Bulletin, 23*, 144–155.

Bailey, D., Rubin, W., Fox, A., & Ley, E. (2007). *The impact of benefits counseling on employment for consumers with severe mental illness*. Columbus, OH: Ohio Department of Mental Health.

Bailey, E., Ricketts, S., Becker, D. R., Xie, H., & Drake, R. E. (1998). Conversion of day treatment to supported employment: One-year outcomes. *Psychiatric Rehabilitation Journal, 22*(1), 24–29.

Bailey, J. (1998). I'm just an ordinary person. *Psychiatric Rehabilitation Journal, 22*(1), 8–10.

Baker, T. B., McFall, R. M., & Shoham, V. (2009). Current status and future prospects of clinical psychology: Toward a scientifically principled approach to mental and behavioral health care. *Psychological Science in the Public Interest, 9*, 67–103.

Bandura, A. (1969). *Principles of behavior modification*. New York: Holt, Rinehart and Winston.

Bartlett, P., Lewis, O., & Thorold, O. (2006). *Mental disability and the European Convention on Human Rights*. Leiden: Martinus Nijhoff.

Beard, J. H., Propst, R. N., & Malamud, T. J. (1982). The Fountain House model of psychiatric rehabilitation. *Psychosocial Rehabilitation Journal, 5*(1), 47–53.

Beauchamp, T. L., & Childress, J. F. (2001). *Principles of medical ethics* (Vol. 5th). New York: Oxford University Press.

Bebout, R. R., Becker, D. R., & Drake, R. E. (1998). A research induction group for clients entering a mental health research project: A replication study. *Community Mental Health Journal, 34*, 289–295.

Becker, D. R., Baker, S. R., Carlson, L., Flint, L., Howell, R., Lindsay, S., et al. (2007). Critical strategies for implementing supported employment. *Journal of Vocational Rehabilitation, 27*, 13–20.

Becker, D. R., Bebout, R. R., & Drake, R. E. (1998). Job preferences of people with severe mental illness: A replication. *Psychiatric Rehabilitation Journal, 22*(1), 46–50.

Becker, D. R., Bond, G. R., McCarthy, D., Thompson, D., Xie, H., McHugo, G. J., et al. (2001). Converting day treatment centers to supported employment programs in Rhode Island. *Psychiatric Services, 52*, 351–357.

Becker, D. R., & Drake, R. E. (1993). *A working life: The Individual Placement and Support (IPS) Program*. Concord, NH: New Hampshire-Dartmouth Psychiatric Research Center.

Becker, D. R., & Drake, R. E. (2003). *A working life for people with severe mental illness*. New York: Oxford University Press.

Becker, D. R., Drake, R. E., & Bond, G. R. (2011). Benchmark outcomes in supported employment. *American Journal of Psychiatric Rehabilitation, 14*, 230–236.

Becker, D. R., Drake, R. E., Bond, G. R., Nawaz, S., Haslett, W. R., & Martinez, R. A. (2011). A mental health learning collaborative on supported employment. *Psychiatric Services, 62*, 704–706.

Becker, D. R., Drake, R. E., Bond, G. R., Xie, H., Dain, B. J., & Harrison, K. (1998). Job terminations among persons with severe mental illness participating in supported employment. *Community Mental Health Journal, 34*, 71–82.

Becker, D. R., Drake, R. E., Farabaugh, A., & Bond, G. R. (1996). Job preferences of clients with severe psychiatric disorders participating in supported employment programs. *Psychiatric Services, 47*, 1223–1226.

Becker, D. R., Smith, J., Tanzman, B., Drake, R. E., & Tremblay, T. (2001). Fidelity of supported employment programs and employment outcomes. *Psychiatric Services, 52*, 834–836.

Becker, D. R., Swanson, S., Bond, G. R., & Merrens, M. R. (2008). *Evidence-based supported employment fidelity review manual*. Lebanon, NH: Dartmouth Psychiatric Research Center.

Becker, D. R., Whitley, R., Bailey, E. L., & Drake, R. E. (2007). Long-term employment outcomes of supported employment for people with severe mental illness. *Psychiatric Services, 58,* 922–928.

Becker, D. R., Xie, H., McHugo, G. J., Halliday, J., & Martinez, R. A. (2006). What predicts supported employment program outcomes? *Community Mental Health Journal, 42,* 303–313.

Bedell, J. R., Draving, D., Parrish, A., Gervey, R., & Guastadisegni, P. (1998). A description and comparison of experiences of people with mental disorders in supported employment and paid prevocational training. *Psychiatric Rehabilitation Journal, 21*(3), 279–283.

Bejerholm, U., Larsson, L., & Hofgren, C. (2011). Individual placement and support illustrated in the Swedish welfare system: A case study. *Journal of Vocational Rehabilitation, 35,* 59–72.

Bell, M. D., Greig, T. C., Zito, W., & Wexler, W. (2007). An RCT of neurocognitive enhancement therapy with supported employment: Employment outcomes at 24 months. *Schizophrenia Bulletin, 33,* 420–421.

Bell, M. D., & Lysaker, P. H. (1997). Clinical benefits of paid work activity in schizophrenia: 1-year followup. *Schizophrenia Bulletin, 23,* 317–328.

Bell, M. D., Lysaker, P. H., & Milstein, R. M. (1996). Clinical benefits of paid work activity in schizophrenia. *Schizophrenia Bulletin, 22,* 51–67.

Bero, L., & Drummond, R. (1995). The Cochrane Collaboration: Preparing, maintaining, and disseminating systematic reviews of the effects of health care. *Journal of the American Medical Association, 274,* 1935–1938.

Bertram, M., & Howard, L. E. (2006). Employment status and occupational care planning for people using mental health services. *Psychiatric Bulletin, 30,* 48–51.

Beveridge, S., & Fabian, E. (2007). Vocational rehabilitation outcomes: Relationship between individualized plan for employment goals and employment outcomes. *Rehabilitation Counseling Bulletin, 50,* 238–246.

Bhugra, D. (2006). Severe mental illness across cultures. *Acta Psychiatrica Scandinavica Supplementum, 429,* 17–23.

Biggs, D., Hovey, N., Tyson, P. J., & MacDonald, S. (2010). Employer and employment agency attitudes towards employing individuals with mental health needs. *Journal of Mental Health, 19,* 505–516.

Bilder, S., & Mechanic, D. (2003). Navigating the disability process: Persons with mental disorders applying for and receiving disability benefits. *Milbank Quarterly, 81,* 75–106.

Black, B. J. (1988). *Work and mental illness: Transitions to employment.* Baltimore: Johns Hopkins Press.

Bleuler, E. (1911). *Dementia praecox or the group of schizophrenias* [*Translated by Zinkin, J., 1950*]. New York: International Universities Press.

Blustein, D. L. (2008). The role of work in psychological health and well-being: A conceptual, historical, and public policy perspective. *American Psychologist, 63,* 228–240.

Bodenheimer, T. (1999). The American health care system: the movement for improved quality in health care. *New England Journal of Medicine, 340,* 488–492.

Bogira, S. (2009). Starvation diet: Coping with shrinking budgets in publicly funded mental health services. *Health Affairs, 28,* 667–675.

Bond, G. R. (1992). Vocational rehabilitation. In R. P. Liberman (Ed.), *Handbook of psychiatric rehabilitation* (pp. 244–275). New York: Macmillan.

Bond, G. R. (1994). Applying psychiatric rehabilitation principles to employment: Recent findings. In R. J. Ancill, S. Holliday & J. Higenbottam (Eds.), *Schizophrenia: Exploring the spectrum of psychosis* (pp. 49–65). Chichester, England: John Wiley.

Bond, G. R. (1998). Principles of the Individual Placement and Support model: Empirical support. *Psychiatric Rehabilitation Journal, 22*(1), 11–23.

Bond, G. R. (2004). Supported employment: Evidence for an evidence-based practice. *Psychiatric Rehabilitation Journal, 27,* 345–359.

Bond, G. R. (2007). Modest implementation efforts, modest fidelity, and modest outcomes. *Psychiatric Services, 58,* 334.

Bond, G. R. (2011, May 10). *J&J Fidelity-Outcome Project: progress report.* Paper presented at the Johnson & Johnson-Dartmouth Community Mental Health Program Annual Meeting, Burlington, NH.

Bond, G. R. (work in progress). A randomized controlled trial of two vocational models for individuals with psychiatric disabilities and criminal justice involvement: National Institute on Disability and Rehabilitation Research: Field Initiated Program. Grant # H133G100110.

Bond, G. R., Becker, D. R., & Drake, R. E. (2011). Measurement of fidelity of implementation of evidence-based practices: Case example of the IPS Fidelity Scale. *Clinical Psychology: Science and Practice, 18,* 126–141.

Bond, G. R., Becker, D. R., Drake, R. E., Rapp, C. A., Meisler, N., Lehman, A. F., et al. (2001). Implementing supported employment as an evidence-based practice. *Psychiatric Services, 52,* 313–322.

Bond, G. R., Becker, D. R., Drake, R. E., & Vogler, K. M. (1997). A fidelity scale for the Individual Placement and Support model of supported employment. *Rehabilitation Counseling Bulletin, 40,* 265–284.

Bond, G. R., & Boyer, S. L. (1988). Rehabilitation programs and outcomes. In J. A. Ciardiello & M. D. Bell (Eds.), *Vocational rehabilitation of persons with prolonged mental illness* (pp. 231–263). Baltimore: Johns Hopkins Press.

Bond, G. R., & Campbell, K. (2008). Evidence-based practices for individuals with severe mental illness. *Journal of Rehabilitation, 74*(2), 33–44.

Bond, G. R., Campbell, K., & Drake, R. E. (2012). Standardizing measures in four domains of employment outcome for Individual Placement and Support. *Psychiatric Services,* in Advance, June 1, 2012; doi: 10.1176/appi.ps.201100270.

Bond, G. R., Dietzen, L. L., McGrew, J. H., & Miller, L. D. (1995). Accelerating entry into supported employment for persons with severe psychiatric disabilities. *Rehabilitation Psychology, 40,* 91–111.

Bond, G. R., & Dincin, J. (1986). Accelerating entry into transitional employment in a psychosocial rehabilitation agency. *Rehabilitation Psychology, 31,* 143–155.

Bond, G. R., & Drake, R. E. (2008). Predictors of competitive employment among patients with schizophrenia. *Current Opinion in Psychiatry, 21,* 362–369.

Bond, G. R., Drake, R. E., & Becker, D. R. (2008). An update on randomized controlled trials of evidence-based supported employment. *Psychiatric Rehabilitation Journal, 31,* 280–290.

Bond, G. R., Drake, R. E., & Becker, D. R. (2010). Beyond evidence-based practice: Nine ideal features of a mental health intervention. *Research on Social Work Practice, 20,* 493–501.

Bond, G. R., Drake, R. E., & Becker, D. R. (2012). Generalizability of the Individual Placement and Support (IPS) model of supported employment outside the US. *World Psychiatry*, *11*, 32–39.

Bond, G. R., Drake, R. E., Becker, D. R., & Mueser, K. T. (1999). Effectiveness of psychiatric rehabilitation approaches for employment of people with severe mental illness. *Journal of Disability Policy Studies*, *10*, 18–52.

Bond, G. R., Drake, R. E., Mueser, K. T., & Becker, D. R. (1997). An update on supported employment for people with severe mental illness. *Psychiatric Services*, *48*, 335–346.

Bond, G. R., Drake, R. E., Mueser, K. T., & Latimer, E. (2001). Assertive community treatment for people with severe mental illness: Critical ingredients and impact on patients. *Disease Management & Health Outcomes*, *9*, 141–159.

Bond, G. R., Evans, L., Salyers, M. P., Williams, J., & Kim, H. K. (2000). Measurement of fidelity in psychiatric rehabilitation. *Mental Health Services Research*, *2*, 75–87.

Bond, G. R., & Kukla, M. (2011a). Impact of follow-along support on job tenure in the Individual Placement and Support model. *Journal of Nervous and Mental Disease*, *199*, 150–155.

Bond, G. R., & Kukla, M. (2011b). Is job tenure brief in Individual Placement and Support (IPS) employment programs? *Psychiatric Services*, *62*, 950–953.

Bond, G. R., McHugo, G. J., Becker, D. R., Rapp, C. A., & Whitley, R. (2008). Fidelity of supported employment: Lessons learned from the National Evidence-Based Practices Project. *Psychiatric Rehabilitation Journal*, *31*, 300–305.

Bond, G. R., Miller, L. D., & Dietzen, L. L. (1992). *Final report on SSA Supported Employment Project for SSI/SSDI Beneficiaries with Serious Mental Illness (Social Security Administration Grant No. 12-D-70299-5-01)*.

Bond, G. R., Peterson, A. E., Becker, D. R., & Drake, R. E. (2012). Validating the revised Individual Placement and Support Fidelity Scale (IPS-25). *Psychiatric Services*, in Advance, June 1, 2012; doi: 10.1176/appi.ps.201100476..

Bond, G. R., Resnick, S. G., Drake, R. E., Xie, H., McHugo, G. J., & Bebout, R. R. (2001). Does competitive employment improve nonvocational outcomes for people with severe mental illness? *Journal of Consulting and Clinical Psychology*, *69*, 489–501.

Bond, G. R., Salyers, M. P., Dincin, J., Drake, R. E., Becker, D. R., Fraser, V. V., et al. (2007). A randomized controlled trial comparing two vocational models for persons with severe mental illness. *Journal of Consulting and Clinical Psychology*, *75*, 968–982.

Bond, G. R., Xie, H., & Drake, R. E. (2007). Can SSDI and SSI beneficiaries with mental illness benefit from evidence-based supported employment? *Psychiatric Services*, *58*, 1412–1420.

Bourgois, P. (2003). *In search of respect: Selling crack in El Barrio*. Cambridge: Cambridge University Press.

Boyce, M., Secker, J., Floyd, M., Schneider, J., & Slade, J. (2008). Factors influencing the delivery of evidence-based supported employment in England. *Psychiatric Rehabilitation Journal*, *31*, 360–366.

Brabban, A., & Kelly, M. (2008). A national survey of psychosocial intervention training and skills in early intervention services in England. *Journal of Mental Health Training, Education and Practice*, *3*, 15–22.

Braitman, A., Counts, P., Davenport, R., Zurlinden, B., Rogers, M., Clauss, J., et al. (1995). Comparison of barriers to employment for unemployed and employed clients in a case management program: An exploratory study. *Psychiatric Rehabilitation Journal*, *19*(1), 3–18.

Brekke, J. S. (1988). What do we really know about community support programs? Strategies for better monitoring. *Hospital and Community Psychiatry, 39,* 946–952.

Brekke, J. S., Ansel, M., Long, J., Slade, E., & Weinstein, M. (1999). Intensity and continuity of services and functional outcomes in the rehabilitation of persons with schizophrenia. *Psychiatric Services, 50,* 248–256.

Brekke, J. S., Levin, S., Wolkon, G. H., Sobel, E., & Slade, E. (1993). Psychosocial functioning and subjective experience in schizophrenia. *Schizophrenia Bulletin, 19,* 599–608.

Browne, D. J., Wright, J., Waghorn, G., & Stephenson, A. (2009). Developing high performing employment services for people with mental illness *International Journal of Therapy and Rehabilitation, 16,* 502–511.

Burkhauser, R. V., Butler, J. S., & Weathers, R. R. (2002). How policy variables influence the timing of Social Security Disability Insurance applications. *Social Security Bulletin, 64*(1), 52–83.

Burns, T. (2000). Models of community treatments in schizophrenia: Do they travel? *Acta Psychiatrica Scandinavica, 102*(Supplement 407), 11–14.

Burns, T., Catty, J., Becker, T., Drake, R. E., Fioritti, A., Knapp, M., et al. (2007). The effectiveness of supported employment for people with severe mental illness: A randomised controlled trial. *Lancet, 370,* 1146–1152.

Burns, T., Catty, J., White, S., Becker, T., Koletsi, M., Fioritti, A., et al. (2009). The impact of supported employment and working on clinical and social functioning: Results of an international study of Individual Placement and Support. *Schizophrenia Bulletin, 35,* 949–958.

Burt, M. R., & Aron, L. Y. (2003). *Promoting work among SSI/DI beneficiaries with serious mental illness: Prepared for the Ticket to Work and Work Incentives Advisory Panel.* Washington, DC: Urban Institute.

Burton, J. D. (2009). Moving towards valued-based supported employment programs. *Psychiatric Rehabilitation Journal, 32,* 257–258.

Bush, P. W., Drake, R. E., Xie, H., McHugo, G. J., & Haslett, W. R. (2009). The long-term impact of employment on mental health service use and costs. *Psychiatric Services, 60,* 1024–1031.

Bushway, S., & Reuter, P. (2002). Labor markets and crime risk factors. In L. Sherman, D. Farrington, B. Welsh & D. MacKenzie (Eds.), *Preventing crime* (pp. 198–240). New York: Rutledge

Butterworth, P., Leach, L. S., Strazdins, L., Olesen, S. C., Rodgers, B., & Broom, D. H. (2011). The psychosocial quality of work determines whether employment has benefits for mental health: results from a longitudinal national household panel survey. *Occupational and Environmental Medicine, 68,* 806–812.

Bybee, D., Mowbray, C. T., & McCrohan, N. M. (1995). Towards zero exclusion in vocational services for persons with psychiatric disabilities: Prediction of service receipt in a hybrid vocational/case management service program. *Psychiatric Rehabilitation Journal, 18*(4), 73–93.

Campbell, K. (2010). Employment rates for people with severe mental illness in the UK not improved by 1 year's individual placement and support. *Evidence-Based Mental Health, 13*(4), 114, doi:10.1136/ebmh1090.

Campbell, K., Bond, G. R., & Drake, R. E. (2011). Who benefits from supported employment: A meta-analytic study. *Schizophrenia Bulletin, 37,* 370–380.

Campbell, K., Bond, G. R., Drake, R. E., McHugo, G. J., & Xie, H. (2010). Client predictors of employment outcomes in high-fidelity supported employment: A regression analysis. *Journal of Nervous and Mental Disease, 198,* 556–563.

Campbell, K., Bond, G. R., Gervey, R., Pascaris, A., Tice, S., & Revell, G. (2007). Does type of provider organization affect fidelity to evidence-based supported employment? *Journal of Vocational Rehabilitation, 27,* 3–11.

Campbell, M. K., Mollison, J., Steen, N., Grimshaw, J. M., & Eccles, M. (2000). Analysis of cluster randomized trials in primary care: a practical approach. *Family Practice, 17,* 192–196.

Carlson, L. (2009). Evidence-based practice supported employment: Implementation in rural and frontier areas. *EBP Times: Supported Employment, June.*

Carlson, L., Smith, G., & Rapp, C. A. (2008). Evaluation of conceptual selling as a job development planning process. *Psychiatric Rehabilitation Journal, 31,* 219–225.

Carpenter, V., & Perkins, D. V. (1997, November 8). *Supported employment as a transition from state hospital to community.* Paper presented at the American Public Health Association, Indianapolis, IN.

Carpenter-Song, E., Alverson, H. S., Chu, E., Drake, R. E., Ritsema, M., & Smith, B. (2010). Ethno-cultural variations in the experience and meaning of mental illness and treatment: Implications for access and utilization. *Transcultural Psychiatry, 47,* 224–251.

Carter, R., Golant, S. K., & Cade, K. E. (2010). *Within our reach: Ending the mental health crisis.* New York: Rodale Books.

Casper, E. S., & Carloni, C. (2007). Assessing the underutilization of supported employment services. *Psychiatric Rehabilitation Journal, 30,* 182–188.

Caspi, A., Wright, B. R., Moffitt, T. E., & Silva, P. H. (1998). Early failure in the labor market: child-hood and adolescent predictors of unemployment in the transition to adulthood. *American Sociological Review, 63,* 424–451.

Catty, J., Lissouba, P., White, S., Becker, T., Drake, R. E., Fioritti, A., et al. (2008). Predictors of employment for people with severe mental illness: results of an international six-centre RCT. *British Journal of Psychiatry, 192,* 224–231.

Chambless, D. L., & Ollendick, T. H. (2001). Empirically supported psychological interventions: Controversies and evidence. *Annual Review of Psychology, 52,* 685–716.

Chandler, D. C. (2011). Work therapy: Welfare reform and mental health in California. *Social Service Review, 85,* 109–133.

Chandler, D. C., Meisel, J., Hu, T., McGowen, M., & Madison, K. (1997). A capitated model for a cross-section of severely mentally ill clients: Employment outcomes. *Community Mental Health Journal, 33,* 501–516.

Chandler, D. C., Meisel, J., Jordan, P., Rienzi, B. M., & Goodwin, S. N. (2005). Mental health, employ-ment and welfare tenure. *Journal of Community Psychology, 33,* 587–610.

Christensen, T. O. (2007). The influence of neurocognitive dysfunctions on work capacity in schizophrenia patients: a systematic review of the literature. *International Journal of Psychiatry in Clinical Practice, 11,* 89–101.

Cimpean, D., & Drake, R. E. (2011). Treating co-morbid chronic medical conditions and anxiety/depression. *Epidemiology and Psychiatric Sciences, 20,* 141–150.

Clark, R. E. (1998). Supported employment and managed care: Can they coexist? *Psychiatric Rehabilitation Journal, 22*(1), 62–68.

Clark, R. E., Bush, P. W., Becker, D. R., & Drake, R. E. (1996). A cost-effectiveness comparison of supported employment and rehabilitative day treatment. *Administration and Policy in Mental Health, 24,* 63–77.

Clark, R. E., Xie, H., Becker, D. R., & Drake, R. E. (1998). Benefits and costs of supported employment from three perspectives. *Journal of Behavioral Health Services and Research, 25*, 22–34.

Clarke, S. P., Crowe, T. P., Oades, L. G., & Deane, F. P. (2009). Do goal-setting interventions improve the quality of goals in mental health services? *Psychiatric Rehabilitation Journal, 32*, 292–299.

Clevenger, N. (2008). In favor of science. *Psychiatric Rehabilitation Journal, 31*, 277–279.

Cohen, M. R., Anthony, W. A., & Farkas, M. D. (1997). Assessing and developing readiness for psychiatric rehabilitation. *Psychiatric Services, 8*, 644–646.

Connell, M., King, R., & Crowe, T. (2011). Can employment positively affect the recovery of people with psychiatric disabilities? *Psychiatric Rehabilitation Journal, 35*, 59–63.

Cook, J. A. (2006). Employment barriers for persons with psychiatric disabilities: Update of a report for the President's Commission. *Psychiatric Services, 57*, 1391–1405.

Cook, J. A. (2008, October 29). *Promoting mental health recovery through evidence-based supported employment* (Webcast: *www.bcm.edu/ilru/html/training/webcasts/archive/2008/10-29-JC.html*). Paper presented at the Independent Living Research Utilization Program, Institute for Rehabilitation and Research, Houston, TX.

Cook, J. A., Blyler, C. R., Leff, H. S., McFarlane, W. R., Santos, A., Goldberg, R. W., et al. (2008). The Employment Intervention Demonstration Program. *Psychiatric Rehabilitation Journal, 31*, 291–295.

Cook, J. A., Leff, H. S., Blyler, C. R., Gold, P. B., Goldberg, R. W., Clark, R. E., et al. (2006). Estimated payments to employment service providers for persons with mental illness in the Ticket to Work Program. *Psychiatric Services, 57*, 465–471.

Cook, J. A., Leff, H. S., Blyler, C. R., Gold, P. B., Goldberg, R. W., Mueser, K. T., et al. (2005). Results of a multisite randomized trial of supported employment interventions for individuals with severe mental illness. *Archives of General Psychiatry, 62*, 505–512.

Cook, J. A., Lehman, A. F., Drake, R., McFarlane, W. R., Gold, P. B., Leff, H. S., et al. (2005). Integration of psychiatric and vocational services: A multisite randomized, controlled trial of supported employment. *American Journal of Psychiatry, 162*, 1948–1956.

Cook, J. A., Mulkern, G., Grey, D. D., Burke-Miller, J., Blyler, C. R., Razzano, L. A., et al. (2006). Effects of local unemployment rate on vocational outcomes in a randomized trial of supported employment for individuals with psychiatric disabilities. *Journal of Vocational Rehabilitation, 25*, 71–84.

Cook, J. A., & Razzano, L. (2000). Vocational rehabilitation for persons with schizophrenia: Recent research and implications for practice. *Schizophrenia Bulletin, 26*, 87–103.

Corbière, M., Zaniboni, S., Bond, G. R., Giles, P., Lesage, A., & Goldner, E. (2011). Job acquisition for people with severe mental illness enrolled in supported employment programs: A theoretically grounded empirical study. *Journal of Occupational Rehabilitation, 21*, 342–354.

Corrigan, P. W., Mueser, K. T., Bond, G. R., Drake, R. E., & Solomon, P. (2008). *Principles and practice of psychiatric rehabilitation: An empirical approach.* New York: Guilford Press.

Corrigan, P. W., Reedy, P., Thadani, D., & Ganet, M. (1995). Correlates of participation and completion in a job club for clients with psychiatric disability. *Rehabilitation Counseling Bulletin, 39*, 42–53.

Courtney, C. (2005). History. In D. W. Dew & G. M. Alan (Eds.), *Innovative methods for providing VR services to individuals with psychiatric disabilities* (*Institute on Rehabilitation Issues Monograph 30*) (pp. 27–45). Washington, DC: George Washington University Center for Rehabilitation Counseling Research and Education.

Crowther, R. E., Marshall, M., Bond, G. R., & Huxley, P. (2001). Helping people with severe mental illness to obtain work: Systematic review. *British Medical Journal, 322*, 204–208.

Cunningham, P., McKenzie, K., & Taylor, E. F. (2006). The struggle to provide community-based care to low-income people with serious mental illness. *Health Affairs, 25*, 694–705.

Danley, K. S., & Anthony, W. A. (1987). The Choose-Get-Keep Model: Serving severely psychiatrically disabled people. *American Rehabilitation, 13*(4), 6–9, 27–29.

Danziger, S., Frank, R. G., & Meara, E. (2009). Mental illness, work, and income support programs. *American Journal of Psychiatry, 166*, 398–404.

Davidson, L., Drake, R. E., Schmutte, T., Dinzeo, T., & Andres-Hyman, R. (2009). Oil and water or oil and vinegar? Evidence-based medicine meets recovery. *Community Mental Health Journal, 45*, 323–332.

Davis, L. L. (2011). *Supported employment for veterans with PTSD*. Paper presented at the Dartmouth Psychiatric Research Center Seminar, Lebanon, NH.

Davis, L. L., Leon, A. C., Toscano, R., Drebing, C. E., Ward, L. C., Parker, P. E., et al. (2012). A randomized controlled trial of supported employment among veterans with posttraumatic stress disorder. *Psychiatric Services, 63*, 464–470.

Deegan, P. E. (1988). Recovery: The lived experience of rehabilitation. *Psychiatric Rehabilitation Journal, 11*(4), 11–19.

Deegan, P. E., & Drake, R. E. (2006). Shared decision making and medication management in the recovery process. *Psychiatric Services, 57*, 1636–1639.

DeSisto, M. J., Harding, C. M., McCormick, R. V., Ashikaga, T., & Brooks, G. W. (1995). The Maine and Vermont three-decade studies of serious mental illness I. Matched comparison of cross-sectional outcome. *British Journal of Psychiatry, 167*, 331–342.

Dewa, C. S., Lin, E., Kooehoorn, M., & Goldner, E. (2007). Association of chronic work stress, psychiatric disorders, and chronic physical conditions with disability among workers. *Psychiatric Services, 58*, 652–658.

Dewa, C. S., McDaid, D., & Ettner, S. L. (2007). An international perspective on worker mental health problems: Who bears the burden and how are costs addressed? *Canadian Journal of Psychiatry, 52*, 346–356.

Dickey, B., & Sederer, L. I. (2001). *Improving mental health care: commitment to quality*. Washington, DC: American Psychiatric Publishing.

Dincin, J. (1975). Psychiatric rehabilitation. *Schizophrenia Bulletin, 1*, 131–147.

Dincin, J., & Witheridge, T. F. (1982). Psychiatric rehabilitation as a deterrent to recidivism. *Hospital and Community Psychiatry, 33*, 645–650.

Dixon, A., McDaid, D., Knapp, M., & Curran, C. (2006). Financing mental health services in low- and middle-income countries. *Health Policy and Planning, 21*, 171–182.

Dixon, L., Hoch, J. S., Clark, R., Bebout, R., Drake, R., McHugo, G., et al. (2002). Cost-effectiveness of two vocational rehabilitation programs for persons with severe mental illness. *Psychiatric Services, 53*, 1118–1124.

Draine, J., Salzer, M. S., Culhane, D. P., & Hadley, T. R. (2002). Role of social disadvantage in crime, joblessness, and homelessness among persons with serious mental illness. *Psychiatric Services, 53*, 565–573.

Drake, R. E., Becker, D. R., & Anthony, W. A. (1994a). The use of a research induction group in mental health services research. *Hospital and Community Psychiatry, 45,* 487–489.

Drake, R. E., Becker, D. R., Biesanz, J. C., Torrey, W. C., McHugo, G. J., & Wyzik, P. F. (1994b). Rehabilitation day treatment vs. supported employment: I. Vocational outcomes. *Community Mental Health Journal, 30,* 519–532.

Drake, R. E., Becker, D. R., Biesanz, J. C., Wyzik, P. F., & Torrey, W. C. (1996). Day treatment versus supported employment for persons with severe mental illness: A replication study. *Psychiatric Services, 47,* 1125–1127.

Drake, R. E., Becker, D. R., Bond, G. R., & Mueser, K. T. (2003). A process analysis of integrated and non-integrated approaches to supported employment. *Journal of Vocational Rehabilitation, 18,* 51–58.

Drake, R. E., Becker, D. R., Goldman, H. H., & Martinez, R. A. (2006). Best practices: The Johnson & Johnson—Dartmouth Community Mental Health Program: Disseminating evidence-based practice. *Psychiatric Services, 57,* 302–304.

Drake, R. E., & Bond, G. R. (2008). The future of supported employment for people with severe mental illness. *Psychiatric Rehabilitation Journal, 31,* 367–376.

Drake, R. E., & Bond, G. R. (2010). Implementing integrated mental health and substance abuse services. *Journal of Dual Diagnosis, 6,* 251–262.

Drake, R. E., Bond, G. R., & Becker, D. R. (in press). *IPS supported employment: An evidence-based approach.* New York: Oxford University Press.

Drake, R. E., Bond, G. R., Thornicroft, G., Knapp, M., & Goldman, H. H. (2011). Mental health disability: An international perspective. *Journal of Disability Policy Studies,* published on December 9, 2011, doi: 10.1177/1044207311427403.

Drake, R. E., Cimpean, D., & Torrey, W. C. (2009). Shared decision making in mental health: Prospects for personalized medicine. *Dialogues in Clinical Neuroscience, 11,* 319, 450–457.

Drake, R. E., & Essock, S. M. (2009). The science-to-service gap in real-world schizophrenia treatment: The 95% problem. *Schizophrenia Bulletin, 35,* 677–678.

Drake, R. E., Essock, S. M., & Bond, G. R. (2009). Implementing evidence-based practices for people with schizophrenia. *Schizophrenia Bulletin, 35,* 704–713.

Drake, R. E., Fox, T. S., Leather, P. K., Becker, D. R., Musumeci, J. S., Ingram, W. F., et al. (1998). Regional variation in competitive employment for persons with severe mental illness. *Administration and Policy in Mental Health, 25,* 493–504.

Drake, R. E., Goldman, H. H., Leff, H. S., Lehman, A. F., Dixon, L., Mueser, K. T., et al. (2001). Implementing evidence-based practices in routine mental health service settings. *Psychiatric Services, 52,* 179–182.

Drake, R. E., McHugo, G. J., Bebout, R. R., Becker, D. R., Harris, M., Bond, G. R., et al. (1999). A randomized clinical trial of supported employment for inner-city patients with severe mental illness. *Archives of General Psychiatry, 56,* 627–633.

Drake, R. E., McHugo, G. J., Becker, D. R., Anthony, W. A., & Clark, R. E. (1996). The New Hampshire study of supported employment for people with severe mental illness: Vocational outcomes. *Journal of Consulting and Clinical Psychology, 64,* 391–399.

Drake, R. E., McHugo, G. J., Clark, R. E., Teague, G. B., Xie, H., Miles, K., et al. (1998). Assertive community treatment for patients with co-occurring severe mental illness and substance use disorder: A clinical trial. *American Journal of Orthopsychiatry, 68,* 201–215.

Drake, R. E., McHugo, G. J., Xie, H., Fox, M., Packard, J., & Helmstetter, B. (2006). Ten-year recovery outcomes for clients with co-occurring schizophrenia and substance use disorders. *Schizophrenia Bulletin, 32,* 464–473.

Drake, R. E., Skinner, J., & Goldman, H. H. (2008). What explains the diffusion of treatments for mental illness? *American Journal of Psychiatry, 165,* 1385–1392.

Drake, R. E., Skinner, J. S., Bond, G. R., & Goldman, H. H. (2009). Social Security and mental illness: Reducing disability with supported employment. *Health Affairs, 28,* 761–770.

Drebing, C. E., Bell, M., Campinell, A. E., Fraser, R., Malec, J., Penk, W., et al. (2012). Vocational services research: Recommendations for next stage of work. *Journal of Rehabilitation Research and Development, 49,* 101–120.

Drebing, C. E., Rosenheck, R. A., Drake, R. E., Penk, W., & Rose, G. (2009). *Pathways to vocational rehabilitation: Enhancing entry and retention.* Bedford, MA: Bedford VHA Hospital.

Dreher, K. C., Bond, G. R., & Becker, D. R. (2010). The creation of the IPS-Q: A measure to assess knowledge of the Individual Placement and Support model. *Psychiatric Rehabilitation Journal, 33,* 181–189.

Dunn, E. C., Wewiorski, N. J., & Rogers, E. S. (2008). The meaning and importance of employment to people in recovery from serious mental illness: results of a qualitative study. *Psychiatric Rehabilitation Journal, 32,* 59–62.

Eack, S. M., Hogarty, G. E., Greenwald, D. P., Hogarty, S. S., & Keshavan, M. S. (2011). Effects of cognitive enhancement therapy on employment outcomes in early schizophrenia: Results from a 2-Year Randomized trial. *Research on Social Work Practice, 21,* 32–42.

Edwards, A., & Elwyn, G. (2009). *Shared decision-making in health care: Achieving evidence-based patient choice* (2nd ed.). New York: Oxford University Press.

Ehrenreich, B. (2001). *Nickel and dimed.* New York: Henry Holt.

Estroff, S. E. (1981). *Making it crazy.* Berkeley, CA: University of California Press.

Estroff, S. E., Patrick, D. L., Zimmer, C. R., & Lachicotte, W. S. (1997). Pathways to disability income among persons with severe, persistent psychiatric disorders. *Milbank Quarterly, 75,* 495–532.

Evans, J., & Repper, J. (2000). Employment, social inclusion and mental health. *Journal of Psychiatric and Mental Health Nursing, 7,* 15–24.

Evans, L. J., & Bond, G. R. (2008). Expert ratings on the critical ingredients of supported employment for people with severe mental illness. *Psychiatric Rehabilitation Journal, 31,* 318–331.

Fabian, E. S. (1989a). Supported employment for severely psychiatrically disabled persons: A descriptive study. *Psychosocial Rehabilitation Journal, 13*(2), 53–60.

Fabian, E. S. (1989b). Work and the quality of life. *Psychosocial Rehabilitation Journal, 12*(4), 39–49.

Fabian, E. S. (1992). Supported employment and the quality of life: Does a job make a difference? *Rehabilitation Counseling Bulletin, 36,* 84–97.

Falloon, I. R., & Talbot, R. E. (1981). Persistent auditory hallucinations: Coping mechanisms and implications for management. *Psychological Medicine, 11,* 329–339.

Farkas, M. D., Rogers, E. S., & Thurer, S. (1987). Rehabilitation outcome of long-term hospital patients left behind by deinstitutionalization. *Hospital and Community Psychiatry, 38,* 864–870.

Federal Register. (1992). *Vocational Rehabilitation Act Amendments of 1992* (No. 29 United States Code 706 (18)). Washington, DC: U.S. Government Printing Office.

Fergeson, D. (1992). In the company of heroes. *The Journal, 3*(2), 29.

Ferron, D. T. (1995). Diagnostic trends of disabled Social Security beneficiaries, 1986–93. *Social Security Bulletin, 58,* 15–31.

Finnerty, M. T., Rapp, C. A., Bond, G. R., Lynde, D. W., Ganju, V. J., & Goldman, H. H. (2009). The State Health Authority Yardstick (SHAY). *Community Mental Health Journal, 45,* 228–236.

Fisher, W. H., Roy-Bujnowski, K. M., Grudzinskas, A. J., Clayfield, J. C., Banks, S. M., & Wolff, N. (2006). Patterns and prevalence of arrest in a statewide cohort of mental health care consumers. *Psychiatric Services, 57,* 1623–1628.

Fixsen, D. L., Naoom, S. F., Blase, K. A., Friedman, R. M., & Wallace, F. (2005). *Implementation research: A synthesis of the literature.* Tampa, FL: University of South Florida.

Flynn, B. G. (1999). Commentary: A business perspective on disability in the workplace. *Rehabilitation Counseling Bulletin, 42,* 370–375.

Fogg, N. P., Harrington, P. E., & McMahon, B. T. (2010). The impact of the Great Recession upon the unemployment of Americans with disabilities. *Journal of Vocational Rehabilitation, 33,* 193–202.

Frank, R. G., & Glied, S. A. (2006). *Better but not well: Mental health policy in the United States since 1950.* Baltimore, MD: Johns Hopkins University Press.

Frank, R. G., Goldman, H. H., & McGuire, T. G. (2009). Trends in mental health cost growth: An expanded role for management? *Health Affairs, 28,* 649–659.

Fraser, V. V., Jones, A. M., Frounfelker, R., Harding, B., Hardin, T., & Bond, G. R. (2008). VR closure rates for two vocational models. *Psychiatric Rehabilitation Journal, 31,* 332–339.

Frey, W. D., Azrin, S., Goldman, H. H., Kalasunas, S., Salkever, D., Miller, A., et al. (2008). The Mental Health Treatment Study. *Psychiatric Rehabilitation Journal, 31,* 306–312.

Frey, W. D., Drake, R. E., Bond, G. R., Miller, A. L., Goldman, H. H., Salkever, D. S., et al. (2011). *Mental Health Treatment Study: Final Report to Social Security Administration.* Rockville, MD: Westat. (http://socialsecurity.gov/disabilityresearch/mentalhealth.htm)

Friedman, M. J., & Rosenheck, R. A. (1996). PTSD as a persistent mental illness. In S. Soreff (Ed.), *The seriously and persistently mentally ill: the state-of-the-art treatment handbook* (pp. 369–389). Seattle: Hogrefe & Huber.

Frounfelker, R. L., Glover, C., Teachout, A., Wilkniss, S., & Whitley, R. (2010). Access to supported employment for consumers with criminal justice involvement. *Psychiatric Rehabilitation Journal, 34,* 49–56.

Frounfelker, R. L., Teachout, A., Bond, G. R., & Drake, R. E. (2011). Criminal justice involvement of individuals with severe mental illness and supported employment outcomes. *Community Mental Health Journal, 47,* 737–741.

Frounfelker, R. L., Wilkniss, S., Bond, G. R., Devitt, T. S., Drake, R. E. (2011). Enrollment in supported employment services for clients with a co-occurring disorder. *Psychiatric Services, 62,* 545–547.

Gaebel, W., & Pietzcker, A. (1987). Prospective study of course of illness in schizophrenia: Part II. Prediction of outcome. *Schizophrenia Bulletin, 13,* 299–306.

Gahnstram-Strandqvist, K., Liukko, A., & Tham, K. (2003). The meaning of the working cooperative for persons with long-term mental illness: a phenomenological study. *American Journal Of Occupational Therapy, 57,* 262–272.

GAO. (2002). *SSA disability: SGA levels appear to affect the work behavior of relatively few beneficiaries, but more data needed (GAO-02-224).* Washington, DC: General Accounting Office.

GAO. (2007). *Vocational rehabilitation: Earnings increased for many SSA beneficiaries after completing VR services, but few earned enough to leave SSA's disability rolls (GAO-07-332) (Report to Congressional Requesters).* Washington, DC: United States Government Accountability Office.

Gates, L. B., Akabas, S. H., & Oran-Sabia, V. (1998). Relationship accommodations involving the work group: Improving work prognosis for persons with mental health conditions. *Psychiatric Rehabilitation Journal, 21*(3), 264–272.

Gervey, R. (2010). Rehabilitation readiness: A construct validity study of the University of Rhode Island Change Assessment for Vocational Counseling (URICA-VC) scale for persons with mental illness. *Journal of Vocational Rehabilitation, 33*, 133–142.

Gervey, R., & Bedell, J. R. (1994). Supported employment in vocational rehabilitation. In J. R. Bedell (Ed.), *Psychological assessment and treatment of persons with severe mental disorders* (pp. 151–175). Washington, DC: Taylor & Francis.

Gervey, R., & Kowal, H. (1994, May). *A description of a model for placing youth and young adults with psychiatric disabilities in competitive employment.* Paper presented at the International Association of Psychosocial Rehabilitation Services Conference, Albuquerque, NM.

Glasgow, R. E., Vogt, T. M., & Boles, S. M. (1999). Evaluating the public health impact of health promotion interventions: the RE-AIM framework. *American Journal of Public Health, 89,* 1322–1327.

Glater, S. I. (1992). The journey home. *The Journal, 3*(2), 21–22.

Glover, C. M., & Frounfelker, R. L. (2011a). Competencies of more and less successful employment specialists. *Community Mental Health Journal,* DOI 10.1007/s10597-011-9471-0.

Glover, C. M., & Frounfelker, R. L. (2011b). Competencies of employment specialists for effective job development. *American Journal of Psychiatric Rehabilitation, 14*, 198–211.

Gold, M., & Marrone, J. (1998). Mass Bay Employment Services (a service of Bay Cove Human Services, Inc.): A story of leadership, vision, and action resulting in employment for people with mental illness. In *Roses and Thorns from the Grassroots* (Vol. Spring). Boston, MA: Institute for Community Inclusion.

Gold, P. B., Macias, C., Barreira, P. J., Tepper, M., & Frey, J. (2010). Viability of using employment rates from randomized trials as benchmarks for supported employment program performance. *Administration and Policy in Mental Health and Mental Health Services Research, 37,* 427–432.

Gold, P. B., Meisler, N., Santos, A. B., Carnemolla, M. A., Williams, O. H., & Kelleher, J. (2006). Randomized trial of supported employment integrated with assertive community treatment for rural adults with severe mental illness. *Schizophrenia Bulletin, 32*, 378–395.

Goldberg, J. F., & Harrow, M. (2004). Consistency of remission and outcome in bipolar and unipolar mood disorders: a 10-year prospective follow-up. *Journal of Affective Disorders, 81,* 123–131.

Goldberg, S. C., Schooler, N. R., Hogarty, G. E., & Roper, M. (1977). Prediction of relapse in schizophrenic outpatients treated by drug and sociotherapy. *Archives of General Psychiatry, 34*, 171–184.

Goldman, H. H., Ganju, V., Drake, R. E., Gorman, P., Hogan, M. F., Hyde, P. S., et al. (2001). Policy implications for implementing evidence-based practices. *Psychiatric Services, 52*, 1591–1597.

Goodwin, A. M., & Kennedy, A. (2005). The psychosocial benefits of work for people with severe and enduring mental health problems. *Community, Work & Family, 8*, 23–35.

Gowdy, E. A., Carlson, L. S., & Rapp, C. A. (2003). Practices differentiating high-performing from low-performing supported employment programs. *Psychiatric Rehabilitation Journal, 26,* 232–239.

Gowdy, E. A., Carlson, L. S., & Rapp, C. A. (2004). Organizational factors differentiating high-performing from low-performing supported employment programs. *Psychiatric Rehabilitation Journal, 28*, 150–156.

Greenhalgh, T., Robert, G., MacFarlane, F., Bate, P., & Kyriakidou, O. (2004). Diffusion of innovations in service organizations: Systematic review and recommendations. *Milbank Quarterly, 82*, 581–629.

Grove, B., Secker, J., & Seebohm, P. (Eds.). (2005). *New thinking about mental health and employment*. Abingdon, UK: Radcliffe Publishing.

Hall, L. L., Edgar, E. R., & Flynn, L. M. (1997). *Stand and deliver: Action call to a failing industry*. Arlington, VA: National Alliance for the Mentally Ill.

Hall, L. L., Graf, A. C., Fitzpatrick, M. J., Lane, T., & Birkel, R. C. (2003). *Shattered lives: Results of a national survey of NAMI members living with mental illness and their families*. Arlington, VA: NAMI/ TRIAD (Treatment/Recovery Information and Advocacy Data Base).

Hannah, G., & Hall, J. (2006). Employment and mental health service utilization in Washington State. *Journal of Behavioral Health Services and Research, 33*, 287–303.

Harding, C. M., Brooks, G. W., Ashikaga, T., Strauss, J. S., & Breier, A. (1987). The Vermont longitudinal study of persons with severe mental illness, II: Long-term outcome of subjects who retrospectively met DSM-III criteria for schizophrenia. *American Journal of Psychiatry, 144*, 727–735.

Harding, C. M., Strauss, J. S., Hafez, H., & Liberman, P. B. (1987). Work and mental illness. I. Toward an integration of the rehabilitation process. *Journal of Nervous and Mental Disease, 175*, 317–326.

Harrison, G., Hopper, K., Craig, T., Laska, E., Siegel, C., Wanderling, J., et al. (2001). Recovery from psychotic illness: A 15- and 25-year international follow-up study. *British Journal of Psychiatry, 178*, 506–517.

Haslett, W. (2011, November 4). *Preliminary findings from a trial of a computerized engagement intervention for IPS Supported Employment*. Paper presented at the Dartmouth Psychiatric Research Center Supported Employment Seminar, Lebanon, NH.

Haslett, W. R., Bond, G. R., Drake, R. E., Becker, D. R., & McHugo, G. J. (2011). Individual Placement and Support: Does rurality matter? *American Journal of Psychiatric Rehabilitation, 14*, 237–244.

Hasson, H., Andersson, M., & Bejerholm, U. (2011). Barriers in implementation of evidence-based practice: Supported employment in Swedish context. *Journal of Health Organization and Management, 25*, 332–345.

Hayes, R. L., & Halford, W. K. (1996). Time use of unemployed and employed single male schizophrenic subjects. *Schizophrenia Bulletin, 22*, 659–669.

Hayes, S. C., Barnes-Holmes, D., & Roche, B. (Eds.). (2001). *Relational frame theory: A post-Skinnerian account of human language and cognition*. New York: Kluwer Academic/Plenum Publishers.

Hayes, S. C., Strosahl, K. D., & Wilson, K. G. (1999). *Acceptance and commitment therapy: An experiential approach to behavior change*. New York: Guilford.

Henry, A. D., & Hashemi, L. (2009, September 9). *Outcomes of supported employment services for adults with serious mental illness in Massachusetts: Findings from the Services for Education and Employment Technical Assistance Project (SEE-TAP)*. Paper presented at the Dartmouth Psychiatric Research Center, Lebanon, NH.

Henry, A. D., & Lucca, A. M. (2002, February 10). *Evaluating the implementation of an evidence-based supported employment program.* Paper presented at the National Association of State Mental Health Program Directors, Baltimore, MD.

Henry, A. D., & Lucca, A. M. (2004). Facilitators and barriers to employment: The perspectives of the people with psychiatric disabilities and employment service providers. *Work: Journal of Prevention, Assessment & Rehabilitation, 22,* 169–182.

Henry, G. T. (1990). *Practical sampling.* Newbury Park, CA: Sage.

Hepburn, B., & Burns, R. (2007, June 22). *Extending the welcome mat: Opening DOoRS to employment for individuals with co-occurring mental health and substance use disorders.* Paper presented at the MHA DORS Annual Conference, Baltimore, MD.

Heslin, M., Howard, L., Leese, M., McCrone, P., Rice, C., Jarrett, M., et al. (2011). Randomized controlled trial of supported employment in England: 2 year follow-up of the Supported Work and Needs. *World Psychiatry, 10,* 132–137.

Hill, A. B. (1965). The environment and disease: association or causation? *Proceedings of the Royal Society of Medicine, 58,* 295–300.

Hoffmann, H., Jäckel, D., Glauser, S., & Kupper, Z. (2012). A randomised controlled trial of the efficacy of supported employment. *Acta Psychiatrica Scandinavica, 125,* 157–167.

Hoffmann, H., & Kupper, Z. (1997). Relationships between social competence, psychopathology and work performance and their predictive value for vocational rehabilitation of schizophrenic outpatients. *Schizophrenia Research, 23,* 69–79.

Hoffmann, H., & Kupper, Z. (2003). Predictive factors of successful vocational re-integration in patients with chronic schizophrenia. *Psychiatrische Praxis, 30,* 312–317.

Hoge, M. A., Huey, L. Y., & O'Connell, M. J. (2004). Best practices in behavioral health workforce education and training. *Administration and Policy in Mental Health, 32,* 91–106.

Hoge, M. A., Paris, M., Adger, H., Collins, F. L., Finn, C. V., Fricks, L., et al. (2005). Workforce competencies in behavioral health: An overview. *Administration and Policy in Mental Health,* 593–631.

Holcomb, P. A., & Barnow, B. S. (2004). *Serving people with disabilities through the Workforce Investment Act's One-Stop Career Centers.* Washington, DC: Ticket to Work and Work Incentives Advisory Panel.

Holzner, B., Kemmler, G., & Meise, U. (1998). The impact of work-related rehabilitation on the quality of life of patients with schizophrenia. *Social Psychiatry & Psychiatric Epidemiology, 33,* 624–631.

Honkonen, T., Stengård, E., Virtanen, M., & Salokangas, R. K. (2007). Employment predictors for discharged schizophrenia patients. *Social Psychiatry and Psychiatric Epidemiology, 42,* 372–380.

Howard, L. M., Heslin, M., Leese, M., McCrone, P., Rice, C., Jarrett, M., et al. (2010). Supported employment: randomised controlled trial. *British Journal of Psychiatry, 196,* 404–411.

Huff, S. W., Rapp, C. A., & Campbell, S. R. (2008). "Everyday is not always Jell-O": A qualitative study of factors affecting job tenure. *Psychiatric Rehabilitation Journal, 31,* 211–218.

Huxley, P., & Thornicroft, G. (2003). Social inclusion, social quality and mental illness. *British Journal of Psychiatry, 182,* 289–290.

Hyde, P. S., Falls, K., Morris, J. A., & Schoenwald, S. K. (2003). *Turning knowledge into practice: A manual for behavioral health administrators and practitioners about understanding and implementing evidence-based practices.* Boston, MA: Technical Assistance Collaborative.

Institute of Medicine. (2002). *The dynamics of disability: Measuring and monitoring disability programs for Social Security Programs*. Washington, DC: National Academy Press.

Institute of Medicine. (2006). *Improving the quality of health care for mental and substance use conditions: Quality chasm series*. Washington DC: National Academies Press.

Isaac, M., Chand, P., & Murthy, P. (2007). Schizophrenia outcome measures in the wider international community. *British Journal of Psychiatry, 191*, s71–s77.

Jacobson, N. S., Roberts, L. J., Berns, S. B., & McGlinchey, J. B. (1999). Methods for defining and determining the clinical significance of treatment effects: Description, application, and alternatives. *Journal of Consulting and Clinical Psychology, 67*, 300–307.

Jamtvedt, G., Young, J. M., Kristoffersen, D. T., O'Brien, M. A., & Oxman, A. D. (2006). Audit and feedback: Effects on professional practice and health care outcomes. *Cochrane Database of Systematic Reviews (Online), 2*(2), http://onlinelibrary.wiley.com/doi/10.1002/14651858.CD000259.pub2/pdf/standard

Johannesen, J. K., McGrew, J. H., Griss, M. E., & Born, D. (2007). Perception of illness as a barrier to work in consumers of supported employment services. *Journal of Vocational Rehabilitation, 27*, 39–47.

Jones, A. M. (2011). Disclosure of mental illness in the workplace: A literature review. *American Journal of Psychiatric Rehabilitation, 14*, 212–229.

Jones, C. J., Perkins, D. V., & Born, D. L. (2001). Predicting work outcomes and service use in supported employment services for persons with psychiatric disabilities. *Psychiatric Rehabilitation Journal, 25*, 53–59.

Kane, J. (work in progress). Recovery After an Initial Schizophrenic Episode study.

Karakus, M., Frey, W., Goldman, H., Fields, S., & Drake, R. (2011). *Federal financing of supported employment and customized employment for people with mental illnesses*. Rockville, MD: Westat.

Kaye, H. S. (2010). The impact of the 2007–09 recession on workers with disabilities (http://www.bls.gov/opub/mlr/2010/10/art2exc.htm,). *Monthly Labor Review, 133*, 19–30.

Kazdin, A. E. (1999). Meanings and measurement of clinical significance. *Journal of Consulting and Clinical Psychology, 67*, 332–339.

Kemmler, G., Holzner, B., Neudorfer, C., Meise, U., & Hinterhuber, H. (1997). General life satisfaction and domain-specific quality of life in chronic schizophrenic patients. *Quality of Life Research: An International Journal of Quality of Life Aspects of Treatment, Care and Rehabilitation, 6*(3), 265–273.

Kendall, P. C., Marrs-Garcia, A., Nath, S. R., & Sheldrick, R. C. (1999). Normative comparisons for the evaluation of clinical significance. *Journal of Consulting and Clinical Psychology, 67*, 285–299.

Kennedy, C., & Manderscheid, R. W. (1992). SSDI and SSI disability beneficiaries with mental disorders. In *Mental Health, United States* (pp. 219–230). Washington, DC: National Institute of Mental Health.

Kiefe, C. I., Allison, J. J., Williams, D., Person, S. D., Weaver, M. T., & Weissman, N. W. (2001). Improving quality improvement using achievable benchmarks for physician feedback: A randomized controlled trial. *Journal of the American Medical Association, 285*, 2871–2879.

Kiefe, C. I., Weissman, N. W., Allison, J. J., Farmer, R., Weaver, M., & Williams, O. D. (1998). Identifying achievable benchmarks of care: Concepts and methodology. *International Journal for Quality in Health Care, 10*, 443–447.

Kilian, R., Lauber, C., Kalkan, R., Dorn, W., Rössler, W., Wiersma, D., et al. (2011). The relationships between employment, clinical status, and psychiatric hospitalisation in patients with schizophrenia receiving either IPS or a conventional vocational rehabilitation programme. *Social Psychiatry and Psychiatric Epidemiology, Online First*.

Killackey, E., Jackson, H. J., & McGorry, P. D. (2008). Vocational intervention in first-episode psychosis: individual placement and support v. treatment as usual. *British Journal of Psychiatry, 193*, 114–120.

Killeen, M., & O'Day, B. (2004). Challenging expectations: How individuals with psychiatric disabilities find and keep work. *Psychiatric Rehabilitation Journal, 28*, 157–163.

Kilo, C. M. (1988). A framework for collaborative improvement: Lessons from the Institute for Healthcare Improvement's Breakthrough Series. *Quality Management in Healthcare, 6*, 1–14.

Kimberly, J., & Cook, J. M. (2008). Organizational measurement and the implementation of innovations in mental health services. *Administration and Policy in Mental Health and Mental Health Services Research, 35*, 11–20.

Kinoshita, Y., Furukawa, T. A., Omori, I. M., Watanabe, N., Marshall, M., Bond, G. R., et al. (2010). Supported employment for adults with severe mental illness (Protocol). *Cochrane Database of Systematic Reviews (www.thecochranelibrary.com), 1. Art. No.: CD008297. DOI: 10.1002/14651858. CD008297* (Published online March 17, 2010).

Kirsh, B., & Cockburn, L. (2007). Employment outcomes associated with ACT: A review of ACT literature. *American Journal of Psychiatric Rehabilitation, 10*, 31–51.

Kirszner, M. L., McKay, C. D., & Tippett, M. L. (1991, October 2). *Homelessness and mental health: Replication and adaptation of the PACT model in Delaware*. Paper presented at the Proceedings from the Second Annual Conference on State Mental Health Agency Services Research, Arlington, VA.

Knapp, M., McCrone, P., Fombonne, E., Beecham, J., & Wostear, G. (2002). The Maudsley long-term follow-up study of child and adolescent depression: impact of comorbid conduct disorder on service use and costs in adulthood. *British Journal of Psychiatry, 180*, 19–23.

Kostick, K. M., Whitley, R., & Bush, P. W. (2010). Client-centeredness in supported employment: Specialist and supervisor perspectives. *Journal of Mental Health, 19*, 523–531.

Kouzis, A. C., & Eaton, W. W. (2000). Psychopathology and the initiation of disability payments. *Psychiatric Services, 51*, 908–913.

Kraemer, H. C., Mintz, M., Noda, A., Tinklenberg, J., & Yesavage, J. A. (2006). Caution regarding the use of pilot studies to guide power calculations for study proposals. *Archives of General Psychiatry, 63*, 484–489.

Kreyenbuhl, J., Nosse, I. R., & Dixon, L. B. (2009). Disengagement from mental health treatment among individuals with schizophrenia and strategies for facilitating connections to care: A review of the literature. *Schizophrenia Bulletin, 35*, 696–703.

Krishnadas, R., Moore, B. P., Nayak, A., & Patel, R. R. (2007). Relationship of cognitive function in patients with schizophrenia in remission to disability: a cross-sectional study in an Indian sample. *Annals of General Psychiatry, 6*, 19 (published online).

Kristof-Brown, A., Zimmerman, R. D., & Johnson, E. C. (2005). Consequences of individuals' fit at work: A meta-analysis of person-job, person-organization, person-group, and person-supervisor fit. *Personnel Psychology, 58*, 281–342.

Krupa, T., McLean, H., Eastabrook, S., Bonham, A., & Baksh, L. (2003). Daily time use as a measure of community adjustment for clients of assertive community treatment. *American Journal of Occupational Therapy, 57,* 558–565.

Kukla, M., & Bond, G. R. (2012). Job match and job tenure in persons with severe mental illness. *Journal of Rehabilitation, 78,* 11–15.

Kukla, M., & Bond, G. R. (submitted). A randomized controlled trial of evidence-based supported employment: nonvocational outcomes.

Kukla, M., Bond, G. R., & Xie, H. (2012). A prospective investigation of work and nonvocational outcomes in adults with severe mental illness. *Journal of Nervous and Mental Disease, 200,* 214–222.

Lachin, J. M. (2000). Statistical considerations in the intent-to-treat principle. *Controlled Clinical Trials, 21,* 167–189.

Larson, J. E., Barr, L. K., Kuwabara, S. A., Boyle, M. G., & Glenn, T. L. (2007). Process and outcome analysis of a supported employment program for people with psychiatric disabilities. *American Journal of Psychiatric Rehabilitation, 10,* 339–353.

Latham, G. P., & Locke, E. A. (2007). New developments in and directions for goal-setting research. *European Psychologist, 12,* 290–300.

Latimer, E. (2005). Economic considerations associated with assertive community treatment and supported employment for people with severe mental illness. *Journal of Psychiatry and Neuroscience, 30,* 355–359.

Latimer, E. (2010). An effective intervention delivered at sub-therapeutic dose becomes an ineffective intervention. *British Journal of Psychiatry, 196,* 341–342.

Latimer, E., Bush, P., Becker, D. R., Drake, R. E., & Bond, G. R. (2004). How much does supported employment for the severely mentally ill cost? An exploratory survey of high-fidelity programs. *Psychiatric Services, 55,* 401–406.

Latimer, E., Lecomte, T., Becker, D., Drake, R., Duclos, I., Piat, M., et al. (2006). Generalisability of the individual placement and support model of supported employment: Results of a Canadian randomised controlled trial. *British Journal of Psychiatry, 189,* 65–73.

Leete, E. (1993). The interpersonal environment: A consumer's personal recollection. In A. B. Hatfield & H. P. Lefley (Eds.), *Surviving mental illness* (pp. 114–128). New York: Guilford.

Leff, H. S. (2005). Evidence in intervention science. In R. E. Drake, M. R. Merrens & D. W. Lynde (Eds.), *Evidence-based mental health practice: A textbook* (pp. 141–164). New York: WW Norton & Company.

Leff, H. S., Cook, J. A., Gold, P. B., Toprac, M., Blyler, C., Goldberg, R. W., et al. (2005). Effects of job development and job support on competitive employment of persons with severe mental illness. *Psychiatric Services, 56,* 1237–1244.

Lefley, H. (1987). Aging parents as caregivers of mentally ill adult children: An emerging social problem. *Hospital and Community Psychology, 38,* 1063–1070.

Lehman, A. F., Dixon, L. B., Kernan, E., & DeForge, B. (1997). A randomized trial of assertive community treatment for homeless persons with severe mental illness. *Archives of General Psychiatry, 54,* 1038–1043.

Lehman, A. F., Goldberg, R. W., Dixon, L. B., McNary, S., Postrado, L., Hackman, A., et al. (2002). Improving employment outcomes for persons with severe mental illness. *Archives of General Psychiatry, 59,* 165–172.

Lehman, A. F., Steinwachs, D. M., & PORT Co-Investigators. (1998). Patterns of usual care for schizophrenia: Initial results from the Schizophrenia Patient Outcomes Research Team (PORT) client survey. *Schizophrenia Bulletin, 24,* 11–23.

Lehrer, P., & Laniol, J. (1977). Natural reinforcement in a psychiatric rehabilitation program. *Schizophrenia Bulletin, 3*, 297–302.

Lerner, D., Adler, D. A., Chang, H., Berndt, E. R., Irish, J. T., Lapitsky, L., et al. (2004). The clinical and occupational correlates of work productivity loss among employed patients with depression. *Journal of Occupational Environmental Medicine, 46*, S46–S55.

Liberman, R. P., DeRisi, W. J., & Mueser, K. T. (1989). *Social skills training for psychiatric patients.* Needham Heights, MA: Allyn & Bacon.

Liberman, R. P., Hilty, D. M., Drake, R. E., & Tsang, H. W. (2001). Requirements for multidisciplinary teamwork in psychiatric rehabilitation. *Psychiatric Services, 52*, 1331–1342.

Lindamer, L. A., Bailey, A., Hawthorne, W., Folsom, D. P., Gilmer, T. P., Garcia, P., et al. (2003). Gender differences in characteristics and service use of public mental health patients with schizophrenia. *Psychiatric Services, 54*, 1407–1409.

Lipsey, M. W. (1990). *Design sensitivity.* Newbury Park, CA: Sage.

Liu, S., & Stapleton, D. (2010). How many SSDI beneficiaries leave the rolls for work? More than you might think. *Disability Policy Research Brief, 10-01*, 1–4.

Livermore, G. A., Goodman, N., & Wright, D. (2007). Social Security disability beneficiaries: Characteristics, work activity, and use of services. *Journal of Vocational Rehabilitation, 27*, 85–93.

Lucca, A. M., Henry, A. D., Banks, S., Simon, L., & Page, S. (2004). Evaluation of an Individual Placement and Support (IPS) model program. *Psychiatric Rehabilitation Journal, 27*, 251–257.

Lurie, S., Kirsh, B., & Hodge, S. (2007). Can ACT lead to more work? the Ontario experience. *Canadian Journal of Community Mental Health, 26*, 161–171.

Lysaker, P., & Bell, M. (1995). Negative symptoms and vocational impairment in schizophrenia: repeated measurements of work performance over six months. *Acta Psychiatrica Scandinavica, 91*(3), 205–208.

MacDonald-Wilson, K. L., Revell, W. G., Nguyen, N. H., & Peterson, M. E. (1991). Supported employment outcomes for people with psychiatric disability: A comparative analysis. *Journal of Vocational Rehabilitation, 1*, 30–44.

MacDonald-Wilson, K. L., Rogers, E. S., Ellison, M. L., & Lyass, A. (2003). A study of the Social Security Work Incentives and their relation to perceived barriers to work among persons with psychiatric disability. *Rehabilitation Psychology, 48*, 301–309.

Macias, C., DeCarlo, L. T., Wang, Q., Frey, J., & Barreira, P. (2001). Work interest as a predictor of competitive employment: Policy implications for psychiatric rehabilitation. *Administration and Policy in Mental Health, 28*, 279–297.

Macias, C., Gold, P. B., Hargreaves, W. A., Aronson, E., Bickman, L., Barreira, P. J., et al. (2009). Preference in random assignment: Implications for the interpretation of randomized trials. *Administration and Policy in Mental Health and Mental Health Services Research, 36*, 331–342.

Macias, C., Jones, D. R., Hargreaves, W. A., Wang, Q., Rodican, C. F., Barreira, P. J., et al. (2008). When programs benefit some people more than others: Tests of differential service effectiveness. *Administration and Policy In Mental Health and Mental Health Services Research, 35*, 283–294.

Macias, C., Rodican, C. F., Hargreaves, W. A., Jones, D. R., Barreira, P. J., & Wang, Q. (2006). Supported employment outcomes of a randomized controlled trial of ACT and clubhouse models. *Psychiatric Services, 57*, 1406–1415.

Malamud, T. J., & McCrory, D. J. (1988). Transitional employment and psychosocial rehabilitation. In J. A. Ciardiello & M. D. Bell (Eds.), *Vocational rehabilitation of persons with prolonged mental illness* (pp. 150–162). Baltimore: Johns Hopkins Press.

Mank, D., Cioffi, A., & Yovanoff, P. (1997). Analysis of the typicalness of supported employment jobs, natural supports, and wage and integration outcomes. *Mental Retardation, 35,* 185–197.

Marrone, J., Foley, S., & Selleck, V. (2005). How mental health and welfare to work interact: The role of hope, sanctions, engagement, and support. *American Journal of Psychiatric Rehabilitation, 8,* 81–101.

Marrone, J., & Golowka, E. (1999). If work makes people with mental illness sick, what do unemployment, poverty, and social isolation cause? *Psychiatric Rehabilitation Journal, 23,* 187–193.

Marshak, L. E., Bostick, D., & Turton, L. J. (1990). Closure outcomes for clients with psychiatric disabilities served by the vocational rehabilitation system. *Rehabilitation Counseling Bulletin, 33,* 247–250.

Marshall, T., Rapp, C. A., Becker, D. R., & Bond, G. R. (2008). Key factors for implementing supported employment. *Psychiatric Services, 59,* 886–892.

Marwaha, S., & Johnson, S. (2004). Schizophrenia and employment: A review. *Social Psychiatry and Psychiatric Epidemiology, 39,* 337–349.

Marwaha, S., Johnson, S., Bebbington, P., Stafford, M., Angermeyer, M. C., Brugha, T., et al. (2007). Rates and correlates of employment in people with schizophrenia in the UK, France and Germany. *British Journal of Psychiatry, 191,* 30–37.

Matthews, W. C. (1980). Effects of a work activity program on the self concept of chronic schizophrenics. *Dissertation Abstracts International, 41*(358b (University Microfilms No. 816281, 98)), 358–359.

McAlpine, D. D., & Warner, L. (2000). *Barriers to employment among persons with mental illness: A review of the literature.* New Brunswick, NJ: Center for Research on the Organization and Financing of Care for the Severely Mentally Ill Institute for Health, Health Care Policy and Aging Research Rutgers, the State University.

McCarney, R., Warner, J., Iliffe, S., van Haselen, R., Griffin, M., & Fisher, P. (2007). The Hawthorne Effect: a randomised, controlled trial. *BMC Medical Research Methodology, 7,* 30doi:10.1186/1471-2288-1187–1130.

McFarlane, W. R. (2002, May 20). *Employment Intervention Demonstration Project (EIDP): Outcome of best practice.* Paper presented at the American Psychiatric Association, Philadelphia.

McFarlane, W. R., Dushay, R. A., Deakins, S. M., Stastny, P., Lukens, E. P., Toran, J., et al. (2000). Employment outcomes in Family-aided Assertive Community Treatment. *American Journal of Orthopsychiatry, 70,* 203–214.

McGlashan, T. H. (1988). A selective review of recent North American long-term followup studies of schizophrenia. *Schizophrenia Bulletin, 14,* 515–542.

McGovern, M. P. (2011, January 7). *Factors associated with change in addiction and mental health program capability to treat co-occurring disorders.* Paper presented at the Dartmouth PRC Research Seminar, Lebanon, NH.

McGovern, M. P., Lambert-Harris, C., McHugo, G. J., Giard, J., & Mangrum, L. (2010). Improving the dual diagnosis capability of addiction and mental health treatment services: Implementation factors associated with program level changes. *Journal of Dual Diagnosis, 6,* 237–250.

McGrew, J. H. (2007). *IPS fidelity survey of 17 supported employment programs in Indiana: Final report to SECT Center.* Indianapolis: Indiana University-Purdue University Indianapolis.

McGrew, J. H. (2008). *Final report to SECT Center: IPS fidelity survey of supported employment programs in Indiana.* Indianapolis: Indiana University-Purdue University Indianapolis.

McGrew, J. H., & Griss, M. (2005). Concurrent and predictive validity of two scales to assess the fidelity of implementation of supported employment. *Psychiatric Rehabilitation Journal, 29,* 41–47.

McGrew, J. H., Johannesen, J. K., Griss, M. E., Born, D. L., & Katuin, C. (2005). Performance-based funding of supported-employment: A multi-site controlled trial. *Journal of Vocational Rehabilitation, 23,* 81–99.

McGuire, A. B., Bond, G. R., Clendenning, D., & Kukla, M. (2011). Service intensity as a predictor of competitive employment in an Individual Placement and Support program. *Psychiatric Services, 62,* 1066–1072.

McGurk, S. R., & Mueser, K. T. (2004). Cognitive functioning, symptoms, and work in supported employment: A review and heuristic model. *Schizophrenia Research, 70,* 147–173.

McGurk, S. R., & Mueser, K. T. (2006). Strategies for coping with cognitive impairment in supported employment. *Psychiatric Services, 57,* 1421–1429.

McGurk, S. R., Mueser, K. T., Harvey, P. D., La Puglia, R., & Marder, J. (2003). Cognitive and symptom predictors of work outcomes for clients with schizophrenia in supported employment. *Psychiatric Services, 54,* 1129–1135.

McGurk, S. R., Wolfe, R., Pascaris, A., Mueser, K. T., & Feldman, K. (2007). Cognitive training for supported employment: 2–3 year outcomes of a randomized controlled trial. *American Journal of Psychiatry, 164,* 437–441.

McGurk, S. R., & Wykes, T. (2008). Cognitive remediation and vocational rehabilitation. *Psychiatric Rehabilitation Journal, 31,* 350–359.

McHugo, G. J., Drake, R. E., & Becker, D. R. (1998). The durability of supported employment effects. *Psychiatric Rehabilitation Journal, 22*(1), 55–61.

McHugo, G. J., Drake, R. E., Whitley, R., Bond, G. R., Campbell, K., Rapp, C. A., et al. (2007). Fidelity outcomes in the National Implementing Evidence-Based Practices Project. *Psychiatric Services, 58,* 1279–1284.

McQuilken, M., Zahniser, J. H., Novak, J., Starks, R. D., Olmos, A., & Bond, G. R. (2003). The Work Project Survey: Consumer perspectives on work. *Journal of Vocational Rehabilitation, 18,* 59–68.

Mechanic, D., Bilder, S., & McAlpine, D. D. (2002). Employing persons with serious mental illness. *Health Affairs, 21*(5), 242–253.

Mellen, V., & Danley, K. (1987). Special issue: Supported employment for persons with severe mental illness. *Psychosocial Rehabilitation Journal, 9*(2, whole issue).

Mellman, T. A., Miller, A. L., Weissman, E. M., Crismon, M. L., Essock, S. M., & Marder, S. R. (2001). Evidence-based pharmacologic treatment for people with severe mental illness: A focus on guidelines and algorithms. *Psychiatric Services, 52,* 619–625.

Menear, M., Reinharz, D., Corbière, M., Houle, N., Lanctôt, N., Goering, P., et al. (2011). Organizational analysis of Canadian supported employment programs for people with psychiatric disabilities. *Social Science and Medicine, 72,* 1028–1035.

Michie, S., Fixsen, D., Grimshaw, J. M., & Eccles, M. P. (2009). Specifying and reporting complex behaviour change interventions: the need for a scientific method. *Implementation Science, 4*(40), doi:10.1186/1748-5908-1184-1140.

Michon, H. W., van Vugt, M., & van Busschbach, J. (2011, June). *Effectiveness of Individual Placement and Support; 18 & 30 months follow-up.* Paper presented at the Enmesh Conference, Ulm, Germany.

Michon, H. W., van Weeghel, J., Kroon, H., & Schene, A. H. (2005). Person-related predictors of employment outcomes after participation in psychiatric vocational rehabilitation programmes: A systematic review. *Social Psychiatry and Psychiatric Epidemiology, 40,* 408–416.

Miller, W. R., & Rollnick, S. (2002). *Motivational interviewing: Preparing people to change addictive behavior* (2nd ed.). New York: Guilford Press.

Mojtabai, R. (2011). National trends in mental health disability, 1997–2009. *American Journal of Public Health, 101*, 2156–2163.

Mojtabai, R., Fochtman, L., Chang, S., Kotov, K., Craig, T. J., & Bromet, E. (2009). Unmet need for care in schizophrenia. *Schizophrenia Bulletin, 35*, 679–695.

Mold, J., & Peterson, K. (2005). Primary care practice-based research networks: Working at the interface between research and quality improvement. *Annals of Family Medicine, 3*, S12–S20.

Möller, H.-J., von Zerssen, D., & Wüschner-Stockheim, M. (1982). Outcome in schizophrenic and similar paranoid psychoses. *Schizophrenia Bulletin, 8*, 99–108.

Morrissey, J., Meyer, P., & Cuddeback, G. (2007). Extending assertive community treatment to criminal justice settings: Origins, current evidence, and future directions. *Community Mental Health Journal, 43*, 527–544.

Mueser, K. T., Aalto, S., Becker, D. R., Ogden, J. S., Wolfe, R. S., Schiavo, D., et al. (2005). The effectiveness of skills training for improving outcomes in supported employment. *Psychiatric Services, 56*, 1254–1260.

Mueser, K. T., Becker, D. R., Torrey, W. C., Xie, H., Bond, G. R., Drake, R. E., et al. (1997). Work and nonvocational domains of functioning in persons with severe mental illness: A longitudinal analysis. *Journal of Nervous and Mental Disease, 185*, 419–426.

Mueser, K. T., Becker, D. R., & Wolfe, R. S. (2001). Supported employment, job preferences, job tenure and satisfaction. *Journal of Mental Health, 10*, 411–417.

Mueser, K. T., Bond, G. R., Drake, R. E., & Resnick, S. G. (1998). Models of community care for severe mental illness: A review of research on case management. *Schizophrenia Bulletin, 24*, 37–74.

Mueser, K. T., Campbell, K., & Drake, R. E. (2011). The effectiveness of supported employment in people with dual disorders. *Journal of Dual Disorders, 7*, 90–102.

Mueser, K. T., Clark, R. E., Haines, M., Drake, R. E., McHugo, G. J., Bond, G. R., et al. (2004). The Hartford study of supported employment for persons with severe mental illness. *Journal of Consulting and Clinical Psychology, 72*, 479–490.

Mueser, K. T., & Drake, R. E. (2005). How does a practice become evidence-based? In R. E. Drake, M. R. Merrens & D. W. Lynde (Eds.), *Evidence-based mental health practice: A textbook* (pp. 217–241). New York: WW Norton & Company.

Mueser, K. T., & Drake, R. E. (2011). Developing evidence-based practices. In G. Thornicroft, G. Szmukler, K. T. Mueser & R. E. Drake (Eds.), *Oxford textbook of community mental health* (pp. 320–324). New York: Oxford University Press.

Mueser, K. T., Salyers, M. P., & Mueser, P. R. (2001). A prospective analysis of work in schizophrenia. *Schizophrenia Bulletin, 27*, 281–296.

Mukherjee, S. (2010). *The emperor of all maladies: a biography of cancer.* New York: Scribner.

Murphy, A. A., Mullen, M. G., & Spagnolo, A. B. (2005). Enhancing Individual Placement and Support: Promoting job tenure by integrating natural supports and supported education. *American Journal of Psychiatric Rehabilitation, 8*, 37–61.

NAMI. (2006). *Grading the states: A report on America's health care system for serious mental illness.* Arlington, VA: National Alliance on Mental Illness.

NAMI. (2011). *State mental health budget cuts: A national crisis.* Arlington, VA: National Alliance on Mental Illness.

National Council on Disability. (2005). *The Social Security Administration's efforts to promote employment for people with disabilities.* Washington, DC: National Council on Disability.

National Council on Disability. (2008). *The Rehabilitation Act: Outcomes for transition age youth.* Washington, DC: National Council on Disability.

New Freedom Commission on Mental Health. (2003). *Achieving the promise: Transforming mental health care in America. Final Report. DHHS Pub. No. SMA-03-3832.* Rockville, MD: Substance Abuse and Mental Health Services Administration.

NIMH. (1999). *Bridging science and service: A report by the National Advisory Mental Health Council's Clinical Treatment and Services Research Workgroup.* Rockville, MD: National Institute of Mental Health.

Noble, J. H., Conley, R. W., Banerjee, S., & Goodman, S. (1991). Supported employment in New York State: A comparison of benefits and costs. *Journal of Disability Policy Studies, 2,* 39–73.

Noble, J. H., Honberg, R. S., Hall, L. L., & Flynn, L. M. (1997). *A legacy of failure: The inability of the federal-state vocational rehabilitation system to serve people with severe mental illness.* Arlington, VA: National Alliance for the Mentally Ill.

Nuechterlein, K. H. (2010, November 29). *Individual placement and support after an initial episode of schizophrenia: The UCLA randomized controlled trial.* Paper presented at the International Conference on Early Psychosis, Amsterdam, the Netherlands.

Nuechterlein, K. H., Subotnik, K. L., Turner, L. R., Ventura, J., Becker, D. R., & Drake, R. E. (2008). Individual Placement and Support for individuals with recent-onset schizophrenia: Integrating supported education and supported employment. *Psychiatric Rehabilitation Journal, 31,* 340–349.

Nunnally, J. C. (1978). *Psychometric theory* (2nd ed.). New York: McGraw-Hill.

O'Connor, A. M., Wennberg, J. E., Legare, F., Llewellyn-Thomas, H. A., Moulton, B. W., Sepucha, K. R., et al. (2007). Toward the 'tipping point': Decision aids and informed patient choice. *Health Affairs, 26,* 716–725.

O'Day, B. L., & Killeen, M. (2002). Does U.S. federal disability policy support employment and recovery for people with psychiatric disabilities? *Behavioral Sciences and the Law, 20,* 559–583.

OECD. (2009). Sickness, disability and work: Keeping on track in the economic downturn (Organisation for Economic Co-operation and Development Directorate for Employment, Labour and Social Affairs), http://www.oecd.org/dataoecd/42/15/42699911.pdf. Retrieved October 31, 2011

Oldman, J., Thomson, L., Calsaferri, K., Luke, A., & Bond, G. R. (2005). A case report of the conversion of sheltered employment to evidence-based supported employment in Canada. *Psychiatric Services, 56,* 1436–1440.

Onken, L. S., Blaine, J. D., & Battjes, R. (1997). Behavioral therapy research: A conceptualization of a process. In S. W. Henggeler & R. Amentos (Eds.), *Innovative approaches for difficult to treat populations* (pp. 477–485). Washington, DC: American Psychiatric Press.

Oshima, I. (2011, August 26). *An update on implementing evidence-based practices in Japan.* Paper presented at the Dartmouth PRC Research Semianr, Lebanon, NH.

Ottomanelli, L., Goetz, L. L., Suris, A., McGeough, C., Sinnott, P. L., Toscano, R., et al. (2012). Effectiveness of supported employment for veterans with spinal cord injuries: results from a randomized multisite study. *Archives of Physical Medicine and Rehabilitation, 93*, 740-747.

Oulvey, G., Carpenter-Song, E., & Swanson, S. J. (submitted). Principles for enhancing the role of vocational rehabilitation in IPS supported employment.

Ozawa, A., & Yaeda, J. (2007). Employer attitudes toward employing persons with psychiatric disability in Japan. *Journal of Vocational Rehabilitation, 26*, 105-113.

Pandiani, J., & Leno, S. (2011). *Vermont Mental Health Performance Indicator Project*. Waterbury, VT: Vermont Agency of Human Services, Department of Mental Health.

Panzano, P. C., & Roth, D. (2006). The decision to adopt evidence-based and other innovative mental health practices: Risky business? *Psychiatric Services, 57*, 1153-1161.

Penk, W., Drebing, C. E., Rosenheck, R. A., Krebs, C., A., V. O., & Mueller, L. (2010). Veterans Health Administration transitional work experience vs. job placement in veterans with co-morbid substance use and non-psychotic psychiatric disorders. *Psychiatric Rehabilitation Journal, 33*, 297-307.

Percudani, M., Barbui, C., & Tansella, M. (2004). Effect of second-generation antipsychotics on employment and productivity in individuals with schizophrenia. *Pharmacoeconomics, 22*, 701-718.

Phillips, S. D., Burns, B. J., Edgar, E. R., Mueser, K. T., Linkins, K. W., Rosenheck, R. A., et al. (2001). Moving assertive community treatment into standard practice. *Psychiatric Services, 52*, 771-779.

Pogoda, T. K., Cramer, I. E., Rosenheck, R. A., & Resnick, S. G. (2011). Qualitative analysis of barriers to implementation of supported employment in the Department of Veterans Affairs. *Psychiatric Services, 62*, 1289-1295.

Priebe, S., Warner, R., Hubschmid, T., & Eckle, I. (1998). Employment, attitudes toward work, and quality of life among people with schizophrenia in three countries. *Schizophrenia Bulletin, 24*, 469-477.

Prince, M., Patel, V., Saxena, S., Maj, M., Maselko, J., Phillips, M. R., et al. (2007). No health without mental health. *Lancet, 370*, 859-870.

Prochaska, J. O., & DiClemente, C. C. (1984). *The transtheoretical approach: Crossing the traditional boundaries of therapy*. Homewood, IL: Dow-Jones/Irwin.

Proctor, E. K., Landsverk, J., Aarons, G., Chambers, D., Glisson, C., & Mittman, B. (2009). Implementation research in mental health services: an emerging science with conceptual, methodological, and training challenges. *Administration and Policy in Mental Health and Mental Health Services Research, 36*, 24-34.

Quimby, E., Drake, R. E., & Becker, D. R. (2001). Ethnographic findings from the Washington, DC, Vocational Services Study. *Psychiatric Rehabilitation Journal, 24*, 368-374.

Ralph, R. O. (2000). *A synthesis of a sample of recovery literature 2000*. Alexandria, VA: National Technical Center for State Mental Health Planning, National Association for State Mental Health Program Directors.

Ramsay, C. E., Broussard, B., Goulding, S. M., Cristofaro, S., Hall, D., Kaslow, N. J., et al. (2011). Life and treatment goals of individuals hospitalized for first-episode nonaffective psychosis. *Psychiatry Research, 189*, 344-348.

Ramsay, C. E., Stewart, T., & Compton, M. T. (2012). Unemployment among patients with newly diagnosed first-episode psychosis: prevalence and clinical correlates in a US sample. *Social Psychiatry and Psychiatric Epidemiology, 47*, 797-803.

Rapp, C. A. (1993). Client-centered performance management for rehabilitation and mental health services. In R. W. Flexer & P. L. Solomon (Eds.), *Psychiatric rehabilitation in practice* (pp. 173–192). Boston: Andover.

Rapp, C. A., Bond, G. R., Becker, D. R., Carpinello, S. E., Nikkel, R. E., & Gintoli, G. (2005). The role of state mental health authorities in promoting improved client outcome through evidence-based practice. *Community Mental Health Journal, 41,* 347–363.

Rapp, C. A., & Goscha, R. J. (2011). *The strengths model: a recovery-oriented approach to mental health services* (2nd ed.). New York: Oxford University Press.

Rapp, C. A., Goscha, R. J., & Carlson, L. S. (2010). Evidence-based practice implementation in Kansas. *Community Mental Health Journal, 46,* 461–465.

Rapp, C. A., Huff, S., & Hansen, K. (2003). The New Hampshire financing policy. *Psychiatric Rehabilitation Journal, 26,* 385–391.

Resnick, S. G. (2009, September 24). *Measuring fidelity in the national dissemination of supported employment in the Veterans Health Administration.* Paper presented at the Festschrift for Gary Bond, Indianapolis, IN.

Resnick, S. G., & Bond, G. R. (2001). The Indiana Job Satisfaction Scale: Job satisfaction in vocational rehabilitation for people with severe mental illness. *Psychiatric Rehabilitation Journal, 25,* 12–19.

Resnick, S. G., & Rosenheck, R. (2007). Dissemination of supported employment in Department of Veterans Affairs. *Journal of Rehabilitation Research & Development, 6,* 867–878.

Resnick, S. G., Rosenheck, R. A., Canive, J. M., De Souza, C., Stroup, T. S., McEvoy, J., et al. (2008). Employment outcomes in a randomized trial of second-generation antipsychotics and per-phenazine in the treatment of individuals with schizophrenia. *Journal of Behavioral Health Services & Research, 35,* 215–225.

Rinaldi, M., Killackey, E., Smith, J., Shepherd, G., Singh, S., & Craig, T. (2010). First episode psychosis and employment: A review. *International Review of Psychiatry, 22,* 148–162.

Rinaldi, M., Miller, L., & Perkins, R. (2010). Implementing the individual placement and support (IPS) approach for people with mental health conditions in England. *International Review of Psychiatry, 22,* 163–172.

Roberts, M. M., & Pratt, C. W. (2007). Putative evidence of employment readiness. *Psychiatric Rehabilitation Journal, 30,* 175–181.

Roberts, M. M., & Pratt, C. W. (2010). A construct validity study of employment readiness in persons with severe mental illness. *American Journal of Psychiatric Rehabilitation, 13,* 40–54.

Robins, L. N. (1966). *Deviant children grown up.* Baltimore: Waverly Press.

Rodriguez, M. N., & Emsellem, M. (2011). *Sixty-five million need not apply.* New York: National Employment Law Project.

Rogers, E. M. (2003). *Diffusion of innovations* (5th ed.). New York: Free Press.

Rogers, E. S., Anthony, W. A., Lyass, A., & Penk, W. E. (2006). A randomized clinical trial of vocational rehabilitation for people with psychiatric disabilities. *Rehabilitation Counseling Bulletin, 49,* 143–156.

Rogers, E. S., MacDonald-Wilson, K., Danley, K., Martin, R., & Anthony, W. A. (1997). A process analysis of supported employment services for persons with serious psychiatric disability: Implications for program design. *Journal of Vocational Rehabilitation, 8,* 233–242.

Rogers, E. S., Martin, R., Anthony, W. A., Massaro, J., Danley, K., Crean, T., et al. (2001). Assessing readiness for change among persons with severe mental illness. *Community Mental Health Journal, 37,* 97–112.

Rogers, E. S., Walsh, D., Masotta, L., & Danley, K. (1991). *Massachusetts survey of client preferences for community support services: Final report.* Boston: Center for Psychiatric Rehabilitation.

Rogers, J. A. (1995). Work is key to recovery. *Psychosocial Rehabilitation Journal, 18*(4), 5–10.

Rollins, A. L., Bond, G. R., Jones, A., Kukla, M., & Collins, L. (2011). Workplace social networks and their relationship with job outcomes and other employment characteristics for people with severe mental illness. *Journal of Vocational Rehabilitation, 35*, 243–252.

Rollins, A. L., Mueser, K. T., Bond, G. R., & Becker, D. R. (2002). Social relationships at work: Does the employment model make a difference? *Psychiatric Rehabilitation Journal, 26*, 51–62.

Rosenfield, S. (1987). Services organization and quality of life among the seriously mentally ill. *New Directions for Mental Health Services, 36*, 47–59.

Rosenheck, R. A., Leslie, D., Keefe, R., McEvoy, J., Swartz, M., Perkins, D., et al. (2006). Barriers to employment for people with schizophrenia. *American Journal of Psychiatry, 163*, 411–417.

Rosenheck, R. A., & Mares, A. S. (2007). Dissemination of supported employment for homeless veterans with psychiatric and/or addiction disorders: Two-year client outcomes. *Psychiatric Services, 58*, 325–333.

Rosenthal, D. A., Dalton, J. A., & Gervey, R. (2007). Analyzing vocational outcomes of individuals with psychiatric disabilities who receive state vocational rehabilitation services: A data mining approach. *International Journal of Social Psychiatry, 53*, 357–368.

Rosenthal, M. B., Frank, R. G., Li, Z., & Epstein, A. M. (2005). Early experience with pay-for-performance: from concept to practice. *Journal of the American Medical Association, 294*, 1788–1793.

Rounsaville, B. J., Carroll, K. M., & Onken, L. S. (2001). A stage model of behavioral therapies research: Getting started and moving on from stage I. *Clinical Psychology: Science and Practice, 8*, 133–142.

Rubin, S. E., & Roessler, R. T. (2001). *Foundations of the vocational rehabilitation process* (5th ed.). Austin, Texas: PRO-ED.

Ruiz-Quintanilla, S. A., Weathers, R. F., Melburg, V., Campbell, K., & Madi, N. (2006). Participation in programs designed to improve employment outcomes for persons with psychiatric disabilities: Evidence from the New York WORKS Demonstration Project. *Social Security Bulletin, 66*, 49–79.

Rupp, K., & Scott, C. (1998). Determinants of duration on the disability rolls and program trends. In K. Rupp & D. Stapleton (Eds.), *Growth in income entitlement benefits for disability: Explanations and policy implications* (pp. 139–176). Kalamazoo, MI: Upjohn Institute.

Rupp, K., & Scott, C. G. (1996). Trends in the characteristics of DI and SSI disability awardees and duration of program participation. *Social Security Bulletin, 59*, 3–21.

Russert, M. G., & Frey, J. L. (1991). The PACT vocational model: A step into the future. *Psychosocial Rehabilitation Journal, 14*(4), 7–18.

Sainsbury Centre. (2003). *Economic and social costs of mental illness in England.* London: Sainsbury Centre for Mental Health.

Sainsbury Centre. (2009). *Commissioning what works: The economic and financial case for supported employment.* London: Sainsbury Centre for Mental Health.

Salize, H. J., McCabe, R., Bullenkamp, J., Hansson, L., Lauber, C., Martinez-Leal, R., et al. (2009). Cost of treatment of schizophrenia in six European countries. *Schizophrenia Research, 111*, 70–77.

Salkever, D. S. (2003). Tickets without takers: Potential economic barriers to the supply of rehabilitation services to beneficiaries with mental disorders. In K. Rupp & S. H. Bell (Eds.), *Paying for results in vocational rehabilitation* (pp. 327–354). Washington, DC: Urban Institute Press.

Salkever, D. S. (2011). *Toward a social cost-effectiveness analysis of programs to expand supported employment services: An interpretive review of the literature.* Rockville, MD: Westat.

Salkever, D. S., Karakus, M. C., Slade, E. P., Harding, C. M., Hough, R. L., Rosenheck, R. A., et al. (2007). Measures and predictors of community-based employment and earnings of persons with schizophrenia in a multisite study. *Psychiatric Services, 58,* 315–324.

Salyers, M. P., Becker, D. R., Drake, R. E., Torrey, W. C., & Wyzik, P. F. (2004). Ten-year follow-up of clients in a supported employment program. *Psychiatric Services, 55,* 302–308.

Salyers, M. P., McGuire, A. B., Rollins, A. L., Bond, G. R., Mueser, K. T., & Macy, V. (2010). Integrating assertive community treatment and illness management and recovery for consumers with severe mental illness. *Community Mental Health Journal, 46,* 319–329.

SAMHSA. (2009). http://www.samhsa.gov/dataoutcomes/urs/urs2009.aspx. Retrieved January 17, 2011

SAMHSA. (2010). *Mental Health, United States, 2008. HHS Publication No. (SMA) 10–4590.* Rockville, MD: Substance Abuse and Mental Health Services Administration.

Sawhill, I. V., & Baron, J. (2010). *We need a new start for Headstart. Brookings Institute http://www. brookings.edu/articles/2010/0301_head_start_sawhill.aspx.*

Saxena, S., Paraje, G., Sharan, P., Karam, G., & Sadana, R. (2006). The 10/90 divide in mental health research: trends over a 10-year period. *British Journal of Psychiatry, 188,* 81–82.

Saxena, S., Thornicroft, G., Knapp, M., & Whiteford, H. (2007). Resources for mental health: scarcity, inequity, and inefficiency. *Lancet, 370,* 878–889.

Scheid, T. L. (1993). An investigation of work and unemployment among psychiatric clients. *International Journal of Health Services, 23,* 763–782.

Schinnar, A., Rothbard, A., Kanter, R., & Jung, Y. (1990). An empirical literature review of definitions of severe and persistent mental illness. *American Journal of Psychiatry, 147,* 1602–1608.

Schneider, J. (2003). Is supported employment cost effective? A review. *International Journal of Psychosocial Rehabilitation, 7,* 145–156 (http://www.psychosocial.com/IJPR_7/empl_costs.html).

Schoenwald, S. K., Hoagwood, K. E., Atkins, M. S., Evans, M. E., & Ringeisen, H. (2010). Workforce development and the organization of work: The science we need. *Administration and Policy in Mental Health and Mental Health Services Research, 37,* 71–80.

Schouten, L., Hulscher, M. E., van Everdingen, J. E., Huijsman, R., & Grol, R. P. (2008). Evidence for the impact of quality improvement collaboratives: Systematic review. *BMJ, 336,* 1491–1494.

Schultheis, A. M., & Bond, G. R. (1993). Situational assessment ratings of work behaviors: Changes across time and between settings. *Psychosocial Rehabilitation Journal, 17*(2), 107–119.

Schutz, L. E., Rivers, K. O., & Ratusnik, D. L. (2009). The role of external validity in evidence-based practice for rehabilitation. *Rehabilitation Psychology, 53,* 294–302.

Scott, S., Knapp, M., Henderson, J., & Maughan, B. (2001). Financial cost of social exclusion: follow-up study of antisocial children into adulthood. *British Medical Journal, 323,* 191–194.

Secker, J., Grove, B., & Seebohm, P. (2001). Challenging barriers to employment, training and education for mental health service users: The service user's perspective. *Journal of Mental Health, 10,* 395–404.

Sengupta, A., Drake, R. E., & McHugo, G. J. (1998). The relationship between substance use disorder and vocational functioning among persons with severe mental illness. *Psychiatric Rehabilitation Journal, 22*(1), 41–45.

Shafer, M. S. (2005). *Employment Intervention Demonstration Project: Arizona site (Unpublished report).* Phoenix, AZ: Arizona State University.

Shannon, H. S., Robson, L. S., & Sale, J. E. (2001). Creating safer and healthier workplaces: Role of organizational factors and job characteristics. *American Journal of Industrial Medicine, 40,* 319–334.

Shortell, S. M., Bennett, C. L., & Byck, G. R. (1998). Assessing the impact of continuous quality improvement on clinical practice: What it will take to accelerate progress. *Milbank Quarterly, 76,* 593–624.

Slade, M. (2009). *Personal recovery and mental illness: A guide for mental health professionals.* New York: Cambridge University Press.

Social Security Advisory Board. (2006). A Disability System for the 21st Century (www.ssab.gov/).

Solinski, S., Jackson, H. J., & Bell, R. C. (1992). Prediction of employability in schizophrenic patients. *Schizophrenia Research, 7,* 141–148.

Sox, H. C., & Greenfield, S. (2009). Comparative effectiveness research: A report from the Institute of Medicine. *Annals of Internal Medicine, 151,* 203–205.

SSA. (2008). Annual statistical supplement, 2007 (released April 2008) (www.ssa.gov/policy/research_sub12.html#sub22). Retrieved June 28, 2009

SSA. (2010). Annual statistical report on the Social Security Disability Insurance Program, 2009 (www.ssa.gov/policy/docs/statcomps/di_asr/#toc). Retrieved February 17, 2011

Stapleton, D., O'Day, B., Livermore, G., & Imparato, A. (2006). Dismantling the poverty trap: Disability policy for the 21st Century. *Milbank Quarterly, 84,* 701–732.

Steele, K., & Berman, C. (2001). *The day the voices stopped.* New York: Basic Books.

Stein, L. I., & Santos, A. B. (1998). *Assertive community treatment of persons with severe mental illness.* New York: W. W. Norton.

Stein, L. I., & Test, M. A. (1980). An alternative to mental health treatment. I: Conceptual model, treatment program, and clinical evaluation. *Archives of General Psychiatry, 37,* 392–397.

Steinwachs, D. M., Kasper, J. D., & Skinner, E. A. (1992). *Family perspectives on meeting the needs for care of severely mentally ill relatives: A national survey.* Baltimore, MD: Center on the Organization and Financing of Care for the Severely Mentally Ill, Johns Hopkins University.

Strauss, J. S., & Carpenter, W. T. (1977). Prediction of outcome in schizophrenia. III. Five-year outcomes and its predictors. *Archives of General Psychiatry, 34,* 159–163.

Strauss, J. S., Hafez, H., Lieberman, P., & Harding, C. M. (1985). The course of psychiatric disorder, III: Longitudinal principles. *American Journal of Psychiatry, 142,* 289–296.

Strickler, D. C., Whitley, R., Becker, D. R., & Drake, R. E. (2009). First person accounts of long-term employment activity among people with dual diagnosis. *Psychiatric Rehabilitation Journal, 32,* 261–268.

Stuart, H. (2006). Mental illness and employment discrimination. *Current Opinion in Psychiatry, 19,* 522–526.

Swain, K., Whitley, R., McHugo, G. J., & Drake, R. E. (2009). The sustainability of evidence-based practices in routine mental health agencies. *Community Mental Health Journal, 46,* 119–129.

Swanson, S. J., & Becker, D. R. (2010). *Supported employment: applying the Individual Placement and Support (IPS) model to help clients compete in the workforce.* Center City, MN: Hazelden.

Swanson, S. J., Becker, D. R., Drake, R. E., & Merrens, M. R. (2008). *Supported employment: A practical guide for practitioners and supervisors.* Lebanon, NH: Dartmouth Psychiatric Research Center.

Swanson, S. J., Burson, K., Harper, J., Johnson, B., Litvak, J., McDowell, M., et al. (2011). Implementation issues for IPS supported employment: Stakeholders share their perspectives and strategies. *American Journal of Psychiatric Rehabilitation, 14,* 165–180.

Swanson, S. J., Langfitt-Reese, S., & Bond, G. R. (in press). Employer attitudes about criminal justice history. *Psychiatric Rehabilitation Journal*.

Swarbrick, M., Bates, F., & Roberts, M. (2009). Peer employment support (PES): A model created through collaboration between a peer-operated service and university. *Occupational Therapy in Mental Health, 25*, 325–334.

Swendsen, J., Ben-Zeev, D., & Granholm, E. (2011). Real-time electronic ambulatory monitoring of substance use and symptom expression in schizophrenia. *American Journal of Psychiatry, 168*, 202–209.

Tarrier, N., Sharpe, L., Beckett, R., Harwood, S., Baker, A., & Yusopoff, L. (1993). A trial of two cognitive behavioural methods of treating drug-resistant residual psychotic symptoms in schizophrenia patients: II. Treatment-specific changes in coping and problem-solving skills. *Psychiatry and Psychiatric Epidemiology, 28*, 5–10.

Tashjian, M. D., Hayward, B. J., Stoddard, S., & Kraus, L. (1989). *Best practice study of vocational rehabilitation services to severely mentally ill persons.* Washington, DC: Policy Study Associates.

Taylor, A. C., & Bond, G. R. (submitted). Employment specialist competencies as predictors of employment outcomes.

Teplin, L. A., Abram, K. M., & McClelland, G. M. (1996). The prevalence of psychiatric disorders among incarcerated women. *Archives of General Psychiatry, 53*, 505–512.

Tessler, R. C., & Goldman, H. H. (1982). *The chronically mentally ill: Assessing community support programs.* Cambridge, MA: Ballinger Press.

Test, M. A. (1992). Training in Community Living. In R. P. Liberman (Ed.), *Handbook of psychiatric rehabilitation* (pp. 153–170). New York: Macmillan.

Test, M. A., Allness, D. J., & Knoedler, W. H. (1995, October). *Impact of seven years of assertive community treatment.* Paper presented at the American Psychiatric Association Institute on Psychiatric Services, Boston, MA.

Test, M. A., & Stein, L. I. (1976). Practice guidelines for the community treatment of markedly impaired patients. *Community Mental Health Journal, 12*, 72–82.

Thornicroft, G. (2006). *Shunned: Discrimination against people with mental illness.* Oxford: Oxford University Press.

Thornicroft, G., Brohan, E., Rose, D., Sartorius, N., & Leese, M. (2009). Global pattern of experienced and anticipated discrimination against people with schizophrenia: a cross-sectional survey. *Lancet, 373*, 408–415.

Thornicroft, G., Tansella, M., Becker, T., Knapp, M., Leese, M., Schene, A., et al. (2004). The personal impact of schizophrenia in Europe. *Schizophrenia Research 69*, 125–132.

Timmons, J. C., & Dreilinger, D. (2000). Time limits, exemption and disclosure: TANF caseworkers and clients with disabilities. *Institute for Community Inclusion: Research to Practice, 6*(3), 1–3.

Torrey, E. F. (2001). *Surviving schizophrenia: A manual for families, consumers, and providers* (4th ed.). New York: Harper-Collins.

Torrey, W. C., Becker, D. R., & Drake, R. E. (1995). Rehabilitative day treatment versus supported employment: II. Consumer, family and staff reactions to a program change. *Psychosocial Rehabilitation Journal, 18*(3), 67–75.

Torrey, W. C., Bond, G. R., McHugo, G. J., & Swain, K. (2011). Evidence-based practice implementation in community mental health settings: The relative importance of key domains of implementation activity. *Administration and Policy in Mental Health and Mental Health Services Research*, DOI: 10.1007/s10488-011-0357-9.

Torrey, W. C., Drake, R. E., Dixon, L., Burns, B. J., Rush, A. J., Clark, R. E., et al. (2001). Implementing evidence-based practices for persons with severe mental illness. *Psychiatric Services, 52*, 45–50.

Torrey, W. C., Lynde, D. W., & Gorman, P. (2005). Promoting the implementation of practices that are supported by research: The National Implementing Evidence-Based Practice Project. *Child and Adolescent Psychiatric Clinics of North America, 14*, 297–306.

Tremblay, T., Smith, J., Xie, H., & Drake, R. E. (2006). Effect of benefits counseling services on employment outcomes for people with psychiatric disabilities. *Psychiatric Services, 57*, 816–821.

Trotter, S., Minkoff, K., Harrison, K., & Hoops, J. (1988). Supported work: An innovative approach to the vocational rehabilitation of persons who are psychiatrically disabled. *Rehabilitation Psychology, 33*, 27–36.

Tsang, H. W., Angell, B., Corrigan, P. W., Lee, Y. T., Shi, K., Lam, C. S., et al. (2007). A cross-cultural study of employers' concerns about hiring people with psychotic disorder: Implications for recovery. *Social Psychiatry and Psychiatric Epidemiology, 42*, 723–733.

Tsang, H. W., Chan, A., Wong, A., & Liberman, R. P. (2009). Vocational outcomes of an integrated supported employment program for individuals with persistent and severe mental illness. *Journal of Behavior Therapy and Experimental Psychiatry, 40*, 292–305.

Tsang, H. W., Fung, K. M., Leung, A. Y., Li, S. M., & Cheung, W. M. (2010). Three year follow-up study of an integrated supported employment for individuals with severe mental illness. *Australian and New Zealand Journal of Psychiatry, 44*, 49–58.

Tsang, H. W., Lam, P., Ng, B., & Leung, O. (2000). Predictors of employment outcome for people with psychiatric disabilities: A review of the literature since the mid '80s. *Journal of Rehabilitation, 66*, 19–31.

Tsang, H. W., Leung, A. Y., Chung, R. C., Bell, M., & Cheung, W. M. (2010). Review on vocational predictors: a systematic review of predictors of vocational outcomes among individuals with schizophrenia: an update since 1998. *Australian and New Zealand Journal of Psychiatry, 44*, 495–504.

Tschopp, M. K., Perkins, D. V., Hart-Katuin, C., Born, D. L., & Holt, S. L. (2007). Employment barriers and strategies for individuals with psychiatric disabilities and criminal histories. *Journal of Vocational Rehabilitation, 26*, 175–187.

Tsemberis, S., McHugo, G. J., Williams, V., Hanrahan, P., & Stefancic, A. (2007). Measuring homelessness and residential stability: The residential time-line follow-back inventory. *Journal of Community Psychology, 35*, 29–42.

Tukey, J. W. (1977). *Exploratory data analysis*. Reading, MA: Addison-Wesley.

Twamley, E. W., Jeste, D. V., & Lehman, A. F. (2003). Vocational rehabilitation in schizophrenia and other psychotic disorders: A literature review and meta-analysis of randomized controlled trials. *Journal of Nervous and Mental Disease, 191*, 515–523.

Twamley, E. W., Narvaez, J. M., Becker, D. R., Bartels, S. J., & Jeste, D. V. (2008). Supported employment for middle-aged and older people with schizophrenia. *American Journal of Psychiatric Rehabilitation, 11*, 76–89.

U.S. Department of Health and Human Services. (1999). *Mental health: A report of the Surgeon General*. Rockville, MD: Substance Abuse and Mental Health Services Administration, Center for Mental Health Services, National Institute of Mental Health.

Van Dongen, C. J. (1998). Self-esteem among persons with severe mental illness. *Issues in Mental Health Nursing, 19*(1), 29–40.

van Erp, N. H., Giesen, F. B., van Weeghel, J., Kroon, H., Michon, H. W., Becker, D., et al. (2007). A multisite study of implementing supported employment in the Netherlands. *Psychiatric Services, 58*, 1421–1426.

Vandergoot, D. (1987). Review of placement research literature: Implications for research and practice. *Rehabilitation Counseling Bulletin, 30*, 243–272.

Vorspan, R. (1992). Why work works. *Psychosocial Rehabilitation Journal, 16*(2), 49–55.

Waghorn, G. R., Collister, L., Killackey, E., & Sherring, J. (2007). Challenges to implementing evidence-based supported employment in Australia. *Journal of Vocational Rehabilitation, 27*, 29–37.

Waghorn, G. R., Lloyd, C., Abraham, B., Silvester, D., & Chant, D. (2008). Comorbid physical health conditions hinder employment among people with psychiatric disabilities. *Psychiatric Rehabilitation Journal, 31*, 243–246.

Wallace, C. J., Tauber, R., & Wilde, J. (1999). Teaching fundamental workplace skills to persons with serious mental illness. *Psychiatric Services, 50*, 1147–1149, 1153.

Wang, C. C., Sung, C., Hiatt, E., Fujikawa, M., Anderson, C., & Rosenthal, D. (2011, April 7). *Effectiveness of supported employment on competitive employment outcomes: a meta-analysis.* Paper presented at the National Council of Rehabilitation Educators, Los Angeles, CA.

Wang, M. C., Hyun, J. K., Harrison, M. I., Shortell, S. M., & Fraser, I. (2006). Redesigning health systems for quality: Lessons from emerging practices. *Joint Commission Journal on Quality and Patient Safety, 32*, 599–611.

Wang, P. S., Demler, O., & Kessler, R. C. (2002). Adequacy of treatment for serious mental illness in the United States. *American Journal of Public Health, 92*, 92–98.

Wang, P. S., Lane, M., Olfson, M., Pincus, H. A., Wells, K. B., & Kessler, R. C. (2005). Twelve-month use of mental health services in the United States: Results from the National Comorbidity Survey replication. *Archives of General Psychiatry, 62*, 629–640.

Warner, R., & Mandiberg, J. (2006). An update on affirmative businesses or social firms for people with mental illness. *Psychiatric Services 57*, 1488–1492.

Warr, P. (1987). *Work, unemployment, and mental health.* Oxford: Oxford University Press.

Watzke, S., Galvao, A., & Brieger, P. (2008). Vocational rehabilitation for subjects with severe mental illnesses in Germany: A controlled study. *Social Psychiatry and Psychiatric Epidemiology, 44*, 523–531.

Wehman, P. (1986). Supported competitive employment for persons with severe disabilities. *Journal of Applied Rehabilitation Counseling, 17*, 24–29.

Wehman, P. (1988). Supported employment: Toward zero exclusion of persons with severe disabilities. In P. Wehman & M. S. Moon (Eds.), *Vocational rehabilitation and supported employment* (pp. 3–14). Baltimore: Paul Brookes.

Wehman, P., & Moon, M. S. (Eds.). (1988). *Vocational rehabilitation and supported employment.* Baltimore: Paul Brookes.

Weiden, P. J., Aquila, R., & Standard, J. (1996). Atypical antipsychotic drugs and long-term outcome in schizophrenia. *Journal of Clinical Psychiatry, 57*(Suppl 11), 53–60.

Weisz, J. R., & Jensen, P. S. (1999). Efficacy and effectiveness of child and adolescent psychotherapy and pharmacotherapy. *Mental Health Services Research., 1*, 125–157.

Wells, K. B. (1999). Treatment research at the crossroads: The scientific interface of clinical trials and effectiveness research. *American Journal of Psychiatry, 156*, 5–10.

Wennberg, J. E. (2010). *Tracking medicine.* New York: Oxford University Press.

West, J. C., Wilk, J. E., Olfson, M., Rae, D. S., Marcus, S., Narrow, W. E., et al. (2005). Patterns and quality of treatment for patients with schizophrenia in routine psychiatric practice. *Psychiatric Services, 56*, 283–291.

Westermeyer, J. F., & Harrow, M. (1987). Factors associated with work impairments in schizophrenic and nonschizophrenic patients. In R. R. Grinker & M. Harrow (Eds.), *Clinical research in schizophrenia: A multidimensional approach* (pp. 280–298). Springfield, Il.: Thomas.

Wewiorski, N. J., & Fabian, E. S. (2004). Association between demographic and diagnostic factors and employment outcomes for people with psychiatric disabilities: A synthesis of recent research. *Mental Health Services Research, 6*, 9–21.

Whitley, R. E., & Drake, R. E. (2010). Dimensions of recovery. *Psychiatric Services, 61*, 1248–1250.

Whitley, R. E., Kostick, K., & Bush, P. (2010). The desirable attributes of supported employment specialists: an empirically-grounded framework. *Administration and Policy in Mental Health and Mental Health Services Research, 37*, 509–519.

Wiltsey Stirman, S., Kimberly, J., Cook, N., Calloway, A., Castro, F., & Charns, M. (2012). The sustainability of new programs and innovations: a review of the empirical literature and recommendations for future research. *Implementation Science, 7*, 17 doi:10.1186/1748-5908-1187-1117.

Woltmann, E. M., Whitley, R., McHugo, G. J., Brunette, M., Torrey, W. C., Coots, L., et al. (2008). The role of staff turnover in the implementation of evidence-based practices in mental health care. *Psychiatric Services, 59*, 732–737.

Wong, K. K., Chiu, R., Tang, B., Mak, D., Liu, J., & Chiu, S. N. (2008). A randomized controlled trial of a supported employment program for persons with long-term mental illness in Hong Kong. *Psychiatric Services, 59*, 84–90.

World Health Organization. (2001a). *World Health Organization International Classification of Functioning, Disability and Health (ICF)*. Geneva: World Health Organization.

World Health Organization. (2001b). *World Health Report 2001. Mental health: New understanding, new hope*. Geneva: World Health Organization.

Xie, H., Dain, B. J., Becker, D. R., & Drake, R. E. (1997). Job tenure among persons with severe mental illness. *Rehabilitation Counseling Bulletin, 40*, 230–239.

Xie, H., Drake, R. E., McHugo, G. J., Xie, L., & Mohandas, A. (2010). The 10-year course of remission, abstinence, and recovery in dual diagnosis. *Journal of Substance Abuse Treatment, 39*, 132–140.

Zadny, J. J., & James, L. F. (1977). Time spent on placement. *Rehabilitation Counseling Bulletin, 21*, 31–35.

Zhang, W., Bansback, N., & Anis, A. H. (2011). Measuring and valuing productivity loss due to poor health: A critical review. *Social Science and Medicine, 72*, 185–192.

Zito, W., Greig, T. C., Wexler, B. E., & Bell, M. D. (2007). Predictors of on-site vocational support for people with schizophrenia in supported employment. *Schizophrenia Research, 94*, 81–88.

Zola, I. K. (1992). Self, identity, and the naming question: Reflections on the language of disability. *Social Science and Medicine, 36*, 167–173.

INDEX